YOU'VE GOT TO K

Would you like your product or name to be recognized by thousands? Are you trying to build and expand your business to increase sales and profits? Are you looking for ways to reach more potential customers than ever before? Promotion is the crucial key to all these goals.

And you don't need a lot of money, a large staff, or a bunch of specialists to produce advertisements, catalogs, commercials—and results. All you really need is the expert advice you'll find in HOW TO PROMOTE YOUR OWN BUSINESS, the nuts-and-bolts guide to doing it all yourself or learning when and how to have others do it for you.

GARY BLAKE is the director of The Communication Workshop, a consulting firm helping business management to improve writing and communications skills. He has been published in such magazines as *Harper's, New York, The New York Times Book Review,* and *Advertising Age*. He is the author of *The Status Book* (Doubleday).

ROBERT W. BLY is an independent copywriter and consultant specializing in industrial advertising and promotion. He has written articles for such publications as *Direct Marketing, Amtrak Express, Business Marketing,* and *Writer's Digest*. He is the author of *A Dictionary of Computer Words* (Dell/Banbury).

Bly and Blake are co-authors of *Technical Writing: Structure, Standards, and Style* (McGraw-Hill).

HOW TO PROMOTE YOUR OWN BUSINESS

Gary Blake and Robert W. Bly

A PLUME BOOK
NEW AMERICAN LIBRARY
NEW YORK
PUBLISHED IN CANADA BY
PENGUIN BOOKS CANADA LIMITED, MARKHAM, ONTARIO

PUBLISHER'S NOTE

This publication is designed to provide accurate and authoritative information in regard to the subject matter covered. It is sold with the understanding that the publisher is not engaged in rendering legal, accounting, or other professional services. If legal advice or other expert assistance is required, the service of a competent professional person should be sought.

NAL BOOKS ARE AVAILABLE AT QUANTITY DISCOUNTS WHEN USED TO PROMOTE PRODUCTS OR SERVICES. FOR INFORMATION PLEASE WRITE TO PREMIUM MARKETING DIVISION, NEW AMERICAN LIBRARY, 1633 BROADWAY, NEW YORK, NEW YORK 10019.

Copyright © 1983 by Gary Blake and Robert W. Bly

All rights reserved

℗

PLUME TRADEMARK REG. U.S. PAT. OFF. AND FOREIGN COUNTRIES
REGISTERED TRADEMARK—MARCA REGISTRADA
HECHO EN HARRISONBURG, VA., U.S.A.

SIGNET, SIGNET CLASSIC, MENTOR, ONYX, PLUME, MERIDIAN and NAL BOOKS are published *in the United States* by NAL PENGUIN INC., 1633 Broadway, New York, New York 10019. *in Canada* by Penguin Books Canada Limited, 2801 John Street, Markham, Ontario L3R 1B4

Library of Congress Cataloging in Publication Data:
Blake, Gary.
How to promote your own business.
Bibliography: p.
Includes index.
1. Advertising.   2. Public relations.   3. Small business.
    I. Bly, Robert W.   II. Title.
HF5823.B59   1983   659.2'81   83-12093
ISBN 0-452-25456-6

First Printing, October, 1983

5   6   7   8   9   10

PRINTED IN THE UNITED STATES OF AMERICA

Dedications

To my mother, who "promoted" my life
—G.B.

To the Rubins—Florence, Ira, Phil, and Gary
—R.W.B.

ACKNOWLEDGMENTS

For those who may think publicity is a thankless task, we'd like to respond by publicly applauding a few of the many people who had faith in this book and who helped contribute to its birth.

Very special thanks to our editor, Channa Taub, who had the sagacity to buy it and the tenacity to help mold it; to Dominick Abel, whose blend of gentleness, tough-mindedness, and patience helped us to do our best; to the small-business owners of the United States, whose creativity in finding new ways to promote their businesses has added variety and fun to this project.

Special thanks also to Eve Blake, Jean Blake, Jack Nathan, Amy Sprecher, and the rest of the "kitchen cabinet" who somehow managed to stay alert even after the tenth time we asked if they'd "mind taking a look at this draft."

We'd also like to thank the following people and organizations for allowing us to use their promotions in our book: Louis Galterio, Abbondanza; Lyla Ward, The Party Place; Tom Okada, Okada Studios; Adele Gross, Bon Bon Travel; Ed Waldman, Ed Waldman Gallery; Bridgford Hunt, The Hunt Company; Philip Magerman, Magerman Associates; Barbara Weinstein, Barbara H. Weinstein & Associates; Contempo Design; Kevin Gormely; Steve Brown; Koch Engineering; Thompson Cigar Co.; Dick and Bert for Weil Olds.

Finally, we thank Alan Cohen at Westwinds for sponsoring the "How to Promote Your Own Business" seminars that provided much of the source material for this book; Jon Isear, who offered numerous helpful comments on many areas of promotion and advertising; and Pauline Yearwood.

Every day is a fishing day,
But every day is not a catching day.
               —Caribbean saying

Some people make things happen,
Some wait for things to happen,
And then there are those that say—what happened?
                         —Anonymous

CONTENTS

Introduction 1

Chapter 1: WHAT PROMOTION IS ALL ABOUT 5
    Promotion: A Key to Success for Small Business 5
    What Is Promotion? 6
    Why You Should Promote Your Business 6
    The Four Types of Promotion 7
    What Promotion Is Best for Your Business 8
    You, Too, Can Promote Your Business 11

Chapter 2: PLANNING YOUR PROMOTIONS 12
    Having a Business Plan 12
    Marketing 12
    Know Your Customer 13
    How Can You Reach Your Customer? 15
    What Do You Want to Say to Your Audience? 18
    The Best Way to Say It 19
    How Do You Want Your Customer to Respond? 20

Chapter 3: HOW TO BUDGET YOUR PROMOTIONS 25
    Promotion Is an Expense 25
    Six Methods for Planning Promotion Budgets 26
    One Sensible Solution 29
    More Budgeting Tips 30
    Promotion Budgets in a Down Economy 31

x • Contents

Chapter 4: WHEN TO HIRE A PROFESSIONAL— AND WHEN TO DO IT YOURSELF ... 33
   Advertising Agencies ... 33
   Should You Use an Advertising Agency? ... 34
   How to Select an Advertising Agency ... 35
   Public Relations Agencies ... 37
   Graphic Design Studios ... 38
   Free-lancers ... 39
   How to Work with Professional Help ... 39
   Where to Find Help ... 40

Chapter 5: HOW TO WRITE COPY THAT SELLS ... 42
   What Is Copy? ... 42
   The Sales Sequence ... 43
   Headlines ... 46
   Characteristics of Good Headlines ... 48
   Body Copy ... 49
   Case History: The Travel-Agency Flyer ... 50
   Ten Tips on Copywriting Technique ... 51
   Effective Body Copy: A Checklist ... 56

Chapter 6: PRODUCING YOUR PROMOTIONAL MATERIAL ... 58
   The Graphic Arts ... 58
   The Elements of Graphic Production ... 58
   Type ... 59
   Alternatives to Type ... 62
   A Glossary of Graphic Arts Terms ... 63
   Ten Tips for Better Layout ... 65
   Photography ... 69
   Illustrations ... 70
   Pulling It All Together ... 72
   A Production Checklist ... 72
   Printing Tips ... 73
   A Quick Paper Primer ... 73
   Printing Techniques ... 74
   Folding ... 76
   Binding ... 77

Contents • xi

Chapter 7: REACHING THE PRESS: PUBLICITY   80
    Why the Media Need Your Help   80
    What Is a Press Release?   81
    The Headline   85
    How to Write a Release   86
    Press Kits   87
    What News Deserves a Press Release?   89
    Why Send Out a Press Release?   89
    Where Do You Send Your Press Release?   90
    Following Up Your Release   92

Chapter 8: SPEAK UP FOR YOURSELF—AND YOUR BUSINESS   95
    Radio and TV: The Not-So Impossible Dream   95
    Radio: The Listening Audience   97
    By-Lined Articles: The Recognition Game   101
    The Query Letter   102
    Speaking Up for Your Business   106
    Where Can You Speak?   107
    Community Relations   108
    Teaching: A Textbook Example of Publicity   110

Chapter 9: ADVERTISING BY LETTER: DIRECT MAIL   112
    What Is Direct Mail?   112
    Advantages of Direct Mail   112
    Use of Mailings   113
    Elements of Direct Mail   114
    Tips on Writing Direct Mail That Pulls   120
    Selecting Mailing Lists   121
    Keeping Your Own Lists   125
    Doing the Mailing   126
    Direct Response Postcards   128
    Measuring the Response   130

Chapter 10: SELLING BY LETTER: MAIL ORDER   132
    Mail Order: A $100 Billion Market   132
    What Sells by Mail?   133
    How to Select Mail-Order Merchandise   133
    How to Promote Mail-Order Merchandise   136

Fifteen Tips for Effective Mail-Order Promotions 139
Measuring the Results of Mail-Order Promotion 144

Chapter 11: NO FEAR OF FLYERS—AND OTHER SALES LITERATURE 146
Why You Need Sales Literature 146
Types of Sales Literature 149
Eleven Tips for Creating Better Brochures 152

Chapter 12: ADVERTISING IN PRINT: NEWSPAPERS, MAGAZINES, DIRECTORIES, AND THE GREAT OUTDOORS 157
Newspapers: The Number One Advertising Medium 157
Running a Newspaper Ad 158
Magazines: The Medium for On-Target Advertising 162
Anatomy of a Magazine Ad 164
Selecting the Magazine 165
The Yellow Pages and Other Directories 166
Outdoor Advertising: Billboards 168
Transit Advertising 169
Other Printed Media 170
Cooperative Advertising 170

Chapter 13: BROADCAST ADVERTISING: RADIO AND TV 172
Radio 172
How Radio Reaches Listeners 172
Eight Tips for Writing Radio Commercials 175
Television 179
When to Use Television 181
Nonbroadcast Commercials 182

Chapter 14: MAYBE YOU SHOULD BE A PUBLISHER: NEWSLETTERS 185
What Is a Newsletter? 185
Types of Newsletters 185
How to Decide If a Newsletter Is Right for You 188

How to Publish a Newsletter	188
How to Write a Newsletter That Will Be Read	190
Tie-ins with the Newsletter	191
How Newsletters Fail	191
Case History: An Art Gallery Newsletter	192

Chapter 15: ON WITH THE SHOW: TRADE SHOWS AND EXPOSITIONS

	195
Trade Shows: A $7 Billion Industry	195
Selecting Trade Shows	196
What to Show at a Show	196
Successful Trade-Show Selling	198
Trade Shows vs. Expositions: Some Definitions	202
Producing the Display	202
A Checklist for Exhibit Managers	204

Chapter 16: A MISCELLANY OF PROMOTIONS

	208
Sales Promotion	208
Business Gifts	212
In-Store Displays	214
Personal Selling	215

Chapter 17: HOW TO MEASURE THE RESULTS OF YOUR PROMOTION

	216
The Purpose of Promotion: Sales	216
What Kind of Results to Expect	217
How to Monitor Your Promotions	218
Case Study: The Handbag Promotion	220
Follow-up	221
How to Test a Promotion Before You Use It	223
Testing Promotions: A Checklist	225
Building a Prospect List	227
Classifying Prospects	229

Appendix: WHERE TO FIND MORE INFORMATION ON MANAGING, FINANCING, AND PROMOTING SMALL BUSINESS

231

INTRODUCTION

"Why are my competitors the ones who always get written about in magazines and newspapers?"

"How can I write a press release that will get the editor's attention?"

"How can I learn some basics about graphic design, printing, brochure writing, and photography so that when I hire someone I'll know what to look for?"

"How can direct mail and mail order help my business?"

"What's the difference between advertising and publicity?"

"Do I need a newsletter?"

"In my newspaper advertising, should I run a big ad once or a small ad many times?"

"How can I bring in new business quickly on a limited promotion budget?"

• • •

These are just some of the questions that entrepreneurs ask us over and over again. Naturally, you'll add some of your own to the list. *How to Promote Your Own Business* was written to give you the answers.

Whether you're a novice or an old hand at running a small business, effective advertising and publicity can be the key to your success. By planning your promotions carefully, and by taking into consideration what has been tried in the past, you can significantly improve your chances of getting publicity—leads—orders—*money!*

How to Promote Your Own Business is a practical, do-it-yourself guide to advertising, publicity, and sales promotion for the small-business owner or manager. The book's numerous examples are drawn from real promotions carried out by real companies, so you can learn from their successes—and failures. We've written the book for the layman, and we've arranged it in an easy-to-use, easy-to-read format. There are numerous step-by-step case histories, checklists, tips, and lists of promotional "dos and don'ts," plus a number of helpful illustrations showing what a finished ad, brochure, or press release looks like. We've collected these examples and illustrations from a wide variety of small businesses—drugstores, florist shops, restaurants, consultants, publishers, travel agents, photographers, caterers, art galleries, and many, many more.

Here's how the book is organized:

Chapters 1–3 present the basics of promotion. They'll help you plan and budget your advertising and publicity program.

Chapters 4–6 tell you how to create your own promotions. They provide tips on copywriting, graphic design, photography, printing, and working with professionals—ad agencies, PR firms, and free-lancers.

Chapters 7–8 explain how you can influence the media to gain free publicity for your product and your business.

Chapters 9–10 cover the basics of direct mail and mail order—today's fastest-growing area of marketing.

Chapter 11 is devoted to sales literature—the brochures, flyers, circulars, and catalogs that almost every business must have in order to sell its products and services.

Chapters 12–13 tell you how to advertise effectively in newspapers, magazines, and directories, and on radio and television.

Chapters 14–16 cover newsletters, trade shows, expositions, and a miscellany of other useful promotional techniques.

Chapter 17 sums it all up, and tells you how to measure the *results* of your promotions so you'll know whether they were successful or not.

Finally, the Appendix lists some further reading in small-business promotion, management, finance, and start-up.

How to Promote Your Own Business will give you the

know-how you need to turn your ideas into action—action that will produce new prospects, new customers, new sales. Simply add your own imagination—and a lot of hard work.

We believe that the hundreds of examples, ideas, tips, and case histories provided in this book will help you gain the recognition that you and your business deserve. We believe that the quality of your promotions reflects the quality of your business and will, in time, lead to success.

Take a look at the sales letters, ads, catalogs, and brochures that cross your desk every day. Some are sharp, clear, crisp, and original. Others are sloppy, or dull and boring, or ill-timed, or misdirected. We want *your* promotions to be the best. We want *you* to have the edge. And that's why we wrote *How to Promote Your Own Business*.

Now, it's up to you.

Chapter 1

WHAT PROMOTION IS ALL ABOUT

Promotion: A Key to Success for Small Business

Each year, American entrepreneurs start a quarter of a million new small businesses—everything from bookstores and bake shops to computer companies and catering services to restaurants and real estate agencies.

Today, there are more than 10.8 million small businesses in the United States.* These growing companies employ 58% of our work force and account for 43% of the U.S. Gross National Product. Small business provides, directly or indirectly, for the livelihood of more than 100 million Americans.

Now for some bad news: Three out of four of the 250,000 new small businesses that start up each year will fail within their first five years, and nine out of ten will fail within ten years. *Of every ten companies going into business today, only one will make it.*

According to Dun & Bradstreet, 95% of these small-business failures are the result of poor management. Many of them are the result of poorly managed—or neglected—*promotion.*

For the small business, a well-planned, properly executed

---

* The U.S. Small Business Administration defines (for the purpose of making loans) small businesses by their income or number of employees. To be defined as "small business," a service business can take in up to $8 million; retail, up to $7.5 million; construction, up to $9.5 million; and wholesale, up to $22 million. A "small" manufacturer must not employ more than 1,500 people.

promotional program can mean the difference between success and failure.

What Is Promotion?

Promotion is communication. It is you telling your potential customers and clients about your business so they will buy your product or service.

Promotion is providing information about those products and services in a way that *persuades* people that they want, need, can use, and should buy them. Promotion is salesmanship—in person, in print, and on the air.

Why You Should Promote Your Business

For the small business, the bottom line of promotion is greater profit through increased sales. Most small-business people feel that any promotion that does not pay for itself many times over (in the profit it brings in from sales) is a waste of time, money, and effort. Fortunately, many promotions *can* justify their expense.

Promotions can benefit you and your business in several different and exciting ways:

- Promotion can sell products directly and immediately. A price-off coupon for orange juice in the Sunday newspaper is a promotion designed to generate a direct sale.
- Promotion can also build awareness among consumers of a company, product, service, idea, or brand name. When you decide to rent a car, you probably think of Hertz, Avis, and possibly Budget—because they *advertise*. Awareness builds sales and businesses over the long run.
- Promotion can establish or change your image. Through promotion, A&P supermarkets became known for high quality and reasonable prices—"Price & Pride." Coca-Cola is "the real thing," GE "brings good things to life," and Westinghouse is "a powerful part of your life." How many small businesses in your area have built their image and rep-

utation using similar slogans and promotions on a smaller scale?
- Promotion can reach many prospects and bring in thousands of qualified sales leads. Sometimes, promotion does not result in a direct sale, but instead helps salespeople make a sale.
- Promotions remind, inform, and persuade your audience.

The Four Types of Promotions

There are four basic types of promotion: personal selling, advertising, publicity, and sales promotion.

1. Personal selling

"Personal selling" is just what the words imply: selling done person-to-person. It is a presentation made by the salesperson to one or more prospects for the purpose of making a sale. The presentation can be made in face-to-face conversation, over the phone, by personal letter, or by wire. When the Avon lady rings your doorbell, *that's* personal selling.

2. Advertising

According to the textbook definition,* advertising is "any paid form of nonpersonal presentation and promotion of ideas, goods, or services by an identified sponsor."

Unlike a letter from your accountant or insurance agent, a local auto dealer's newspaper advertisement is *not* a personal message created for your eyes only. It is a *mass* communication, designed to reach a broad audience. The dealer is identified as an advertiser (the sponsor of the ad). He created the message. And he paid for the space.

Advertising takes many forms. Print advertisements appear

---

* In this case, the textbook is *Marketing Principles: The Management Process,* 2nd ed., by Ben M. Enis (Santa Monica: Goodyear Publishing Company, 1977), pp. 360–365.

in newspapers, magazines, local shoppers, the telephone book, catalogs, directories, programs, menus, and circulars. Signs appear as highway billboards, posters, on buses and subways, and in train stations. The written word can even be delivered as skywriting. And the spoken word is aired as commercials for television and radio.

3. Publicity

Publicity is a kind of free advertising. By providing editors and program directors with news and other information, you can get your business coverage in the media. You do not pay for the coverage, and are not identified as the source of the story—and you have no control over the timing and content of your free publicity. The basic tool of publicity is the press release, and Chapter 7 tells you how to use it to get your name in newspapers and magazines and on radio and television.

4. Sales promotion

Sales promotion encompasses a miscellany of promotional activities. Sales promotion is everything that is not personal selling, advertising, or publicity. Trade shows, product samples, premiums, contests, demonstrations, coupons, "price-off" deals, dealer incentives, point-of-purchase displays, sales brochures, flyers, and direct mail* are all sales promotion.

What Promotion Is Best for Your Business?

Not every business can profit equally from all the different types of promotion. A dry cleaner would benefit very little from sending out a press release, since dry cleaning is not of great interest to the press. An advertisement in a neighbor-

---

* Some authorities classify direct mail as sales promotion; others call it advertising. While it is true that direct mail is a kind of advertising by mail, it doesn't usually require the purchase of space in any media, and so we have chosen to list it under sales promotion.

hood newspaper, however, could bring new customers to the store.

Below we've listed different types of promotions and a few of the types of businesses that have used them with success.

Newspaper ads:
Health care
Apparel
Restaurant
Entertainment
Dry cleaner
Real estate
Tutor
Jeweler
Barber
Beauty parlor
Home furnishings
Limousine service
Gifts
Tailor
Typing service
Bookstore

Local shopper ads:
Kitchenware
Vitamins
Beauty parlor
Exercise clinic
Car rental
Picture framing
Interior design
Clothing
Antiques
Music lessons
Bookstore
Boutique
Optician
Travel agent
Accountant
Liquor store
Bake shop
Locksmith

Local magazine ads:
Department store
Real estate
Clothing
Hotel
Furniture
Restaurant
Entertainment
Exercise clinic
Private club
Auto dealer
Plastic surgeon
Bar or tavern
Disco
Limousine service
Dating service
Stereo systems
Résumé writing
Personal instruction

Telephone directory ads:
Insurance agent
Exterminator
Printer
Photographer
Stationer
Phone answering service
Travel agent
Mover

10 • HOW TO PROMOTE YOUR OWN BUSINESS

Telephone directory ads: (cont.)
Auto dealer
Take-out food
House painter
Physician
Attorney
Pet shop
Roofing contractor
Typing service

Air-conditioning repair
Locksmith
Laundry
Karate instructor
Hardware store
Dentist
Carpet cleaning
Bicycle shop

Television commercials:
Auto dealer
Stereo systems
Restaurant
Racetrack
Vocational training
Home video equipment

Marine equipment
Department store
Tires
Mufflers
Record store
Mail order

Radio commercials:
Furniture
Auto dealer
Ice cream parlor
Entertainment
Bank
Accountant

Restaurant
Health club
Travel agent
Department store
Home improvement
Health care

Direct mail:
Magazine
Newsletter
Consultant
Free-lance artist
Office equipment
Insurance
Advertising agency
Seminar

Coins and stamps for collectors
Clothing
Gifts
Driver training
Cleaning service
Public relations agency

Publicity:
Acupuncturist
Gourmet store
Art gallery
Consultant
Restaurant
Gift shop

Boutique
Handbags
Consumer newsletter
Home-cleaning service
Dating service
Interior design

Brochures, catalogs, or flyers:
Medical products	Industrial manufacturer
Consultant	Handcrafts
Travel agent	Mail order
Advertising agency	Engineering design
Typing service	Construction
Computer store	Educational seminar
Office equipment	Publisher

Newsletters:
Management consultant	Gift shop
Bank	Trade association
Publisher	Business cooperative
Art gallery	Engineering firm

Trade shows and expositions:
Craftsperson	Industrial manufacturer
Antique dealer	Farmer
Jeweler	Automobile dealer
Artist	Boat dealer

You, Too, Can Promote Your Business

Promotion can get your message across and bring in business. It can improve your image, build recognition, and increase sales and profits.

You do not need a great deal of money to succeed at promotion. Hathaway Shirts began advertising with a budget of $30,000; Wrigley's Gum began with only $30.

Promotions work best when they are done to achieve some specific sales or marketing goal. That takes some planning, and planning your promotions is the subject of our next chapter.

• Chapter 2 •

PLANNING YOUR PROMOTIONS

Having a Business Plan

Every business begins with a plan—usually an idea that forms in the mind of an entrepreneur. One idea leads quickly to another, and, before long, a sketch of what the business will be, and who the prospects are, begins to take shape.

This initial flow of ideas is invigorating and may spawn numerous other ideas about how the business will run, but, inevitably, the ideas need to be refined, arranged, and acted upon. A business plan helps form the ideas into a workable program, a systematic way of viewing and reaching your prospects, planning promotions, and defining your business goals.

A simple business plan should cover such points as why the product or service is needed, its potential market, competitors, estimated earnings, and so forth.

Our purpose in this chapter is to discuss some of the marketing aspects of an informal business plan. Using several typical businesses as examples—a gourmet food store called Abbondanza, a typing service, a photography studio, a newsletter publisher—we'll look at key areas of marketing that may help you decide how best to promote your business.

Marketing

Marketing is an aggregate of functions involved in moving goods or services from producer to consumer. This important function involves four elements—the four P's of marketing:

product, price, place (distribution), and promotion. Your marketing strategy will depend on how you define each of these P's in terms of your own business.

Owners of small businesses have limited resources to spend on marketing activities. Concentrating the marketing efforts on one or more key marketing segments is the basis of target marketing. The major ways to segment a market are:

- *Geographic segmentation.* People located close to your place of business are more likely to become customers than those who are far away.
- *Demographic segmentation.* You may choose to market to groups of prospects based on age, race, sex, social class, marital status, or income.
- *Type-of-business segmentation.* Your market may be specific types of businesses (car dealers, hotels, steelmakers, restaurants, computer companies) and organizations (hospitals, universities, federal agencies).
- *Product segmentation.* The market for your products may be determined by how customers will use your product, and what benefits they derive from it. For example, beer brewers know that there are "heavy" beer drinkers who purchase 90% of all beer, and light (not "Lite") drinkers who buy an occasional six-pack. The heavy beer drinkers drink for taste and develop loyalty to a brand; light beer drinkers are likely to buy the low-priced brand.

Know Your Customer

Marketing begins with knowing your customer. A *customer* is someone who purchases your product or service; a *prospect* is a prospective customer. And, although luck may play a role in determining the *actual* people who eventually become your customers, you should nevertheless form a detailed picture of your *typical* customer.

For example, a new gourmet store will primarily appeal to people with a refined palate. The owner would be very foolish if he reasoned that since everyone has to eat, my store has thousands of potential customers. Most people, either because of taste or budget, do not include pâté, French roasted duck, smoked salmon, or watercress dip in their daily menu!

A gourmet store appeals to people who are affluent enough to afford luxury food items and who choose these delicacies over simpler (often less caloric) foods. Naturally, a fine presentation of the food will entice even those on a budget to indulge in the occasional Smithfield ham, caviar spread, or Amaretto cheesecake, but these people are not the devotees, the people who a gourmet store owner hopes will be his steady customers.

In the same way, a photographer who is just starting out may stay alive by shooting the occasional photograph of a child or a wedding, but his real market may be commercial customers. In his business plan, he should estimate the numbers of people whom he can reach who are actively engaged in purchasing the services of a commercial photographer (advertising agencies, public relations agencies, corporations, catalog producers).

When it comes to a neighborhood typing service, the "typical" steady customer is harder to define. Businesspeople may stop in to have a report, manual, or proposal typed quickly and accurately; students want term papers and book reviews typed; writers need their book manuscripts, plays, and screenplays typed in proper form. Each of these customers cares only about his particular needs, and your promotion to each group should speak primarily to those needs.

It may be helpful for you to think of these separate markets in terms of their relative value. Students may bring in the most repeat business, but screenplay writers, page for page, may be your most lucrative market. Also, you may wish to think about which of your submarkets is easiest to service. As with so many businesses, the most lucrative business often requires the most time. For a typing service, businesspeople may be a better market than either students or writers.

After you've been in business awhile, you'll come to have a clearer picture of your typical customer, and that information can be used to focus your promotions. So, if the typing service discovered that the office manager typically was the person at each company who brought in the office's reports, manuals, and proposals, the typing service's owner might think about a promotion aimed at reaching office managers throughout the neighboring business district.

A versatile neighborhood photographer who discovers that his work derives from a variety of sources should define his customers in terms of steadiness as well as how lucrative their business is. If he is engaged to shoot photos of an annual banquet, he should know that it is hardly "bread-and-butter" business. Unless he chooses to specialize in doing banquets, he must orient his business to ongoing clients, people who can be counted on for regular assignments.

Think about each type of customer who purchases your products or services. What do you know about your customers? Where do they live? Are they married or single? How much money do they make each year? You don't have to do a sophisticated marketing survey to help make a realistic assessment as to whether the people you need for your business need you. The better you define your customers' "demographics" and "geographics," the less chance you have of kidding yourself into thinking that, to paraphrase Will Rogers, "I never met a person who didn't like my product."

How Can You Reach Your Customer?

Try to outline realistic methods of reaching your customer. Each business reaches its audience in a variety of ways. For some businesses, a sign over the door is the only way in which they let their potential customers know of their existence. However, considering the unlimited ways in which to use advertising, press releases, articles, flyers, brochures, radio, TV, newspapers, and magazines to help us communicate our message to the public, it seems foolish not to at least explore many possible avenues for exposure.

In the case of our fledgling photographer, he may choose to stimulate interest in his work by circulating a press release focusing on one aspect of his work. In his press release (Fig. 2-1), photographer Tom Okada used his past associations as well as the opening of his new studio as "pegs" upon which to construct the release. By circulating the press release to local newspapers and magazines involved with photography, advertising, and the media, Okada was able to generate interest in his work and gain some publicity.

After writing (or having a publicity-minded friend write) the release, Tom must choose places to send it. If his goals were purely to gain recognition in artistic circles, he might send it only to photographic "arts" magazines. But if he is interested in stimulating business, he will select magazines that reach people who have the power to make a decision to hire him for an assignment, such as fashion magazines or women's magazines.

In the same way, a gourmet-store owner has a variety of promotional options, and must decide upon his goals for a particular promotion. A great deal of care must go into a promotional decision, because the goals sometimes conflict with each other. For example, it would be easy to print 10,000 flyers announcing the store's opening and hire high school students to hand the flyers out throughout the neighborhood. That would certainly get the word out, and it might well bring in customers. But an inexpensively produced flyer might tacitly label the store as "cheap" or, worse, as just another "takeout place." So, although you might gain customers, you wouldn't be gaining the "right" customers—people who are motivated to buy good food, not just curiosity-seekers.

A gourmet-store owner may have to take a long-range view. The owner may want to throw a grand-opening party for the press or try to line up corporate catering business, reasoning that in these ways he will be building a continuing market for his store's food. The critics, once they know of the store, may review the food; if the reviews are good, customers will follow. In the same way, a promotion aimed at food-service people at corporations might result in the catering of several business luncheons or office parties. After that, word of mouth might well take over.

A stenography service that has determined that its prime customers are (1) local businesspeople, (2) out-of-town businesspeople staying at local hotels, (3) screenwriters or playwrights, and (4) job seekers who wish to dictate cover letters to accompany résumés has taken the first step toward reaching these people.

Client:
Tom Okada
45 West 18th Street
New York, NY 10011

Contact:
THE COMMUNICATION WORKSHOP
207 East 85th Street
New York, NY 10028
(212) 794-1144

For Immediate Release:

FORMER APPRENTICE TO MASTER PHOTOGRAPHERS
W. EUGENE SMITH AND ARNOLD NEWMAN
OPENS MANHATTAN STUDIO

NEW YORK, NY—"When you work with a good photographer, you get a lot of good information; when you work with a great one, you receive inspiration." So says Tom Okada, who gained not only inspiration but earned the respect and affection of top photographers Arnold Newman and W. Eugene Smith.

Now, with a versatility and experience few photographers achieve, Okada, 29, has just opened his own photographic studio at 45 West 18th Street in New York.

Since a Newman or a Smith can have his pick of eager photographic assistants, Okada had to prove himself in a number of areas. His portfolio established him as an expert in a number of photographic formats. He's at ease with tungsten as well as strobe lighting; in studio as well as location settings. Okada is also a fine carpenter, and is as exacting building sets as he is in photographing them.

Specializing in "fine-image" still-life photography, Okada hopes to broaden his experience in candid photography, catalog work and general advertising. Says Okada, "A photographer is one artist who can't afford to be a prima donna

—more—

Fig. 2-1 This excerpt from a three-page release shows how a press release arranges thematic material. The central idea (the studio opening) is blended with the photographer's background to give importance to the event.

In the same way, a dating service segments its market by recognizing that there are a number of subgroups within its market, and by approaching each subgroup with a unique angle.

For example, a dating service might wish to send one type of message to gays who are single and a completely different one to senior citizens. Another message could be fashioned for middle-aged singles or recently divorced or widowed singles—assuming that you can separate these people and address them as special groups of people. Mailing lists of people who fit each category may be available from mailing-list brokers, specialty magazines, or associations. By addressing the particular needs of each group separately, you give the impression that your organization specializes in that group's needs. That will go a long way toward making gays or senior citizens or the recently divorced respond to your message.

Direct mail and sales promotion worked for the dating service; a press release worked for Tom Okada; a grand-opening press party helped gain attention for the gourmet store. Other businesses might make use of late-night radio, advertising, or phone calls to prospects. In any case, you should consider the risks, costs, and time demands of all types of promotions before deciding which ones to pursue.

What Do You Want to Say to Your Audience?

The answer: anything that might stimulate them to buy your product or service! You are arranging your product or service's "sales points" in a clear, careful manner. You hope that your customer will seize upon one or more of them and keep them in mind when it comes time to make a purchase.

A dating service that stressed its empathy with being alone and aging might well be remembered by a single senior citizen. On the other hand, a food store or a photography service might have to work hard to truly separate itself from the crowd. Tom Okada drew attention by talking about his unique experience and the singular event of opening his own studio; the food store also uses its opening as an occasion to introduce its products to the public. Perhaps the chef is famous, or the store has a new concept in takeout food. It might be that the store has a dazzlingly beautiful interior or that it specializes in salads or cheesecakes or baby back ribs. To entice the media into writing about the store, the owner must keep in mind that his is one of many similar stores, all craving media attention. Attention will be paid, therefore, to the store that presents itself in the most newsworthy light.

It's not hard to gain publicity for an odd business such as a love-letter-writing service or a breakfast-in-bed catering service that features a strolling violinist, but it is often difficult to gain ongoing publicity for more mundane businesses—beauty parlors, or locksmiths, or plumbers. Therefore, you should consider not just the uniqueness or "sexiness" of the concept of your business, but its ability to grow, to gain new customers, to entice ongoing media coverage or consumer interest.

For many businesses, a sale or a new item or a new location provides the spark for a new promotion. Perhaps a personnel change—a new chef, decorator, or administrator—is noteworthy. The thrust of your promotion remains steady: You are selling quality or service or low cost or all three, and you need to keep reminding the public that you, among your competitors, are best equipped to handle its business. It also helps to just say "thank you" to past customers. A Christmas card is one of the easiest and nicest ways of keeping your name in front of your customers without making a blatant sales pitch.

The Best Way to Say It

Christmas cards lead us to the idea of finding the best way to say what you want us to say. Do you want subtlety or do you want to bang the drum loudly? Subtlety doesn't work for everyone. A new pizza place doesn't want subtle promotion; it wants to tell people that its prices are reasonable, the mozzarella is fresh, and the crust is crusty. A flyer dropped strategically near the mailboxes at a few hundred large apartment buildings in the neighborhood can do the trick. So can posting the flyer at nearby laundromats, supermarkets, and community bulletin boards. Since anyone might crave a pizza, there need not be any targeting of the market, except that the flyers will pull best if they are delivered within walking distance of the pizza place. It would be absurd to spread the flyer to other neighborhoods, because they are likely to have their own pizza parlors.

However, a business selling an expensive service must take great care to hone its promotional messages, and even greater pains to target them to decision-makers. For example, a consultant who sells training seminars in writing or presentation skills must make sure that his written promotions are especially well written, concise, and clear. He, above all others, must avoid redundancy, antiquated phrases, clichés, and self-serving statements. When preparing his promotional message, the consultant must tailor his ideas to fit the interests of his audience.

And who are the audience? They may be training directors who purchase training seminars from outside vendors. Or his message may go to people with similar titles or corporate functions: manager of management development, vice-president of human resources, or vice-president of manpower planning. These people receive numerous sales messages every day, and a consultant must catch attention before he can present his full message. An example of a consultant's sales letter is shown in Fig. 2-2.

How Do You Want Your Customers to Respond?

When a pizza parlor delivers flyers to an apartment house, the pizza purveyor hopes that the flyer will stimulate the reader's appetite, and that the message will translate into the sale of a pizza or at least a meatball hero.

But sometimes sales are not that simple. It would be unreasonable for the writing consultant to expect a person receiving his mailing to pick up a phone and, without gaining more information, order one writing seminar "to go." The writing consultant's package—brochure, cover letter, and return postcard (Figs. 2-3 and 2-4 show a sample brochure cover and return postcard)—aims at stimulating a request for additional information. That's all. There's no expectation of an immedi-

Planning Your Promotions • 21

This year, my business writing seminars will save a large insurance company $50,000. Next year, they'll save the company even more.

Here's how:

Recently I designed and implemented a writing program for twelve supervisors at Mutual of New York. Among the many skills they learned was how to edit the "fat" out of their letters, memos and reports.

We figured out that if each of the twelve trainees cut just one paragraph out of each of their communications, MONY would save 2,400 paragraphs per year. Since each paragraph takes an average of 20 minutes to write, edit, type, read and understand, MONY would save 800 man-hours a year.

Since corporate time costs about $60 per hour, the savings could amount to as much as $50,000 in the first year. And that's a conservative figure.

Why? Because _extra_ dividends are paid in an employee's greater confidence, improved productivity and sharper communication skills as well as in a better corporate image.

Next year, these same twelve people will again save their company $50,000 in wasted words, effort and time–and it won't cost MONY another penny. And, if MONY trains another twelve people, they'll probably save an _additional_ $50,000 a year... every year.

Insurance companies such as MONY and The American Re-Insurance Company, for whom I designed a similar program, must feel I'm doing something right: they've invited me back to help train new groups of employees.

Please take a moment to review the enclosed brochure. If you'd like more information about how improved writing can make your company more productive, just fill out the enclosed card and mail it.

Gary Blake, Ph.D.
Director

**THE
COMMUNICATION WORKSHOP**

207 East 85th Street
New York 10028
(212) 794-1144

Fig. 2-2 Aimed solely at training managers at insurance companies, this cover letter attempts to translate improved writing skills into tangible benefits.

ate sale. If the training manager returns the postcard, he is taking the first step in what may be many steps between the first contact and the final sale. Considering that the price of a seminar is several thousand dollars, it would be foolish to expect a purchase to take place before the prospect calls references, sees the consultant in action at another organization, or asks for a proposal. The true value of a return postcard is its help in building a reliable mailing list of qualified prospects.

When a mail or TV solicitation is used solely to generate immediate sales, we call that direct-response advertising. In this type of advertising, products such as subscriptions, records, books, and cutlery are sold directly to a consumer who, upon hearing or reading the solicitation, writes a check. Perhaps he'll be induced to act quickly because he's been promised a "premium" or gift for speedy action. Keep in mind that the more money your product or service costs, the more so-

THE
COMMUNICATION WORKSHOP

Communication Seminars
for Business

207 East 85th Street
New York, NY 10028
(212) 794-1144

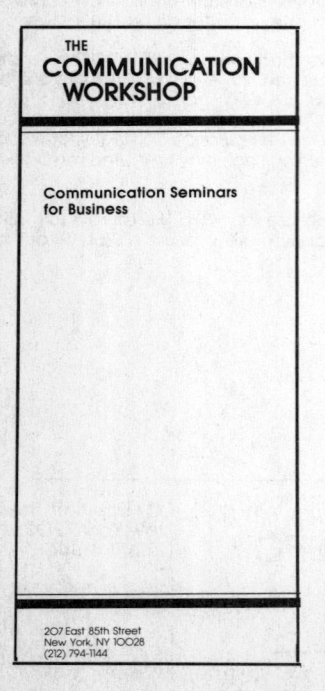

Fig. 2-3 This front panel of a consultant's brochure uses lots of white space to attain a "clean" look. White space also helps the eye rivet on the company name.

```
┌─────────────────────────────────────────────────────┐
│  ☐ We are currently offering training in writing.   │
│  ☐ We are not currently offering training in writing.│
│  Please send me additional information about:       │
│    ☐ The Writing Audit      ☐ Stress Management     │
│    ☐ Effective Business Writing ☐ Persuasive Speaking│
│    ☐ Technical Writing      ☐ Successful Business Meetings│
│  Name_____Organization_____ │
│  Address_____ │
│  Telephone_____ │
└─────────────────────────────────────────────────────┘

┌─────────────────────────────────────────────────────┐
│                                                     │
│                                                     │
│                                                     │
│         THE COMMUNICATION WORKSHOP                  │
│         207 East 85th Street                        │
│         New York, NY 10028                          │
│                                                     │
│                                                     │
└─────────────────────────────────────────────────────┘

Fig. 2-4  The front and back of a return postcard. This card provides the sender with valuable information about an organization's training needs and at the same time helps build a specific mailing list of prospects.

phisticated the promotion must be, and the more times you'll have to contact your prospect before completing the sale.

Your business plan, therefore, charts a course for your business and your promotions. It makes you face the primary question of your business life: What can I do with limited time and money and unlimited imagination and enthusiasm?
```

A plan forces you to think carefully about your product and your prospects, and this chapter has raised a few questions that may arise in your own business plan. A plan forces you to evaluate the number of prospects you have as well as to confront the difference between steady customers and the occasional customer. In order for your business to flourish, you'll probably need to build a base of ongoing customers.

A business plan is the foundation upon which your promotions will be built. If you understand your customer, his needs, his spending habits, and his awareness of the competition, you have taken a step toward leading him to your door.

• Chapter 3 •

HOW TO BUDGET YOUR PROMOTIONS

Promotion Is an Expense

You know you will have to spend some money to execute your advertising and publicity plan. The question is: How much?

Promotion is a gamble. You never know for sure that a given promotion will bring in enough new business to justify the time and money spent to execute the project. When you're running a small operation on a shoestring budget, it takes real guts to allocate a large sum for advertising when you've never advertised before.

Without guidance, setting the annual promotion budget is a task fraught with uncertainty. How do you know that you're not spending too much on promotion? How do you know that you're spending enough? Why not just spend as little as you can get away with? What rational basis do you have for this decision? These are the questions which gnaw at the promotional novice.

There is no magic formula that can easily and precisely set the proper promotion budget for your company. There *are*, however, six time-tested methods that other businesses have used throughout the years to plan their promotion budgets.

Below, we list each budgeting method, and describe its advantages and disadvantages. Each has some merit, and at the end of the list, we suggest how to combine the best of several techniques to plan your budget effectively.

Six Methods for Planning Promotion Budgets

1. Percentage of sales

The most widely used budgeting technique is to set your promotion budget as a fixed percentage of your sales.

Let's say you sell $50,000 in handwoven baskets every year. If you set the promotion budget at 2% of sales, you will allocate $1,000 for promotion.

What sales do you base the percentage on? It's up to you. You can base it on past sales (either last year's sales or an average of the past several years), on future sales (as predicted by your sales forecast), or some combination of past and predicted sales.

What percentage of sales should you choose as the promotion budget? It varies from industry to industry. Defense contractors spend very little on promotion—about 0.15% of sales. Some large consumer companies spend 15%—and more. In 1975, General Motors' advertising budget was 0.6% of sales; General Foods', 6.8%; Carter-Wallace's, 31.4%; Revlon's, 9.2%; Pepsi's, 3.9%; Sears', 1.9%; Procter & Gamble's, 7.9%.

Listed below are some types of small businesses and their typical promotion budgets as a percentage of sales:*

Type of Business	Advertising Budget as a Percentage of Sales
Apparel stores	2.5–3.0%
Auto supply stores	0.5–2.0%
Bars and cocktail lounges	1.0–2.0%
Bookstores	1.5–1.7%
Coin-op laundries	0.6–2.0%

---

* The source for most of these figures is "Advertising Small Business: Small Business Reporter," Bank of America, 1981, vol. 15, no. 2, pp. 10–11.

Type of Business	Advertising Budget as a Percentage of Sales
Gift stores	1.5–2.5%
Hairgrooming/beauty salons	2.5–3.0%
Industrial manufacturers	0.15–3.0%
Printers	0.4–1.0%
Restaurants	0.8–3.0%

As you can see, most small businesses spend between 1% and 3% of their income from sales on advertising and promotion.

The percentage-of-sales method is simple to use, and its major benefit to small business is that these percentage guidelines can tell you whether your budget is reasonable or way out of line.

On the negative side, basing promotional expenditures on sales is somewhat illogical—it implies that promotion is the result of sales when, in fact, sales are the result of promotion.

Also, the percentage-of-sales method does not take into account the economy, the market, the competition, and your own planned sales objectives. Therefore, it is, at best, a rough guideline only—and not the final word.

2. Unit of sales

This variation of the percentage-of-sales method bases promotional expenditures on units of product sold rather than on the gross dollar amount of sales.

Say past experience has taught you that it takes 5 cents worth of promotion to sell one can of baked beans. If your goal is to sell 100,000 cans of beans, you will need to spend $5,000 on promotion.

This method can be helpful when you are selling durable goods of high value, such as television sets and washing machines, or goods of small unit value, such as canned food, toilet paper, and motor oil. It is not a valid approach to setting a budget for a service business.

3. Match the competition

Some companies play follow-the-leader by basing their promotion budget on what their competitors are spending.

It is good business sense to recognize the importance of competition. But, by matching your competitors' promotions dollar for dollar,* you assume they are trying to achieve the same sales and marketing objectives as you are—and that is probably false. Besides, your competitors may not know how to budget and execute promotions effectively, in which case you would be mimicking their errors.

By all means, pay attention to the competition. But don't follow them automatically. Instead, come up with a plan that suits your goals, your company, your products, and your marketing philosophy.

4. All you can afford

With the all-you-can-afford method, you first appropriate money for essential operating expenses: rent, raw material, taxes, insurance, labor, postage, inventory. Whatever is left over is allocated to the promotion budget.

This technique can help fledgling business ventures survive. But if you are past the stage where you're struggling just to pay the landlord, avoid the all-you-can-afford method, because it implies that promotion is a luxury and not an essential part of running a growing business. And chances are, if you are reading this book, that is not the case.

5. Historical

The easiest way to set a promotion budget is to say, "Let's spend what we spent last year—plus 10% for inflation."

This method has essentially the same advantages and disadvantages as the percentage-of-sales method. Use it as a rough guideline only.

---

* Of course, if a competing firm is much larger than you are, you can't possibly match its budget dollar-for-dollar. But you *could* spend what it's spending on a percentage-of-sales basis.

6. Objective and task

This is the most effective method: to define the sales and marketing objectives that promotion should accomplish, and then appropriate the budget needed to achieve these objectives.

Let's say a free-lance graphic artist wants to promote his services, and that his *sales objective* is to earn $30,000 by getting assignments from a dozen or so different advertising agencies.

The *task* that can best accomplish this objective is a direct-mail campaign aimed at ad-agency creative directors. Thus, his simple promotion budget would look like this:

Sales Objective	Task	Cost
To get $30,000 in work from 10–15 different ad agencies	Direct mail to 1,000 creative directors	$500
	Phone follow-up	$50
	Second mailing to 1,000 creative directors	$250
	TOTAL BUDGET:	$800

Methods 1 through 5 set a budget, and then allocate funds for specific tasks. The objective-and-task method takes the more logical approach of building a budget based on the tasks you want to complete. It ensures that promotional dollars are spent on those projects that will most benefit your business.

A disadvantage of the objective-and-task method is that the budget will probably be much more than you can afford. If that happens, you must rank objectives in order of importance, and concentrate on those at the top of your list.

One Sensible Solution

None of these six methods—percentage of sales, unit of sales, match the competition, all you can afford, historical, or objective and task—is the absolute ideal way of setting a promotion budget.

Rather, a combination of several techniques seems to work best. We recommend the following three-step method for budgeting promotions:

1. Use the percentage-of-sales method (number 1) to set upper and lower limits on your budget. An industrial manufacturer with sales of $600,000 should, according to the list given earlier, be spending somewhere between $900 (0.15% of sales) and $18,000 (3% of sales) on promotion.

2. Pay attention to what your competitors are doing, but don't copy them blindly. If one widget maker triples his trade-journal advertising, the others may lose sales to him unless they do something. This something may be an increase in advertising. Or it may be a price reduction, a product improvement, a penetration into a new market or application, or any one of a number of non-advertising items.

3. Now that you know what the competition is doing and have established a minimum and maximum budget, allocate money to complete tasks that will achieve your planned objectives (objective-and-task, method number 6). Be sure not to spend more than you can afford, and don't underspend, either.

More Budgeting Tips

Here are some more helpful hints on how to set a promotion budget:

- *Be flexible.* If the economy fluctuates, if you develop a new product, or if your major competitor goes out of business, you may change your promotion strategy—and your promotion budget—in midyear. Remember, a budget is not a commandment cast in stone; it is a tool to help you control promotional expenditures. Don't be afraid to change the budget to suit your changing needs.

- *Set priorities.* The majority of small businesses can't afford to do even half the promotions they'd like to do. Therefore, you need to rank your objectives, and concentrate on high-priority projects.

- *Make it manageable*. Large promotion budgets can be broken down by product, department, division, store, sales territory, or market. Or any combination of these.
- *Use the calendar*. Some small businesses set budgets by the year; others by the quarter; a few by the month. Don't neglect seasonal promotions when setting the budget. A greeting-card wholesaler would spend more money in December than in any other month, because Christmas-card sales are the lifeblood of that industry.
- *Spend money to make money*. Be prepared to spend more than the usual percentage of sales if you are introducing a new product or trying to break into a new market. It costs more to promote the new than to maintain the status quo. In Holland, a food company coming out with a new salad dressing set a promotion budget that was *three times* the product's projected sales for the next two years.
- *Expect the unexpected*. Put a 10% contingency fund in the promotion budget. It is difficult to estimate all promotion costs precisely, and many companies find themselves going over budget by as much as 10%.

Promotion Budgets in a Down Economy

When money is tight, it is only natural to cut back on expenses; after all, the employees must be paid and the shelves filled with merchandise before you can indulge in a costly radio campaign.

However, *Magazine Age* reports that in 1982, a year of severe recession, nearly 60% of all industrial manufacturers planned to *increase* their advertising budgets by an average of 27%. Only 6% of the manufacturers planned to cut back on their advertising expenditures.

Although it is tempting to panic at the first sign of a slump in the economy, there is wisdom in not slashing the promotion budget when money becomes tight. Consider, for example, these findings from some recent articles in the *Harvard Business Review:*

- Increased advertising during a recession will still result in increased sales. The increase in sales will be greater than that of competitors who do not increase their ad budgets.

- If you choose to reduce your advertising budget, your sales will probably fall off *even more sharply than the sales of those firms which do no advertising at all!*
- Promotion can stimulate consumer demand for products even in hard times.

Surprisingly, the nation's total "disposable income" (the amount of money consumers can spend on products and services) does not fall more than a percentage point or so during a recession.

• • •

Should it become necessary to cut the budget, eliminate low-priority items. Concentrate on the promotions vital to your continued sales success. Stick with proven promotions you know will work, and save experimentation for better times.

Also, see if you can find a less expensive way of doing things—a thinner paper stock for your brochures, a smaller newspaper ad, a shorter television commercial.

• Chapter 4 •

WHEN TO HIRE A PROFESSIONAL—AND WHEN TO DO IT YOURSELF

Few of us in small business have the time to become expert in the many skills needed to produce effective advertising and promotions, and so the question is raised: Should you hire an advertising agency or public relations firm to handle all this, or can you do it yourself?

There are some small businesses that use such agencies to handle their promotions. Other entrepreneurs create the bulk of their promotions in-house. Most small businesses, however, use a combination of staff and outside services. These outside services are provided by advertising and public relations agencies, graphic design studios, and free-lance writers, artists, photographers, and publicists.

Advertising Agencies

Advertising agencies provide advertisers with a wide range of communications services: copywriting, art, production, media planning and buying, market research, sales promotion, and public relations.

The very words "advertising agency" are a turn-off to most small-business managers. They conjure up images of Madison Avenue at its worst: three-martini lunches, plush conference rooms, elaborate creative presentations, golf-playing account executives, and other evils that waste clients' time and money.

Yes, it's true that Madison Avenue agencies probably aren't for you. For starters, their "creative time" (copywriting, artwork, planning) goes for about $125 an hour and more. (Even medium-size New York agencies are getting $75 an hour.)

Worse, your company will get lost in the shuffle at a large agency. Let's say the agency does $20 million a year. Assuming the agency would even talk to you, how much attention will you get if you spend $200,000 or $20,000?

(As an interesting aside, industry sources note that major advertising agencies will devote three members of their staff to your account full-time for every *million* dollars you spend.)

This doesn't mean that there isn't an ad agency out there that's right for you. The advertising business has more than its fair share of entrepreneurs—small agencies ranging from one- or two-person shops to those with perhaps a dozen or so employees. Many of these small advertising agencies do work that rivals the creative excellence of Madison Avenue—and costs far less. A six-man agency in New York, for example, bills creative time at $60 an hour, while a one-man shop in Akron charges $20 an hour. In addition, small agencies often distinguish themselves from their giant competitors by specializing in a particular area such as medical, financial, dental, corporate, retail, fashion, or industrial advertising. A small specialty agency can be ideal for a small business.

Should You Use an Advertising Agency?

Do you need the highly professional and somewhat costly services of an advertising agency? Or can you do things less expensively and better yourself? Here's a list of dos and don'ts to help you decide:

• *Do* use an agency if effective advertising is crucial to your success, and if you feel you can afford the going rates.

• *Do* consider using an agency if you spend $10,000 or more a year on promotion. That's probably the minimum amount it will take to interest even the smallest agency in handling your account.

• *Don't* hire an agency because you're trying to cut costs. Getting outside help is almost always more expensive than doing it yourself.

When to Hire a Professional—and When to Do It Yourself • 35

- *Don't* hire an agency solely because "you don't have time to do it yourself." Yes, the agency will free your time for other tasks. But when you hire an agency, you're hiring creativity coupled with marketing expertise—and not just another pair of hands.
- *Do* hire an agency if your company is marketing-oriented.
- *Do* hire an agency if you intend to use its services to full advantage.
- *Do* hire an agency for fresh thinking, outside objectivity, and a more creative approach to promotions.
- *Do* hire an agency if you need help planning promotions, introducing new products, and selecting target markets.
- *Do* hire an agency to do things "first-class."
- *Don't* hire an agency if you are certain that only *you* know the best way to promote your business, and that outsiders can *never* make useful suggestions in this area.
- *Don't* avoid hiring an agency because you want to save its 15% commission by placing your ads and commercials with the media yourself. Studies show that after taking into account administrative and staff costs, buying media yourself saves only 4.5%—not 15%.
- *Don't* feel you must hire an outside agency for prestige when your company becomes big. Ralston Purina, General Electric, Pfizer, Scott Paper, and Lever Brothers all have sizable in-house advertising departments.

If you decide to hire an agency, you need to know how to select the one that's right for your business.

How to Select an Advertising Agency

Here are six useful tips for selecting the advertising agency that can best serve your company:

1. **Choose an ad agency with expertise in your area.**

Accountants, brokers, and banks should select an advertising agency that specializes in financial accounts. A manufacturer of globe valves for petroleum refineries should choose an agency with industrial-advertising expertise. A designer of men's swimwear would do best to seek counsel from an agency with other fashion accounts.

By insisting that your agency already be somewhat expert in your industry, you save yourself the costly and time-consuming process of educating its staff from scratch. One warning: Make sure the agency does not have any of your competitors as clients. A conflict would surely arise.

2. Do not hire an agency with more capabilities than you need.

Do you really need an agency with overseas branch offices, television-production capabilities, a market research department, and clout with nationwide print and broadcast media? All of an agency's clients pay to support its complete operations—so, to save money without sacrificing service or quality, select an agency that offers only those communications services you need. Which, at the very least, will likely be copywriting, print production, and media buying.

3. Make sure the agency is the right size for you.

A $20,000 account represents only 0.1% of a $20 million agency's income, and consequently will receive only 0.1% of its management attention and 0.1% of its creative effort. Make sure your agency is small enough to consider your account profitable and worth its best efforts.

4. Ask to see the agency's work.

Examine a prospective agency's portfolio of ads, brochures, and catalogs. Do you like what you see? Is it the kind and caliber of work you want done? Avoid agencies whose work is either too shabby or too elegant for your market, business, and taste.

When to Hire a Professional—and When to Do It Yourself • 37

5. Make sure the agency is sympathetic with the needs of small business.

Explain to prospective agencies that your goal is to create promotions that increase sales—and not to win advertising awards.

Tell them your money is limited. Tell them you want an ad to pull inquiries or generate sales, not to look pretty on the page or read like a poem.

Let them know what you expect. If you want the agency to design and produce letterhead, business cards, signs, brochures, price sheets, mail stuffers, and flyers, say so. Not every agency will handle these small assignments.

6. Check out the price.

Most smaller agencies collect a 15% commission for placing ads with the media, and charge a flat project fee for creating advertisements and other promotions. This fee is usually based on some hourly rate for agency time.

Ask what they typically charge to produce a quarter-page black-and-white newspaper ad, a four-page brochure, a 30-second radio commercial. It may be more than you want to pay.

Public Relations Agencies

Public relations agencies are the professionals to turn to when you want to get coverage in the media.

Now, sending out a press release or calling up a local editor are two things anyone can do—you don't need to be a specialist to practice public relations. So why hire a PR agency? Here's what you buy when you contract for their services:

• *Media contacts.* Frequently, a PR man will wink slyly and promise that he can "get you" the *Wall Street Journal* or the *Boston Globe.* This is an unprofessional attitude and an exaggeration; editors are not tools of PR agents, and no PR pro can guarantee favorable coverage of your story in the press. Nevertheless, most PR professionals do have relationships with members of the press, and they can use their contacts to place stories in the media. This is what makes them valuable to you, the client.

• *Expertise.* Public relations agents are expert at writing, planning, timing, and executing publicity campaigns. While novices tend to be unstructured and haphazard in their PR efforts, professionals can plan and execute a campaign that supports marketing strategy.

Most public relations firms charge their clients a monthly retainer for their services; a typical monthly retainer can be $1,000 and up. Therefore, most small businesses are better off finding a small PR agency to do work on a project basis, or handling public relations in-house.

Graphic Design Studios

Most small businesses rely on print promotions—posters, signs, pamphlets, ads, point-of-purchase displays, coupons, and brochures—to reach their customers and prospects.

Graphic design studios do not, as a rule, offer media, marketing, writing, and PR services. They are simply the experts in designing and producing print material. (For more information on producing print promotions, see Chapter 6.)

Some small-business managers have a good grasp of sales and marketing, know their business well, write lucid copy, and understand the basic promotional tools. They just need help turning their ideas into polished print material, and the graphic design studio can provide that help.

Graphic design studios usually offer two hourly rates: a "design" rate for the creative work of designing the format and special look of your promotions, and a lower "mechanical" rate for the more straightforward task of physically pasting up type, illustrations, and photos for the printer.

The rates vary according to where your business is located. In Manhattan, a city that may have more working graphic artists than anywhere in the United States, the design rate ranges from $40 to $60 an hour and up and the mechanical rate from $10 to $25 an hour or so.

Free-lancers

Many creative types in promotion—especially writers, artists, photographers, and publicists—work as free-lancers serving both advertisers and advertising agencies.

Free-lancers are capable of delivering the same high-quality work as advertising and PR agencies at a fraction of the cost. Using free-lancers can be the least expensive way of getting professional help to create your promotions.

Before hiring a free-lancer, check his résumé, portfolio, and client list. Find out his rates, and get a written estimate in advance. Most important, make sure you like (or at least can tolerate) the free-lancer *as a person*. With advertising agencies, an account executive separates you from the writer or artist. With free-lance help, you deal with the creator of your promotion directly. If you are to have a successful collaboration with the free-lancer, you must be able to work well together.

How to Work with Professional Help

You've looked at your checkbook, looked with dismay at your current promotion campaign, and made a major decision: You want your promotions to be first-class, and you've decided to get professional help—an advertising agency, a PR firm, a graphic design studio, or a free-lancer.

Here, then, are some helpful hints for getting the best work out of your outside supplier with the least amount of trouble:

1. Brief your agency.

The more your advertising agency knows about your product, your company, and your markets, the better. Tell your agency what makes your product unique. Explain its advantages over the competition's products. Explain your marketing strategy. Provide background material in the form of current ads and press releases, brochures, articles on your industry, and market-research reports. The best clients prepare comprehensive agency briefings *in writing*.

2. Do not compete with your agency in the creative area.

Certainly you can disapprove of the brochure copy your copywriter turns in. Make helpful criticisms, and turn it back to him for a revision. But do not tell outside talent how to do the job. If you can write better than the writer and take better pictures than the photographer, then fire them and do it yourself.

3. Don't strain your promotions through many layers of approval.

You, and possibly your business partner, should approve or disapprove the work submitted by the outside agency. But don't look for approval from your purchasing agent, your accountant, your cashier, and your mother-in-law. Too many levels of approval will muddy clear writing and water down the impact of the message. Worse, it will dampen the creative spirit of your writers or artists so that the next thing they do will be mediocre enough to get your company's approval *instantly*.

4. Be reasonable about paying.

It is difficult to make a good profit in advertising, and many agencies and free-lancers have gone out of business waiting for late payments from their clients. Be fair to your agencies and free-lancers, and pay them promptly.

By all means, watch expenses carefully and don't pay for something you never asked for in the first place. On the other hand, too much haggling over money can cause your outside professionals to put forth less effort on your account. You will get, then, a competent promotion, but not a great one.

Where to Find Help

You want to hire an agency or free-lancer, but don't know where to turn. The following mini-directory of creative talent should be of some assistance:

- *Standard Directory of Advertising Agencies: The Agency Red Book,* published by the National Register Pub-

When to Hire a Professional—When to Do It Yourself • 41

lishing Company, Inc., 5201 Old Orchard Road, Skokie, IL 60077. This directory lists 4,400 advertising agencies here and overseas. For each agency, the *Red Book* reports agency income, number of employees, key accounts, and the addresses and phone numbers of its offices. There is also a useful index listing agencies by state. The *Red Book* is available in most libraries.

• *O'Dwyer Directory of Public Relations Firms,* 271 Madison Avenue, New York, NY 10016. Lists 1,200 PR firms. Available in most libraries.

• *The Creative Black Book,* published by Friendly Publications, Inc., 401 Park Avenue South, New York, NY 10016. Lists thousands of photographers, illustrators, graphic designers, printers, TV producers, ad agencies, and other creative resources. Available by mail order through the publisher and in some major bookstores.

• *Adweek Creative Services Directories,* published by *Adweek,* 820 Second Avenue, New York, NY 10017. Similar in scope to the *Black Book,* the *Adweek Creative Services Directories* list photographers, artists, illustrators, designers, printers, and other creative resources. The *Adweek Directories* are published in five regional editions (East, Southeast, Midwest, Southwest, and West), and can be purchased from the publisher.

• *Public Relations Journal,* a monthly magazine published by the Public Relations Society of America, 845 Third Avenue, New York, NY 10022. Many PR agents offer their services each month in the classified ads section of this journal.

• Also, check your local Yellow Pages for listings under "Advertising Agencies," "Public Relations Agencies," "Graphic Design Studios," "Illustrators," "Writers," "Copywriters," "Artists," and "Photographers."

• Chapter 5 •

HOW TO WRITE COPY THAT SELLS

What Is Copy?

The word "copy" refers to the text of an article, advertisement, press release, brochure, flyer, or almost anything else that is written.

Copy is writing. It is used to inform, to entertain, to persuade, and to sell. Although advertising copywriters are paid to write copy that will catch attention and sell products, they do not have a monopoly on copywriting skill. In fact, with a little practice, you can write copy for your promotions.

Good copy sets your promotions apart from the crowd, and therefore it's easy to understand why professionals are often needed to add their talents to a commercial, a brochure, a solicitation letter, or a flyer. Yet, if you are willing to take a look at what makes for good copy, and are willing to learn to distinguish effective copy from uninteresting, sloppy, or boring copy, you'll be taking the first long step toward creating your own promotions.

In this chapter, we'll concentrate on how style, taste, structure, and human insight—as well as the specific sales points of your product or service—can be united to make exciting, original copy that helps motivate people to buy whatever you're selling.

All of the hints and ideas we'll discuss are mentioned in the context of persuading people to take an interest in a product or service. Although one could spend a chapter focusing solely on beer-advertisement headlines or press releases announcing sales at retail stores, this chapter attempts to discuss elements of persuasive writing as they apply to a wide gamut of promotions.

The Sales Sequence

Meeting a person, dating, and getting engaged are parts of a sequence of activities resulting in a wedding. In the same way, a sale is the final step in a sequence of activities. Recognizing this fact, we should attempt to understand just what steps compose the sequence, and how one step leads to another. The steps usually involved are:

1. Getting attention for your product or service
2. Showing that a need exists for it
3. Convincing prospects that your product or service satisfies the need
4. Requesting action or belief for the ideas you've set forth

Let's examine each part of this sequence:

1. Getting attention

People get attention in a variety of ways. Some ask questions; others shout. Other people say startling things, or use humor, conflict, sex, or suspense. Your job is to capture the attention of your reader, suggest an element of your sales message, and motivate the reader to continue reading. It would certainly capture attention if an air-conditioner manufacturer used a semiclad woman to gain attention for his ad, but it would also be irrelevant and perhaps even tasteless.

However, a bold thought or a "teaser" may well "hook" a reader. A travel agent used the following headline in a flyer: "When You Travel, You Don't Need a 'Super-Saver,' You Need a Super Travel Agent." That headline caught people's attention and led them naturally to the *body copy* (text following the headline). Another headline that is bound to catch attention is "You've Just Taken Your Last Food Binge." It practically compels the reader to read on and learn more about the diet plan being advertised.

2. Showing a need

After you've gained attention, you need to show your readers that they have a need for your product. You do this by empathizing with their situations, their feelings. A public relations firm found a way to gain attention and show a need in the opening passage from the letter to an executive search firm (Fig. 5–1).

This opening waves a red flag in front of the executive recruiter, a person who is probably sensitive to the word "headhunter." Using this highly charged word, the writer carefully allies himself with the reader. After accomplishing that, he can then pose, subtly, a hypothetical question, one which he'll delight in answering.

3. Convincing Prospects

Once you've pointed to a customer's need—for a book, a subscription, a pizza, photographs, anything—you must be prepared to step forward and *convince* him that you can *satisfy* the need. In simplified form, here is how a pizza parlor's flyer convinces you that Tony's pizza will satisfy you:

(Attention)	TONY'S PIZZA—OLD-FASHIONED FLAVOR YOU'LL LOVE
(Showing a Need)	Tired of pizza with soggy crust, skimpy cheese, and too few pepperonis?
(Conviction)	At Tony's, you'll love our pizza because the crust is thick. So's the cheese. And the pepperoni!

You have stepped forward to answer a need and to help the reader better visualize how your product will meet the need. Tony's pizza answers his neighborhood's need for good pizza, but it also paints a picture of how his pizza achieves perfection.

Similarly, if you were applying for a job, your cover letter would go beyond stating your belief that you could do the job. You'd probably point out several things you could do that would make you an asset to the employer. It gives the em-

Dear Mr. Thomas:

Some people think of all executive search firms as "headhunters." They're wrong. The only heads you search for are attached to people who have talent, experience, and the will to succeed. But how do you tell corporate recruiters, job-seekers, and other professionals that your firm is a cut above the rest?

Sales letters are a simple, inexpensive, attention-getting method of keeping your name in front of the people you want to reach. And that's where we come in.

We're Mann & Mann, a publicity and sales promotion company with special expertise in direct mail for executive search firms. We know that whether you're sending a cover letter to accompany a recent article in <u>Business Week</u> or a "keep in touch" letter to current clients, every word counts—as you can see by reading this letter and our flyer.

If you'd like to see samples of our work, call us. We think you'll like our style.

Sincerely,

Fred A. Heyward
Director of Sales

Fig. 5-1 This letter follows the sales sequence and culminates in a call for action: "Call us."

ployer an image of exactly how you would help him solve his business problems.

The sales points of a typing service's flyer were selected, arranged, and bulleted to allow the customer to make a mental picture of each service:

- Work guaranteed when promised
- Pickup and delivery
- Experience with proofreaders' marks
- Typists who specialize in financial and legal typing as well as in tape transcriptions

The public relations agency that was pitching its services to the executive recruiting firm used the following passage to help the reader gain an image of the writer's potential value:

... whether you're sending a cover letter to accompany a recent article in *Business Week* or a "keep in touch" letter to current clients, every word counts ...

4. Requesting action

Practically every flyer, TV commercial, sales letter, or catalog ends with an appeal to take action. A sales letter from a consultant may ask the reader to send for more information. A TV ad for a set of recordings or books might end with the phrase "Call this toll-free number." A magazine solicitation letter might ask you to fill out a coupon and place an order. Other promotions may call for other responses, but the message is the same: Believe us! Take action!

Just as a wedding invitation ends with an RSVP, an ad for a restaurant might conclude: "Come tonight and let us make your dinner a real feast!" A brochure for a new directory might be more abrupt: "Complete the reverse side of this form and mail to ..."

Headlines

Just as a newspaper headline catches our attention, the headline of an advertisement, flyer, or direct-mail piece is meant to capture the prospect's attention. The only difference is that advertising headlines may use a wide assortment of interesting gambits that would be inappropriate for gaining attention in the non-advertising sections of newspapers.

After capturing our attention, an effective headline will make us want to read further. It will make us hungry for more information.

Also, a headline selects prospects; it sends a signal to your customer. A headline involving "The Great American Cannoli" will whet the appetite of pastry-lovers. A dating service will attract a single person's attention with a headline like "Need a Date?" A newspaper scored a success with the inventive headline: "You can't judge a book by its cover but you should judge a newspaper by its coverage." Not every headline focuses on a particular type of prospect, but many concentrate on specific purchasers: women, children, smokers, beer drinkers, swingers, housewives, business people.

Here are a few generic types of headlines:

1. The how-to headline

A how-to headline offers the promise of specific, practical information: how to eat and still stay slim, how to choose a writing consultant, how to turn your old coins into new gold. The how-to headline need not contain the words "how-to." A how-to headline might be phrased: "Five Secrets of Successful Pasta," "The Secret of Solar Power," or "Advice to Halloween Party Givers."

The how-to headline is informational, even educational, and it offers the reader the allure of real information instead of ballyhoo.

2. The question headline

Just as rhetorical questions help a speaker gain attention, a question headline pulls the reader into the ad copy.

You're probably familiar with headlines that go "Tired of the Same, Boring Breakfast Cereal?" or "Would You Like to Make $500 Per Week Operating a Word Processor?" If the headline raises a question that will be explored in the body copy, and if the headline is not designed to mislead the reader, a question headline can be very effective.

3. The reason-why headline

"Three Reasons Why Small Businesses Avoid Public Relations Firms" is an example of the reason-why headline. This type of headline is effective for new companies that must explain their product or service in short order. It is also wise to use this type of headline when you are trying to distinguish your service from those of your competitors.

Essentially, this is the same type of headline as those that guarantee a service. Take the famous Lee Myles slogan "You'll Never Pay for Another Muffler as Long as You Own Your Car." The ad goes on to explain the reasons why Lee Myles can make this claim, and the reasons why you should choose Lee Myles.

4. The command headline

The command headline commands you to take notice by telling you to take action. A hair stylist might use a command headline such as "Take Care of Your Hair and It Will Take Care of You"; a copy shop announces, "Be a Copy Cat"; a dental group's headline reads, "Save Your Teeth."

5. The direct headline

This type of declarative headline has a news feeling to it, and it promises the reader something fresh and important. It can be as simple as "Sale! Everything Marked Down 50 Percent" to "Wait! You Can Earn Money in Your Spare Time" or "The Future Card: Never Spend Cash Again."

6. The indirect headline

As the name suggests, the indirect headline sneaks up on you. It could be a predicament: "You're alone in a city and you've lost your wallet . . ." Or it could be a word play such as that used by the co-authors of a book on technical writing: "When It Comes to Technical Writing, We Wrote the Book."

Characteristics of Good Headlines

How do you know when you've written a good headline? You'll know. You'll know through experience and through instinct. You'll know because the people you show it to will respond well to it.

Let's recapitulate some of the characteristics of good headlines:

Good headlines send a signal to particular prospects for the kind of product or service you are advertising. They also promise the reader that he will benefit from your business; they do this by building a bridge to your reader's self-interest.

If possible, you should include the selling promise in your headline ("Are You Sick and Tired of Being Sick and Tired?") and you should try to end your headline with a lure to read on ("An Effective Business Writing Program Will Save Your Organization Time and Money. Here's How:").

Avoid "blind" headlines—the kind that mean nothing unless you read the body copy underneath them. (Examples of blind headlines are "Britannia Waves the Rules" and "What's Black and White and Read All Over?") Studies show that 80% of your readers will read only the headline and not the body copy. Therefore, ads with blind headlines waste 80% of your advertising dollars.

Headlines are usually stated in the affirmative, and for good reason: Negative words, no matter what they are leading up to, set a negative tone. Examples of negative headlines are "Don't Rely on Just Any Security System" and "We Have Never Had a Complaint About Our Food."

Finally, keep obscure references out of your headline altogether. Here are two examples of obscure headlines, or, at least, headlines that test a reader's knowledge of a particular allusion: "See Rodney Dangerfield—the Mouth That Roared" and "At LeDisco, You Can Always Depend Upon the Kindness of Strangers" (a reference to the last line of Tennessee Williams' play *A Streetcar Named Desire*).

Body Copy

Body copy can take a variety of approaches; it can be factual, or fanciful, or descriptive. It can rely on testimonials, or it can tell a story. It can even be written in dialogue. It all depends on what you're selling, who your audience is, and what approach will catch attention and be persuasive.

Body copy has no predetermined length, but conciseness is always a virtue.

You can't afford to waste the impact of the headline by taking your time to get to the point in the body copy. As you would in other writing, it's wise to be as specific and concrete as possible, putting an enthusiastic, factual, and friendly tone into the words and ideas.

As for gaining believability, your promotions may be helped by the use of testimonials. When Joe DiMaggio speaks up for Mr. Coffee or for New York City's Bowery Savings Bank, he is lending his personal persuasion to the product. Why Joe DiMaggio for a bank? Perhaps it's because DiMaggio seems prosperous thirty years following his retirement from baseball. The reader or listener makes the subtle connection that Joe saved wisely for his golden years . . . at the Bowery. Also, the Bowery is a part of New York City, while Joe DiMaggio also has a strong identification as part of New York City.

Finding that best person to give a testimonial for your product or service is an art. There is no rule of thumb, except that the person must be trustworthy and be recognized by your prospects. Joe DiMaggio would not make a good pitchman for candy because the youngsters today might not know his name half as well as they know the names of Reggie Jackson, George Foster, and Sugar Ray Leonard.

Three other tips on writing effective body copy: Don't try to be entertaining (it often doesn't work); write your ads in everyday language (so that everyone understands), and give the reader advice that is both helpful and useful.

CASE HISTORY: The Travel-Agency Flyer

A travel agency commissioned a small PR firm to write a flyer to help stimulate new business. The one-page flyer had one purpose: to attract business. But how could the agency make itself distinctive when all travel agencies offer the same basic services?

When the public relations people started learning about the breadth of those services, they decided to write a flyer stressing the services. They designed a flyer that made no outrageous claims, nor did it try to distinguish the travel agency from its competitors. What it did do was concisely list the main services provided by good travel agencies, and then end the flyer with the travel agent's name, company name, address, and phone number. It was felt that an upbeat, specific, and educational flyer would prompt people to hold on to it, to tack it to bulletin boards and keep it in desk drawers.

The flyer (Fig. 5-2) shows an effective use of a headline, and a thoughtful arrangement of sales points, even though the sales points pertain to all agents. The flyer relies on short sentences and short paragraphs to keep the reader reading.

The flyer has yielded dozens of responses.

Ten Tips on Copywriting Technique

The following tips will help you sharpen your copywriting skills and create more effective promotions:

1. **Have a "you" orientation.**

Copywriters know that the word "you" may well be the most important word in their vocabulary. By thinking of the *reader's needs* first, a good copywriter never confuses his own biases or irrelevant sales points with appeals that will touch the lives of his audience. An acting teacher who, in a sales flyer, goes into a detailed description of where he studied acting before even describing the class he's offering is hardly taking a "you" orientation. He's simply flexing his ego. In the same way, when a school for reflexology presents a program called "Diagnoses East/West," it has lost sight of the fact that people need to be *introduced* to what reflexology is before they can absorb the implications of the program's title.

2. **Slogans help readers and listeners remember.**

"Pan Am Makes the Going Great," "GE: We Bring Good Things To Life," and "American Express: Don't Leave

When You Travel, You Don't Need A "Super-Saver," You Need A Super Travel Agent.

Here's Why:
1. **Their service is free.**
   You don't pay one penny more for your trip when you let a travel agent arrange it. Travel agents earn their fees from hotels and airlines, not travelers.
2. **They'll take the confusion out of complex fares.**
   Their job is to help you understand your travel alternatives, and discover which is truly the most economical and convenient.
3. **They save you time and money.**
   They make all your reservations. You save time and don't run up your phone bill. They'll contact the hotels, arrange for a car and even help you choose a cabin on a cruise ship.
4. **They're travel experts.**
   They know about most destinations because they've been there themselves. So they'll help you decide what to pack, where to stay, what to see, and where to eat.
5. **They're aware of money-saving travel plans.**
   They have up-to-the-minute information about mid-week excursions, night flights and a variety of special "package" vacations.
6. **They do the ticketing.**
   A travel agent can write your ticket for you—whether you're going to Madison, Wisconsin or Madagascar. They can also arrange for a pre-paid ticket to be left for you at the airport.
7. **They'll arrange for special service.**
   Don't feel limited to the usual airline menu. If you like, a travel agent will arrange a vegetarian, seafood, dietetic or kosher meal, as well as arrange for a seat in a smoking or non-smoking section.
8. **They're sensitive to special business needs.**
   They know that executives of each industry have specific travel requirements. Travel agents are able to provide the type of V.I.P comforts busy travelers demand.
9. **They accept all major credit cards, and are available during business hours.**
   Like your lawyer or your doctor, your travel agent is a consultant, someone you can trust with the personal details of your travel arrangements.

"We believe in going the extra mile"

BON BON TRAVEL, INC.
Roger Smith Hotel ● Suite 205 ● 501 Lexington Avenue ● New York, N.Y. 10017 ● (212) 752-7384

Fig. 5-2 This flyer takes a low-key, informative approach. By giving the reader useful information instead of mere sales talk, the flyer suggests that the owners of the agency are not just travel agents but highly informed spokespeople of the travel industry.

Home Without It" are examples of catchy slogans. These pithy phrases have permeated our minds, becoming part of a national idiom, while reminding consumers of each company's spirit and services.

A clever slogan continually reverberates in the mind. The phrase "Coffee-er coffee" came to Savarin in a verse submitted by a free-lance writer (who, by the way, is still writing and editing at age ninety). The simplicity and directness of phrases like "I Love New York" or "You Deserve a Break Today" help make them memorable.

The phrase "Perfect Typing" became a slogan for a typing service, and the slogan was used on all of the typing service's promotions. The owner of the service even became known as the "Perfect Typing" lady. Sometimes a slogan will be more a byword than a fancy phrase. A paperhanger in New Jersey uses the phrase "All work done with craftsmanship and integrity" on his flyers. A gourmet shop has imprinted the phrase "catering with an Italian accent" on its letterhead. These phrases, when repeated through advertising and sales literature, provide a uniformity and unity to your promotions. They not only help your customers remember you, but they help form a single, identifiable symbol in their minds. Just as a logo is unique, a slogan attempts to capture the essence of what you do in a single, succinct phrase.

3. Carefully arrange your selling points.

It is not just the sales points that are important, it's their arrangement. You must develop a feel for which points deserve top billing, and which are extra added attractions. The typing-service owner knew that "Perfect Typing" was a more important idea than "24 Hours a Day" and so she put them in just that order on her flyers. To help readers absorb more than a few sales points, you may wish to use "bullets," numbers, or subheads (as we do in this book).

4. Avoid sexism.

The women's liberation movement has had a great impact on our language. For one thing, we can no longer blithely use the word "man" as a stand-in for "person." Since women share almost all occupations with men, writers must be ready to search for ways to recast sentences so that they do not have sexist connotations. When you reach for a phrase like "the man who sells ice cream," or "an advertising man's salary," an alarm should sound in your brain. "The person who sells ice cream" is more generic, since the field isn't limited to males, and should be used unless you are describing a particular male ice cream sales*person*. "Ad man" is one of a storehouse of stock phrases that now must be rethought and reworded. You might recast the phrase to read "an advertising professional's salary."

How about a sexist phrase like "the doctor uses *his* car"? Using the plural form is one way to avoid the male pronoun "his." The phrase would then read, "doctors use their cars."

5. Be tasteful.

No one can teach you about taste; you either have it or you don't. But you can become more sensitive to exactly what constitutes bad taste by studying the ads you see all around you. We once saw an ad for a beautician specializing in electrolysis. The ad featured a line drawing of a ballet dancer in a spotlight. The copy read, "Why share the spotlight with unwanted hair?" Something about hair in the spotlight strikes us as unfortunate . . . the kind of image you want to forget, not remember. Taken literally, it's not a very pretty picture.

6. Use graphics.

Don't be dissuaded from using graphics. Photographs, line drawings, charts, maps, tables, and other illustrations attract the reader. Graphics should be of high quality and should blend harmoniously with the body copy. Don't just use a graphic because it's handy or free; use it when it will communicate an idea well. A photo of two people dancing helps communicate the nature of a dance studio as well as or better than any copy.

7. Avoid jargon.

Technical advertisements and promotions speak to technical people and therefore require the use of technical terms.

Indeed, technical terms such as "CPU," "binomial theorem," or "biodegradable" seem hard to avoid under such circumstances. What you should avoid are the catch phrases, the words that have been bandied about in the media: *stagflation, meltdown, feedback, state of the art, hands-on, on-line, supply-side economics.* Use your best judgment. Many people, for example, have some understanding of the word "cholesterol," but how many truly understand terms like "polyunsaturated," "emulsified," or "rack-and-pinion steering"?

8. Keep sentences and paragraphs short.

People are scared off by lengthy sentences and paragraphs; they view them with the trepidation with which a light eater views a 12-ounce sirloin. The words seem to blend into a formidable chunk of type. The solution? Loosen it up. Break up lengthy sentences and paragraphs. Allow the reader to grasp your message in short, easy-to-understand blocks.

Very brief sentences (two or three words) and paragraphs (one sentence or two), if used sparingly, can add a touch of drama to your copy.

9. Don't forget the obvious.

Sometimes you're so busy writing an ad or a press release that you forget to include obvious information. You may remember to put your telephone number in an ad but neglect to put in the area code. Similarly, you may give your address but forget the zip code. If your address is one that does not readily conjure up a specific locale—even to people who live just across town—you can sometimes clarify things by adding more information. For example, instead of just putting "1665 Second Avenue" on your business cards, you might say "1665 Second Avenue (between 79th and 80th Streets)." And don't forget store hours, prices, branch locations, and other essential information.

10. Add an additional inducement.

Just as a P.S. adds an additional thought to a letter, a flyer or ad is sometimes enhanced by a "bonus" sales point, another reason to buy the product or service. On TV commercials for various kitchen appliances, a voice excitedly tacks on, "And, if you act *now,* you'll receive, free of charge . . ." These added inducements do tip the scales in favor of the sale.

Your company's added inducement may take the form of mentioning an award you've won ("Voted One of the Five Best Seafood Restaurants in the County"), or a brand-new service you're offering ("Free Delivery"), or a premium item that you'll give away along with another product or service (a shoe store that offers a free shoeshine kit with all repairs over $20). Other examples: "Now available in the New Economy Size," "Special Discount for Newlyweds," and "10% Off for New Customers."

Effective Body Copy: A Checklist

When you write copy, make sure it is:
- *Interesting.* Does it keep your attention and make you want to keep reading?
- *Specific.* Specificity is the heart of all effective writing. Don't ever settle for general or vague words when you can be specific and concrete.
- *Simple.* A good ad uses simple language because, in a world of advertising messages competing for attention, simplicity reaches people on a "gut" level. It doesn't overburden them.
- *Concise.* As in all types of writing, there should be no wasted words. Economy of words is as much of a virtue as using the right words.
- *Believable.* People are skeptics when it comes to promotion. They've been burned many times and they don't like to be plied with phony claims. You have to earn the reader's respect and credibility in every bit of copy you write.
- *Relevant.* Your product or service may have a variety of selling points, but you should try to keep your copy focused on matters that pertain to the particular audience you're trying to reach. One promotion may stress economy, while another stresses status. Keep your ideas consistent by

remembering that you should not be trying to please everyone at once.

- *Persuasive*. Your copy must motivate readers to take an interest. It must present compelling evidence that will show consumers how products and services meet their most vital needs. According to Yale University researchers, the twelve most persuasive words are: *discovery, easy, guarantee, health, love, money, new, proven, results, safety, save,* and *you.*

• Chapter 6 •

PRODUCING YOUR PROMOTIONAL MATERIAL

The Graphic Arts

This chapter will tell you how to take the copy you've written and turn it into a brochure, a flyer, a poster, or any other print promotion.

We don't expect you to design and illustrate your print material yourself. Most of us can't draw well enough to do the job professionally. And frankly, we're too busy running our businesses to take the time to become skilled graphic artists.

Fortunately, there are many places to turn to for help. Advertising and PR firms, graphic design studios, free-lance artists, local art schools, and even the corner print shop can handle most of the graphic work you need done.

This chapter presents the basics of graphic design and production: type, layout, photography, illustration, printing, and binding. By knowing something about graphics, you can work with the experts more effectively and gain a realistic sense of what can be accomplished within your budget.

The Elements of Graphic Production

There are five basic elements that go into the making of any print promotion:

1. Type—the text, including headlines, body copy, and captions
2. Layout—positioning of the components of a printed page (headline, body copy, art, and blank space)

3. Art—illustrations and photographs
4. Printing—reproduction of an original printed page
5. Folding or binding

Type

Type is text to be reproduced by the printer. When you buy type, you buy words.

Today, most type is produced or "set" by electronic phototypesetting machines. The typesetter takes your typescript and transcribes the copy onto an electronic CRT terminal, and the machine produces the words as black images on strips of white photographic paper. A graphic artist will then take the type and arrange it on an "art board" for reproduction on the printing press.

There are more than 8,000 different styles of type to choose from; a few of these are shown in Fig. 6–1.

Specifying type is a complex procedure that requires a knowledge of such esoteric things as point size, letterspacing, line spacing, line length, and type justification. But don't worry about it—that's what the printer or graphic artist is for. All you need to recognize in type are two things: style and readability.

1. Style

Take another look at the typefaces in Fig. 6–1. Megaron Light has a clean, modern look. Souvenir medium has a warmer appearance. Eurostile Extended looks futuristic and technical. And Nuptial Script seems just right for a wedding invitation.

Obviously, type style is an important design element in the overall look of your advertising and print promotion campaign. Select a type that fits your image—elegant or plain, high-tech or old-fashioned, corporate or folksy, loud or quiet. Try to stick with the same type in all your promotions; a consistent graphic style will help build your image and recognition of your company.

60 • HOW TO PROMOTE YOUR OWN BUSINESS

This is Megaron Light
This is Megaron Light Italic
This is Megaron Medium
This is Megaron Medium Italic
This is Megaron Bold
This is Megaron Bold Italic
This is Souvenir Medium
This is Souvenir Medium Italic
This is Souvenir Demi-Bold
This is Souvenir Demi-Bold Italic
This is Times Roman
This is Times Roman Italic
This is Times Bold
This is Times Bold Italic
This is Colonial
This is Colonial Italic
This is Eurostile Extended
This is Eurostile Bold Extended
This is Friz Quadrata Medium
This is Friz Quadrata Bold
This is Bauhaus Light
This is Bauhaus Medium
This is Bauhaus Demi-Bold
This is Bauhaus Bold
THIS IS ENGRAVERS ROMAN
THIS IS ENGRAVERS BOLD
This is Caslon Openface
This is Univers Light
This is Univers Light Italic
This is Univers Light Condensed
This is Univers Light Condensed Italic
This is Univers Condensed Medium
This is Univers Condensed Medium Italic
This is Univers Condensed Bold
This is Univers Condensed Bold Italic

This is Avant Garde Extra Light
This is Avant Garde Medium
THIS IS COPPERPLATE GOTHIC LIGHT
THIS IS COPPERPLATE GOTHIC HEAVY
This is Stymie Light
This is Stymie Medium
This is Franklin Gothic Condensed
This is Bodoni Medium
This is Bodoni Medium Italic
This is Bodoni Bold
This is Bodoni Bold Italic
This is Highland Medium
THIS IS ALSO HIGHLAND MEDIUM
This is Highland Medium Italic
This is Highland Bold
THIS IS ALSO HIGHLAND BOLD
This is Gothic Outline
This is Helenna Script
This is Kaylin Script
This is Park Avenue
This is P.T. Barnum
This is Murray Hill Bold
This is Broadway
This is Broadway Bold
THIS IS BROADWAY ENGRAVED
This is Hobo
THIS IS KARTOON
This is Wedding Text
This is Commercial Script
This is Formal Script
This is Nuptial Script
This is Wintergreen
This is Bernhard Fashion
This is Brush
This is Francine
This is Bernhard Tango
á è ï ô ü ñ ç å œ ß

Fig. 6-1   Typefaces. (Credit: Emery Printing Co.)

2. Readability

Your message will be lost if an ad or brochure is difficult to read. Make things easy on your readers by following these simple dos and don'ts of typography:

- *Do* select a typeface that is easy to read. There are two basic kinds of type: *serif* types have little crossbars on the tops or bottoms of certain letters; *sans serif* types do not. Most graphic artists feel that serif type is more readable for body copy. Headlines are set in either style.
- *Don't* SET TYPE IN ALL CAPITAL LETTERS. ALTHOUGH IT MAY GET ATTENTION, IT IS DIFFICULT TO READ IF USED IN BODY COPY.
- *Do* set type large enough to read. Type size is measured, from top to bottom of the letters, in *points* (a point is 1/72 of an inch). This book is set in 11-point type. The body copy of your promotional material should be set in 9-point type or larger.
- *Don't* set any promotional body copy in type that is less than 8-point; it will be difficult to read.
- *Do* set type in narrow columns. On an 8½-by-11-inch flyer, for example, the type should be broken up into two or three columns. Columns should generally not exceed 40 characters (letters and spaces) in width; most newspapers use columns of approximately 26 characters. Wider columns cause the eye to wander across the page.
- *Do* leave plenty of blank space ("white space") on the page. A page jam-packed with solid copy scares readers away.
- *Do* leave space between the paragraphs. It will increase readership by as much as 12%.
- *Do* leave sufficient spacing between individual letters and between lines in a paragraph. A little breathing space will make things easy on the reader.
- *Don't* set long sections of body copy in reverse (white text on black background), and don't set it over a colored tint. Occasionally, black or colored type on a colored paper can be attractive and elegant, and white copy on a black background can be attention-getting. But more often than not, the old standard—black print on white paper—is best.

- *Don't mix typefaces*. For variety, you can use several typefaces in the same family—for example, you might use Megaron Bold for headlines, Megaron Medium for subheads, Megaron Light for body copy, and Megaron Light Italic for captions. But don't mix typefaces from different families (Megaron with Souvenir or Times Roman with Colonial) in the same document; it would result in a jumbled, amateurish appearance.

Alternatives to Type

Typesetting is far more expensive than producing text on an ordinary typewriter. To typeset 100 words of 10-point body copy, for example, could cost between $10 and $75, depending on the typeface. Therefore, the budget-minded entrepreneur is tempted to ask his graphic designer, "Isn't there a way to produce my flyer *without* a fancy typesetting charge?"

The answer is: "Yes—*but* . . ." *Yes,* because there are several techniques—hand lettering, rub-on type, and typewriter type—that can yield reproducible text. And *but,* because in most instances these methods are not satisfactory substitutes for the style and reproduction quality of phototypesetting.

Let's take a quick look, then, at these three options:

1. Hand lettering

Writing headlines and body copy in freehand is time-consuming work that usually produces unsatisfactory results: Freehand writing looks amateurish and reproduces poorly. It can be appropriate for certain signs and posters, and a fine handwriting such as calligraphy will add a touch of class to menus, business cards, letterhead, and invitations. In general, though, it is best to avoid hand lettering.

2. Rub-on type (also known as transfer type)

Rub-on lettering is transferred from a plastic sheet to the page by pressure; rubbing causes the ink to adhere to paper or art board. Using rub-on type is a slow, tedious process, and the letters often develop cracks that cause them to reproduce poorly. Aside from an occasional headline, rub-on type is best used in items that will not be reproduced at the printer's—signs, posters, quickie flyers, and other "throwaway" pieces. Rub-on type can be purchased at any art supply store.

3. Typewriter

An electric typewriter with a fresh black ribbon can produce text that will reproduce cleanly. Unfortunately, even the most sophisticated electric typewriter is limited in choice of type size and style. Typewriters are ideal for producing sales letters, press releases, newsletters, and simple flyers (especially if it's a flyer for a typing service!). For more sophisticated print promotions—advertisements, brochures, and catalogs—typesetting is the better choice.

A Glossary of Graphic Arts Terms

Like doctors, lawyers, and engineers, graphic arts people have a jargon all their own, and words like *comprehensive, mechanical, score,* and *cut* take on entirely new meanings in their lingo.

Half the battle in working with graphics people is learning to understand their language. The glossary of terms presented below should get you off to a good start:

Art   an illustration or photograph

black-and-white   originals or reproductions in a single color, as opposed to multicolor

blue-line (blueprint or blues)   a photoprint used as a final proof to check the position of layout elements before reproducing the piece on the press

color separation   the process used to prepare color art for full-color printing

comprehensive (comp)   an artist's drawing of the layout of a printed piece. The comp is used for review purposes and as a guide for the printer.

copy   headline, body, and caption text, usually set in type

cut   a photograph

design   the creative process of putting together a print piece to achieve some specific look, style, or effect

dummy   a sample brochure or other piece made of blank pages. The dummy is used to indicate the weight and feel of the finished piece.

four-color printing   there are four primary colors in printing: black, magenta (red), yellow, and cyan (blue). A four-color printing job uses all four color inks to reproduce art in natural full color.

halftone   reproduction of continuous-tone artwork (such as a photograph) through a screen which converts the image into dots of various sizes

layout   the positioning of the elements of the print piece

line art   art suitable for reproduction without using a halftone screen

logo (logotype)   the name of a company or product in a special design used as a trademark in promotion

mechanical   camera-ready pasteup of artwork. The mechanical includes type, photos, and illustrations all on a single piece of art board.

rough   a crude sketch of the layout, used for showing the basic idea

score   to impress a mark with a rule in the paper to make folding easier

stock   the paper on which the piece will be printed

Producing Your Promotional Material • 65

Fig. 6-2a The *rough* is a crude sketch of the print piece. It is used to approve the basic concept.

tissue   a thin, translucent paper placed as an overlay on the mechanical. Used for protection, and to indicate colors, corrections, and other special instructions.

white space   blank area on a page

Ten Tips for Better Layouts

Your artist is the expert in art; you are the expert in your business. Here are ten tips on layout that will help both of you produce effective print promotions:

1. Always ask to see a rough sketch first.

Steve Brown, a free-lance graphic artist, designed and produced the ad "A Prescription for Profits" for Magerman Associates, Incorporated. First, Steve submitted a *rough* (Fig. 6–2a) to his client for approval of the basic concept. Then he created a *comp* (Fig. 6–2b) to show the exact positions of the headline, body copy, illustrations, and logo as they would appear in the final version. After the comp was approved, Steve bought type and produced the finished ad (Fig. 6–2c).

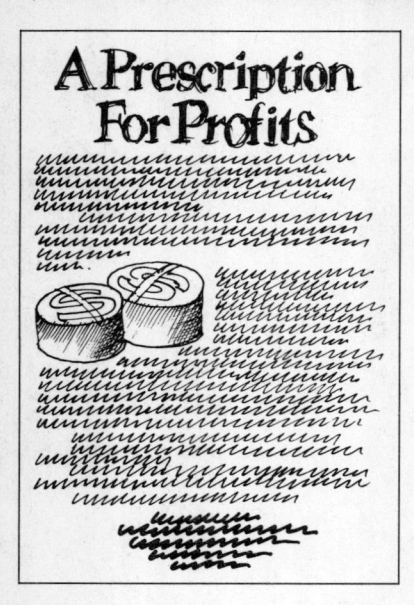

Fig. 6-2b A *comprehensive* or *comp* is a "fine-tuned" version of the rough. It shows the exact positions of the headline, body copy, art, and logo as they will appear on the final print piece.

Fig. 6-2c The finished ad. Note how closely it follows the layout of the comp.

"I always show my client a sketch of the layout first," says Steve. "That way, the client knows what I'm going to do before I spend his money to do it."

Ask to see a rough. It helps you avoid costly surprises.

2. Make the headline big.

Be bold. Set the headline in large type to capture the reader's eye and attention.

3. Illustrate your writing.

Good illustrations can add interest to print promotions. And photographs are even better than drawings—they're more real, more believable (provided the quality of the reproduction is good). Using photos instead of drawings can increase reader recall of your brochure by up to 26%.

4. Make the artwork big.

A single large photo gains more attention than several smaller ones. Also, a page with one large halftone is less expensive to produce than a page with multiple halftones.

5. Use captions.

Put a caption under every photo and drawing, and write captions that make a selling point. The readership of captions is twice that of body copy.

6. Find a consistent style.

Give all your promotions a uniform graphic look. Consistency is the key to building recognition in your prospects' minds.

7. Make the design portray your image.

Typeface, layout, art, and paper stock can create an image of your business in the mind of the reader.

Graphic arts novices don't realize that a one-color piece does not *have* to be black ink on white paper. You could, for example, use a dark-brown ink on a textured, off-white paper to convey a warm and friendly yet dignified image—perfect for an art gallery or small accounting firm. A supermarket, on the other hand, might use black ink on brightly colored stock —orange, blue, red, or yellow—to make its coupon sheets stand out.

8. Leave plenty of white space.

Pages crammed with words and pictures fatigue readers. Large, unbroken chunks of text intimidate them.

Plenty of open ("white") space will make your brochure inviting, attractive, and easy to read.

Koch Engineering used white space in its brochure (Fig. 6-3) to make highly technical information seem less formidable. The blank space, headline, table, photo, captions, and body copy blend together to make a handsome page that's a pleasure to look at—and to read.

9. Make the logo big.

A logo helps readers to tune in quickly to what a promotion is all about. Why not make the logo big enough to be noticed?

10. Design with the reader in mind.

If you are opening a health clinic in Spanish Harlem, print your flyer in English and Spanish. If you market to senior citizens, make the type larger on all your promotions. Always design print promotions with the special needs of your audience in mind.

Photography

There are three ways to obtain photographs to use in your promotions: buy them, hire a photographer, or take them yourself.

Stock photo houses will sell you photographs they already have on hand. Tell the stock photo suppliers what photos you need—a fighter plane, a mountain range, a sunset—and they'll supply it, for a price.

HEAT EXCHANGERS

In an empty pipe, the thermal boundary layer that builds up along the pipe wall inhibits heat transfer. The Koch SMXL static mixing unit induces a strong transversal flow that virtually eliminates this boundary layer, raising the heat transfer coefficient. And by inducing radial flow, the SMXL unit maintains a uniform temperature over a given cross section of pipe. This prevents "hot spots" caused by exothermic reactions and insufficient cooling at the center of the pipe.

The Koch viscous heat exchanger achieves efficient heat transfer with a minimal surface area. So it takes less space, reduces residence time, and offers significant savings in construction costs for units fabricated from exotic materials.

Some applications of this unique viscous heat exchanger include:
- Food—pasteurizing temperature-sensitive foodstuffs
- Plastics—heating and cooling polymer melts, e.g. cellulose acetate, polystyrene, PVC
- Adhesives—heating and cooling at various process stages in adhesives production
- Chemical—removing heat from exothermic reactions in laminar flow

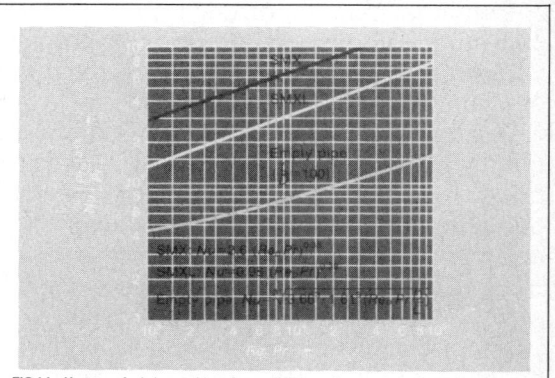

FIG.14 Heat transfer is boosted by a factor of three to six when Koch SMX or SMXL elements are placed in an empty pipe.

FIG.15 The Koch multitube viscous heat exchanger is used for large volumetric flow rates where space and residence time must be kept to a minimum.

FIG.16 The Koch monotube heat exchanger is the simple, low-cost solution to viscous heating or cooling problems.

Page 8

Fig. 6-3 Page from a technical sales brochure showing how white space can be an effective element in a layout. (Credit: Koch Engineering Co., Inc.)

Retailers, manufacturers' representatives, insurance agents, and other middlemen can obtain photos (and many other advertising support materials) from the companies whose products and services they sell.

Hiring a professional photographer is the surest way of obtaining high-quality photographs. Day rates for photographers range from $100 to $500 and up. A simple black-and-white publicity shot may be commissioned for as little as $50, while a sophisticated fashion shot can cost several thousand dollars. Your needs will probably fall somewhere in between.

If you are the do-it-yourself type, you may elect to take your own photographs. Purchase a 35mm camera and a good book on basic photography. We recommend Tom Grimm's *The Basic Book of Photography* (Revised Edition, Plume, 1979).

What makes for a good promotional photo?

First, the photo should make a selling point. A photograph of a slim bikini-clad girl has no relevance to a piece of industrial equipment. It can, however, make a selling point about a health spa, a beach resort, or a fashion boutique specializing in swimwear.

Second, *people* add interest to photographs. If you are selling a luxury car, put a driver behind the wheel in the photo.

Third, keep the photo simple. Photos are often reduced in reproduction, and fine detail will be lost.

Fourth, use photographs that arouse the reader's curiosity. When the photo raises a question in the reader's mind, he will read your copy in search of an answer.

Illustrations

Can you draw? If not, you can obtain drawings for your print promotions from one of three sources: a commercial art studio, a local art school, or a "clip book."

Commercial artists can draw or paint whatever you need. Their services are apt to be expensive, so get a firm price quotation in writing before you commission a piece of art.

Students at local art schools can provide excellent illustrations at a fraction of the cost of a professional illustrator.

Look over the student artist's portfolio to see if he or she can indeed handle the assignment.

Art supply stores sell "clip books" containing a wide variety of drawings you can cut out and use in your promotions. Clip-book art is inexpensive, but it is unlikely that the clip book will contain a drawing directly related to your product. Clip art is no substitute for custom-made art.

Illustrations can enhance print promotions in many ways. A cutaway drawing grabs an engineer's attention and makes the message of a technical brochure immediately clear. A map in a hotel brochure guides tourists to the resort. A series of bar charts sums up an annual report at a glance. The cover of a mailer for "YOUR MAGIC BODY: A Health and Science Magic Show" (Fig. 6–4) uses an illustration that tells the whole story and lures you into the body of the piece. (The Magic Show uses magic and other entertainment techniques to teach children about science and the human body.)

It is best to avoid abstract art in promotion. Abstract art

Fig. 6-4 The cover illustration graphically tells the story of this mailer on a health and science magic show for children. (Illustration by Gary Allen. Credit: Kevin Gormley.)

does not communicate selling messages quickly and directly enough to be effective in an ad, brochure cover, or mailer.

Pulling It All Together

Let's review briefly the steps the artist takes in creating print promotions:
1. The artist produces a rough sketch of the proposed layout.
2. Upon your approval of the rough, the artist sets the type and produces the necessary art.
3. Type and art are pasted up on the mechanical—a single art board with all the elements of the print piece in place.

At this stage, the job is ready for the printer. But before you send it off to have hundreds (or thousands) of copies made, look over the mechanical thoroughly to make certain it is as you want it to be. The checklist presented below covers ten items you should check for.

A Production Checklist

Before you release a mechanical to the printer, ask yourself:
- Has all type on the mechanical been proofread against the original manuscript?
- In proofreading, have you checked for punctuation, spelling, and capitalization?
- Are the logos properly drawn, sized, and positioned?
- Have all logos, trademarks, and proprietary names been given registration marks or trademark designations where appropriate?
- Have all addresses and phone numbers been checked for accuracy?
- Have all form numbers, dates, and copyright lines been set and placed according to requirements?
- Have all elements been securely mounted on the mechanicals?

- Have all smudges, pencil marks, and excess rubber cement been removed?
- Are all elements properly sized and positioned?
- Does the tissue overlay indicate the proper instructions for the printer?

Printing Tips

Printing can be an expensive proposition. To make sure you pay a fair price, get bids from at least three different printers.

In order to ask for bids, you should put, in writing, the exact specifications of your job—number of pages, weight and type of paper stock, number of halftones, number of colors, type of folding or binding, number of copies to be printed, and any other special instructions.

There are dozens of variables in the printing process. Be as precise as possible in your specifications to eliminate any chance of misunderstanding or error.

Order as many copies of the piece as you think you will need. It is better to order too many rather than too few, since the biggest expense in printing is creating the plates, and running off extra copies is a simple and inexpensive matter.

For example, 1,000 copies of a pamphlet might cost $300 to print—30 cents each. Now, 2,000 copies might run you $350—17½ cents each. Ordering an additional 1,000 pamphlets added only $50 to the bill and reduced the unit cost considerably.

A Quick Paper Primer

Your printer or graphic artist will guide you in the selection of the paper stock used in your printed pieces. This section will help you understand the basics of paper selection.

Paper is graded by weight. Heavy papers are stiff and thick, lighter papers are thinner.

Paper weight is measured using the term "pound." Newspapers are printed on 30-pound stock. "Quick print" shops use 50- or 60-pound stock to run off letters, résumés, and flyers. Magazines are printed on 80- or 90-pound stock.

Paper may be smooth and uniform in composition, or it may have an interesting weave or texture running through it.

The surface of the paper may be dull, highly glossy, or somewhere in between.

Below, we list a few of the grades of paper commonly used in printing, along with some of their applications:

- *Bond papers* are used in stationery and business forms. Bond paper is easy to write on.
- *Coated stock* has a glossy finish. It receives ink well, and is used for high-quality printing jobs such as sales brochures.
- *Text papers* have a rich texture and feel to them. They are used in booklets, brochures, and other print promotions.
- *Cover stock* is a heavier paper used mainly for brochure covers. It is easy to cut, fold, and emboss.
- *Book stock* is a less expensive grade of paper used for trade books and textbooks.
- *Offset* is similar to book stock and is used on most small offset lithography presses.

Although it helps to know the lingo, do not spend your time fretting over the complex world of paper. Instead, ask for the recommendation of your printer or artist, and *ask to see samples of the various papers he suggests*. Then select a stock you like—and can afford.

Printing Techniques

There are five basic reproduction techniques to choose from: copier, offset lithography, letterpress, gravure, and silk screen.

1. Copier

Copiers make what we call a *xerox** or *photocopy*.

This technique is simple and inexpensive—copies cost between 5 and 10 cents apiece at your local library or copy

---

* Actually, the word *xerox* is a trademark of the Xerox Corporation and should *not* be used to refer to any kind of photocopy, even one done on a Xerox copier.

center. And many small businesses can afford to own their own copiers.

Copiers can make adequate reproductions of black-and-white line art and type. But most can't handle halftones or color reproduction.

Use copiers to reproduce small quantities of press releases, reports, proposals, announcements, and day-to-day correspondence. The quality of photocopy reproduction is inadequate for brochures, pamphlets, and other promotion material.

2. Offset lithography

Most local print shops handle small runs of offset printing at reasonable prices. Printing a one-page 8½-by-11-inch sheet costs around $5 per 100 copies.

Offset is rapidly becoming the most popular method of reproducing print promotions. It is likely that 90% of the jobs you have will be handled on an offset press.

The process is termed *offset* because material is not printed from the plate directly. Instead, the plate deposits its design on an intermediate rubber roller which, in turn, acts as the printing surface. *Lithography* means that prints are made from a flat surface—printing ink is transferred chemically, not mechanically.

Offset printing produces extremely clear impressions. It is used for books, folders, flyers, catalogs, print advertising, press releases, and brochures.

3. Letterpress (relief printing)

In letterpress, the printing occurs as the raised surface of the printing plate gives up its ink to the paper. (This is the way a rubber stamp works.)

Although letterpress is losing ground to offset lithography, it is still used in some package and specialty printing, and for printed matter that is mainly text—price lists, parts lists, schedules, and directories.

4. Gravure (intaglio)

Gravure is the opposite of letterpress; in gravure, the printing surface is depressed, not raised. The ink lies in the depressions.

Gravure is used primarily on large runs, because the plates are expensive to produce.

Its main advantage is high-quality reproduction of illustrations and halftones on cheaper grades of paper. It is used to print Sunday magazines for newspapers, color advertising preprints, and large mail-order catalogs.

5. Silk screen (screen printing, serigraphy)

In silk screen, an ink or other pigment is pressed through a fine silk screen to create a design.

Because silk screen can be done on virtually any surface, it is used for trade-show display panels, decals, posters, billboards, and menu covers.

Folding

To save money on paper and binding, smaller pieces can be printed on a single sheet of paper and folded to form pages or "panels." By using the folding techniques illustrated in Fig. 6–5, you can turn a single sheet of paper into a four-page, six-page, or eight-page booklet.

Fig. 6-5 Some popular folding styles are shown here: (1,2) four pages; (3) six pages with flap; (4,5,6) six pages; (7,8) eight pages.

Binding

On large jobs, several sheets of paper must be mechanically bound together to form the printed piece. Fig. 6–6 shows a variety of common binding techniques.

Saddlewire stitching (saddle stitching) is the simplest and least expensive binding method for brochures, small booklets, programs, and catalogs. In saddlewire stitching, staples are forced through the backbone of the booklet to hold the pages together.

78 • HOW TO PROMOTE YOUR OWN BUSINESS

1. **Perfect Binding**
   For a paperback look.

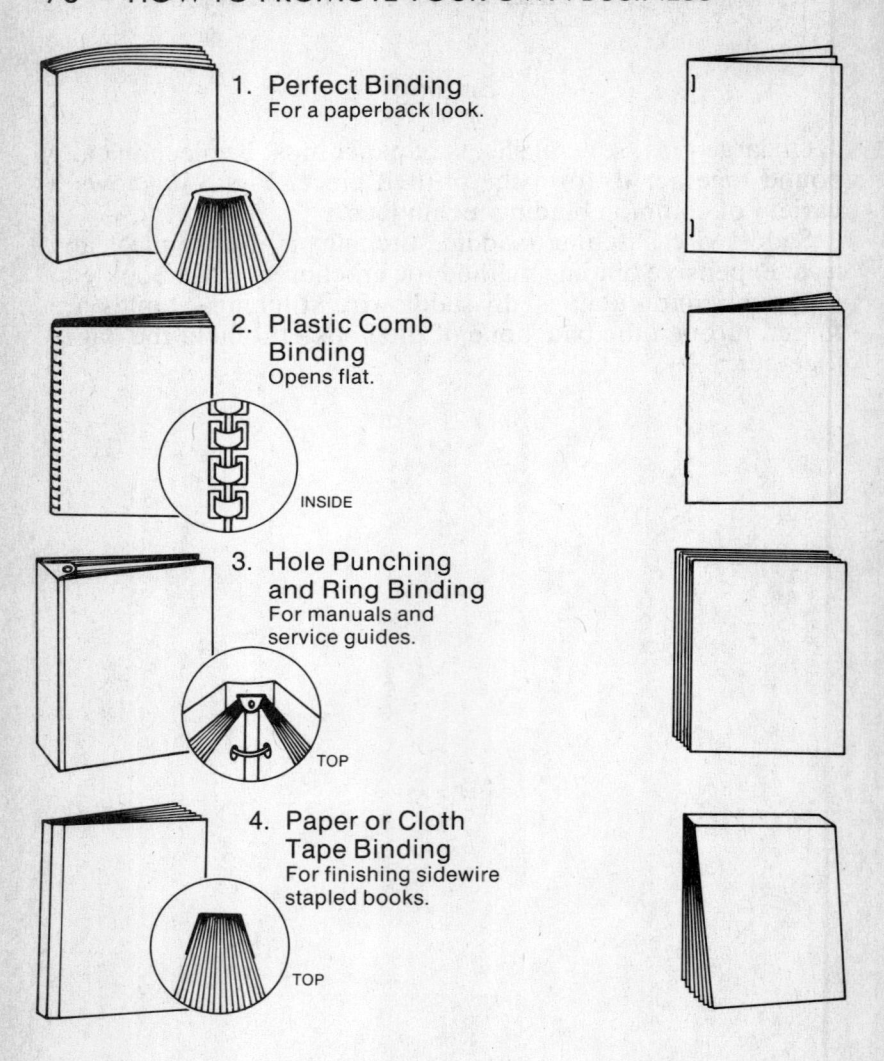

2. **Plastic Comb Binding**
   Opens flat.

   INSIDE

3. **Hole Punching and Ring Binding**
   For manuals and service guides.

   TOP

4. **Paper or Cloth Tape Binding**
   For finishing sidewire stapled books.

   TOP

Fig. 6-6 Binding techniques.

Producing Your Promotional Material • 79

5. **Sidewire Binding**
   For scientific reprints or business reports.

6. **Saddlewire Stitching**
   For small booklets and brochures.

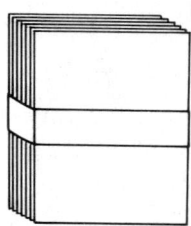

7. **Shrink Packaging**
   For loose pages that require handling or shipping.

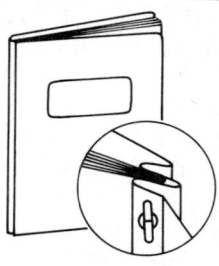

8. **Padded Material**
   For memo pads, telephone messages, order forms, and specification sheets.

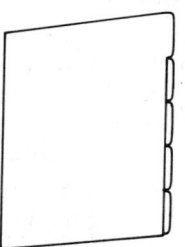

9. **Collating and Corner-Stapling**
   For research notes, newsletters and presentations.

10. **Paper Banding**
    For securing loose pages.

11. **Duo-tang**
    For protection for all printed matter. To allow pages to be added at a later date.

12. **Tabs**
    Can be added for easy division of categories in most binding processes.

• Chapter 7 •

REACHING THE PRESS: PUBLICITY

In Chapter 1, we defined the difference between advertising, sales promotion, and publicity:
- *Advertising* is a paid communication in print or broadcast media in which the sponsor is identified. A McDonald's TV commercial, a billboard on a highway, and a "help wanted" classified in your town paper are all advertisements.
- *Sales promotion* encompasses a broad range of activities that support advertising, publicity, and person-to-person selling. Brochures, cents-off coupons, point-of-purchase store displays, and trade-show exhibits all fall under this category.
- *Publicity* is a *non*paid communication in the media in which the sponsor is *not* identified. If we were to send a copy of this book to Phil Donahue and he talked about it on his show, that would be publicity. A mention on the Donahue show would probably sell many copies of the book. Clearly, we would have prompted the event by sending Mr. Donahue the book and bringing it to his attention. But we would not have had to pay for the air time, nor would we be a sponsor who has control over the time. Mr. Donahue would be allowed to say anything he wished about the book, complimentary or otherwise, and wouldn't even be obligated to mention it at all.

Why the Media Need Your Help

Publicity, then, means generating news and feature stories about yourself, your organization, and your product in newspapers, newsletters, and magazines and on radio and television. This news may be anything from a one-line mention in a fashion column to a full-page feature story in a trade publication.

To say that business "generates news" may sound shocking and somewhat unethical to novices in business and journalism. But the media, especially small newspapers, local radio stations, and specialty trade magazines, cannot always find enough information on their own. Newsworthy items help them fill their publications and broadcasts, while providing a form of "free advertising" for you.

There are several techniques for getting your story to Phil Donahue and other TV and radio shows as well as newspapers and magazines. The basic technique is the press release.

What Is a Press Release?

Generally, a press release is information released to the press, in written form, usually from a source outside the media.

It may be a brief announcement about a change in personnel, a January white sale, or a new branch of a restaurant or bookstore; or it may cover the details of an upcoming speech, graduation ceremony, new Broadway opening, or sporting event.

In a way, a press release makes its writer a potential journalist, because one need not be a professional writer or member of a public relations firm to write, distribute, or place a press release. *Anyone can do it . . . for any purpose.* If your message is newsworthy, accurate, and well written, it stands a chance of being picked up—or "run"—by a newspaper, magazine, or radio show, or even a TV talk or news show.

What does a press release look like? Very much like any typed story: double-spaced, neatly typed, wide margins, paragraph form. A look at a sample release (Fig. 7-1) will show you the generally accepted format.

First, most releases identify the person or organization (or both) the release is about. Generally, the name of this person or company appears in the upper left-hand corner of the page, although this may vary.

If the release is prepared by a professional public relations agency, it also identifies the "contact:" the person or public relations firm responsible for writing the release as well as for responding to any inquiries it may generate. The name of the contact is generally found in the upper right-hand corner of the release.

Client: Contact:

For immediate release:
>   ABBONDANZA, MANHATTAN'S FIRST ROSTICCERIA,
>   OPENS ON UPPER EAST SIDE—ABUNDANT
>   DELICACIES WITH AN ITALIAN ACCENT

NEW YORK, NY, May 18th—In Italian, Abbondanza means abundance. And Abbondanza is the perfect word to describe Manhattan's first "rosticceria," which officially opens on May 18, 1981.

A rosticceria is a store which features cooked foods prepared on the premises, along with a variety of other entrees which may be purchased for eating at home.

Abbondanza offers—for the first time—truly authentic Italian dishes prepared in an open kitchen for all to see. Owner Lou Galterio explains his concept this way: "People think of Italian food as just pizza, pasta and provolone. I want them to see that Italian food is just as sophisticated as French food—if not more."

To ensure that Abbondanza's offerings would be Italian—and not Italian-American—Lou Galterio imported a chef who spent more than 30 years heading up the kitchens of Italy's finest hotels.

Chef Giuseppe Allegra has forged an international reputation at such hotels as the Riviera Grand Hotel in Messina, the Ritz Carleton in Montreal and the Four Seasons in Toronto, where he was sent on special assignment by the Italian government.

In Abbondanza, Chef Allegra works in a kitchen that is in full view of the customers. Since the main kitchen is an integral part of the store, the aromas surround you. And browsers are invited to ask the staff about any of the food preparation.

Like a fine pantry, Abbondanza is decentralized, with sections of the store devoted to cheeses, coffees and teas, Italian desserts, meats and pastas. Each department is staffed by people who are delighted to offer suggestions for meal-planning, serving and entertaining. For example, they'll suggest an unusual menu for a romantic supper or a tempting meal for those who want to eat at home and not cook. Also, Abbondanza is able to prepare a complete buffet for any special occasion.

In addition to the Italian appetizers, entrees and vegetables prepared in the store by Chef Allegra, Abbondanza offers a variety of specialty items. Freshly prepared mozzarella plus tortellinis and gnocchis are available at the pasta department.

The meat department is replete with Italian sausages made on the premises as well as a variety of salamis and hams.

The breads and rolls are baked daily by Frank Vermonti, owner of Vermonti's, one of Greenwich Village's most highly-regarded bakers.

The coffee department, where the beans are displayed in their burlap shipping sacks, boasts a truly Italian espresso, ground to each customer's specifications.

Via closed-circuit television, patrons upstairs can view dishes being readied in the preparation kitchen downstairs. While browsing, customers can watch ice cream, cheesecake, quiches, pastas or Italian pastries being created.

Abbondanza's not a stuffy place where you're too intimidated to ask questions or ask for samples; it's a place with hot food and warm surroundings. Abbondanza is a grand Italian kitchen where you'll discover many joys and bring those joys from our kitchen to your table.

Abbondanza, 1647 Second Avenue (between 85th and 86th Streets), is open 10 a.m. to 10 p.m., seven days a week. Telephone: (212) 879-6060.

Here are a few of the many Italian specialties served at Abbondanza:

> Vitello Aurora Tonnato (Veal with Tuna). Veal stuffed with cooked prosciutto, baked in a tuna, vegetable and sardine sauce.
>
> Impanata di Pescespada (Swordfish in Puff Pastry). Swordfish, cooked in a casserole, with anchovies, artichoke and zucchini. Wrapped in a flaky, brown pastry shell.
>
> Chicken ville Roy (Chicken in Cheese). Breasts of boned chicken, cooked in a blend of melted cheeses.
>
> Flan di Spanaci (Spinach, Mushroom and Cheese Pâté). This unusual vegetarian dish has a mushroom and vegetable sauce in its center.
>
> Fillet of Beef Brasalla. Beef, coated with a layer of pâté de foie gras and sealed with a light shell of puff pastry.

And these special desserts:

> Mandarin Orange Ice Cream. With morsels of fresh mandarin oranges.
>
> Pesche all'Imperiale. Peeled peaches, marinated in champagne and mixed with strawberries and maraschino liquor.
>
> Ricotta alla Romana. Tart with ricotta cheese and assorted fresh berries.

●

Fig. 7-1 This press release uses the word *rosticceria* as a "hook." It stresses the store's atmosphere and originality as much as the food itself. The release became the basis for stories in all of New York City's major daily newspapers.

A press release is not an immediate "turn off" to an editor unless he works for a publication that makes it a policy never to use press releases. Very few of this country's print or broadcast media ever discard all releases unread. *The Today Show, The Tonight Show,* the *New York Times,* and *Time* magazine have all used numerous stories which grew out of press releases.

Your release should be typed on a plain piece of 8½-by-11-inch typing paper. If you wish, you may use paper—usually found at stationery stores—which already has the words "News Release" or "For Immediate Release" printed across each sheet. Your release may be written on letterhead, or it may have the logo of your company. Some releases show the logos and addresses of both the client and the PR firm representing the client.

Usually, as you look down the first page of a news release, you'll see the words "For Immediate Release" close to the top of the page. Many releases are written to be timeless, and the phrase "For Immediate Release" means that the release may be run at any time. Naturally, if your release concerns an event that is timely or carries an element of surprise, you may wish your release to carry a phrase indicating the specific date and time when the release may run. Press releases on grand openings, sales, and other special events are usually dated.

The Headline

A press release, like a news story, should have a headline. A good headline will succinctly announce or describe the main idea of the release, but it must also be written for impact, to gain immediate attention.

The press release's content will be the chief factor in determining just how specific, spicy, or succinct the headline should be.

If, for example, you were to send a press release to announce the opening of a new store, you would probably want to specify the store's name in the headline. The challenge would be to find a new, interesting angle to the store's opening.

For instance, when Abbondanza opened on the Upper East Side of New York City, we had to write a release which would try to suggest this store's unique qualities without playing into the public's perception of Italian takeout food as limited to "pizza, pasta, and provolone." In the course of conversations with the store's owner, we kept hearing him refer to a type of Italian food store called a "rosticceria." We asked him to explain exactly what a rosticceria was, and he went into a detailed description of how in Italy the term "rosticceria" connoted a type of food store where meats, game, and other fresh delicacies were cooked on the premises and sold fresh. Knowing how food journalists love to seize upon new food concepts, we decided to play up the idea of the store as a rosticceria. In fact, we said it was Manhattan's *first* rosticceria. The headline ran: "<u>Abbondanza</u>, Manhattan's First Rosticceria, Opens on Upper East Side—<u>Abundant</u> Delicacies with an Italian Accent." By the way, the release was picked up or served as the basis for stories in all the major New York newspapers, and it even led to a mention on the front page of the *Wall Street Journal*.

How to Write a Release

A well-written release, like a well-written news story, conveys information concisely, tending to capsulize the story in its opening paragraphs. This "lead" carries the who, what, when, where, why, and how of the story. Succeeding paragraphs elaborate on the story stated in the opening paragraph or paragraphs.

Unlike a news story, a release may vary its lead in an attempt to capture the reader's attention and interest before focusing on the facts. The first two paragraphs of the Abbondanza release capture the attention and then swiftly proceed to the facts. They also have the additional task of defining two words—*abbondanza* and *rosticceria*—which must be understood before the facts of the release will make sense.

The rest of the release addresses itself to subordinate ideas such as the store's unique approach to Italian food, the chef, the various departments in the store, and the store's physical layout. It ends with the store's address and phone number, as well as the hours and days it is open.

Naturally, press releases will vary greatly, depending upon the product or service being written about, the publicist's style, and the particular media for which the release is being prepared. However, there are a few tips on writing releases which we feel will help make your release the best release it can be:
- Keep it short.
- Use many quotes (when applicable).
- Keep it factual.
- Keep it focused.
- Keep it neat: no typos, wide margins.
- Offset the release instead of photocopying it.
- Write for the reader, not for yourself.
- Use correct press-release format.
- Single-space the name of the "contact" in the upper right-hand corner along with the person's phone number.
- Before the text of a news release, there is a city and date. It's called a dateline. Every release needs one so that the editor can tell when it was mailed.
- Do not address editorial staff as if they were advertising staff. Even if you are the biggest advertiser in the newspaper, don't put on the bottom, "I advertise frequently in your newspaper." Some editors may be influenced by advertising but most will be affronted. A good story and an interesting angle are your best credentials.

Press Kits

A press kit is an entire package of materials prepared for members of the press. Like a press release, a press kit functions to gain the attention and interest of members of the press. A release is only one part of a press kit. Other elements of a kit may include:
- *Photographs.* Reasoning that a photo is worth at least 1,000 words, some publicists like to circulate a photo or two epitomizing the product or service they are describing. One handsome photograph of savory pasta is far more attention-

catching than even a well-written release. A lovely photo of a new handbag will not only be a fitting accompaniment to a release about new handbags, but it may very well illustrate any story which the editor chooses to pursue. Photos can be expensive to have taken and to produce (more about this in our chapter on production), so, if money is tight, you may want to indicate on your release that photos are "available upon request." In the same way, if you circulate a black-and-white photo with your release, you can indicate that color photos are available upon request. Naturally, if the requests pour in, you can then make a judgment about investing in color shots.

- *Fact Sheet.* A fact sheet is a rundown of factual information, usually in tabular form, allowing readers to gain a synopsis of the facts of the story without having to wade through the release. For example, Abbondanza attached a "Food Facts" sheet (included in Fig. 7-1) which mentions a few of the dishes available and gives a brief description of each dish. This information was not derived from the press release; it was additional information—material which, if included in the release, would have made the release too long.
- *Biography.* Occasionally, a press kit hinges on the credibility of a key individual. In these cases, it's appropriate to include a one- or two-page biography of the person. By breaking out biographical information, you aid the editor in separating an individual from the accomplishment or product or service with which the release links him. Also, a biography may serve to reveal additional interesting facts—any one of which could suggest a new angle to the story.
- *Backgrounder.* A backgrounder supplies the history of an event or a company. It may or may not have a news peg. Often it is included in a press kit merely to suggest that a product, person, or service is well established.
- *Client list.* Occasionally, you add credibility to your organization when you include in your kit a list of people or organizations with whom you have done business. A manufacturer of retail clothing might benefit, for example, by enclosing a one-page list of stores carrying its fashions

(especially if those stores include names that will be instantly recognizable to editors and shoppers alike).

What News Deserves a Press Release?

You may send out press releases on any topic, whether it's a front-page story or not. However, the more news appeal your press release has, the better its chances of gaining an editor's attention.

Here are just a few of the many events and items that may gain your business some publicity if you send out a press release on them:

- Anniversaries of events such as the opening of your store
- Introduction of new products or product lines
- An improvement on an existing product or service
- Changing your company name
- Opening a new business, store, or branch
- Personnel changes (new employees and promotions)
- Special events—sales, parties, demonstrations, open houses, plant tours, charitable acts, other community relations
- Publication of a new brochure, flyer, or catalog
- Expert-opinion stories in which you, as a leader in your business or community, speak out or provide new information on some market trend, controversial issue, or other subject

Why Send Out a Press Release?

There are a number of reasons why you would wish to send out a press release. The first is to gain recognition and acceptance for your business or organization.

People always complain that "the other guy" is always being mentioned in the paper, and that "it isn't fair." True. Being mentioned in the newspaper or on the radio is not an equal-opportunity procedure. Newspapers, like people, have a tendency to reach for whatever is close at hand. If a newspaper or radio show is planning to run a story about new gourmet restaurants and a press release announcing your new gourmet restaurant arrives on the editor's desk that day, you stand a good chance of being included in the article or broadcast.

If a newspaper or a magazine mentions your company in its story, or makes a story out of your release, the public will get to read about *your* business—not the other person's. They'll find out about your offerings, your special features, and where they can find you. If the story has appeal, you may experience a quick and sharp surge in business. The day that the *New York Times* printed its story about Abbondanza, the store was jammed. In fact, Abbondanza had its best day of the year. And what made the day especially welcome was that the article ran in mid-July, a time when most gourmet stores are empty.

Where Do You Send Your Press Release?

The surest way of satisfying every editor's news needs would be to write a customized press release, tailored to his particular editorial requirements.

That's not practical if you want to reach more than one or two publications. That's why we use the press release, a kind of mass-produced news story that each editor can use as the basis for a news item.

Your press release should be distributed to any publication or station that could benefit your business and reach qualified prospects. If you're selling computing systems to small-business people, you'd send your release to *Inc., Venture,* and *Entrepreneur*—three magazines whose readers have a strong interest in small and growing businesses.

But don't stop here. These small-business people are also interested in the complete business picture, not just small business. Pickup of the release in *Forbes, Fortune,* or *Business Week* would help promote your small-business computer.

You begin to get the picture. The bulk of your time and energy went into creating the release; printing and mailing extra copies is relatively inexpensive. So you want to be sure you mail the release to *all* the publications that your key prospects might read. Public relations people call a list of these publications the *media list*.

Most PR novices are surprised and pleased to learn that there is a book that lists most of the major newspapers, popular magazines, and trade journals published in the United States and Canada. The book is *Bacon's Publicity Checker* and it's published annually by Bacon's Publishing Company, 14 East Jackson Boulevard, Chicago, IL 60604. *Bacon's* lists nearly 9,000 newspapers by region and approximately 4,400 magazines by specialty (women's magazines, electronics, computers, and so forth) and has an alphabetical index, too.

Let's say you wanted to send a release on your small business computing system. Here are the steps to take in compiling the media list:

1. Ask yourself, "What kind of publications does my prospect read?" The small-business person probably reads small-business publications, general business publications, and trade publications in his particular industry. If the release was aimed at corporate types, you'd add in-flight magazines to the list, since Fortune 500 managers do a lot of business flying.

2. *Bacon's* lists these publications by specialty. Make a list of the publications, addresses, and the names of the editors who should receive your release.

3. Unfortunately, *Bacon's* is not complete. It doesn't include many newsletters, local newspapers, and other specialized media, such as a weekly TV shopper or advertising mart. If your release has a local flavor, you need to look around to see what people in your town read. Also, there may be specialized magazines, newsletters, circulars, or reports in your particular industry which *Bacon's* doesn't include. Add these to your media list.

4. Some releases may be appropriate for radio and television. While these media are discussed at length in Chapter 13, several major reference books should be mentioned here. The first, *Broadcasting Yearbook* (published by *Broadcasting Magazine*, 1735 DeSales St., NW, Washington, DC 20036) lists 9,000 AM and FM radio stations by state and city. Another section of this book lists the addresses, personnel data,

and other information about shows of a particular format (talk shows, black radio, Top 40). This book will help you compile lists of "call-in shows," radio shows nationwide that, if interested, could interview you via telephone. The interviews, conducted live or on tape, help the show as much as they help you: It's often very difficult for producers to fill up 24 hours of air time each day.

5. For a reference of key network TV shows, consult *New York Publicity Outlets,* a spiral-bound annual reference that includes "key personnel on media located within a 50-mile radius of Columbus Circle." This book, put out by Public Relations Plus, Inc. (Washington Depot, CT 06794; 203-868-0200), also contains information about magazines, news syndicates, radio shows, and trade publications.

6. Time your release for maximum effect. If you know that *Accessories Magazine* has a March issue that regularly features new handbags for spring, make sure that you have your release to the magazine by early December. Remember that the lead time for most monthly magazines is at least three months.

Following Up Your Release

After distributing your release, it's only natural that you'd like to see it picked up in the media. But is it wise to start calling all of the editors and program directors (of radio stations) you've mailed your release to? Do you have the time, the patience, and the telephone budget to make all those calls? And, assuming you do make a few calls, what do you say?

When you send out numerous copies of a release, you may wish to follow up on a *percentage* of them by telephone. For example, if you mailed a hundred copies of a release to editors and program directors, you might wish to choose ten or fifteen of the most valuable media (for your particular product or service) and place calls to the specific individuals who received your release.

If, for example, you're in the handbag industry, you might wish to follow up on a release sent to the accessories editor of *Women's Wear Daily* or *Accessories Magazine.* If you were the owner of Abbondanza, you might wish to follow through on the releases sent to *New York Magazine,* the *Daily News, Gourmet,* or *Food and Wine.*

Obviously, when you call, you don't want to begin your discussion with a plea that the editor use your release. That's a turn-off, as most begging generally is. Perhaps you want first to find out if the material was even received. You'd be surprised how often material arrives later than you could have imagined. Mail moves slowly.

You may then want to ask if the editor has had the opportunity to take a look at the material you sent. That gives the editor a chance to let you know that you're calling too early. If that's the case, simply say that you'll call back later on. Don't reprimand an editor for not getting to read your release as soon as it hits his desk. Your goal is to elicit information, and not to be judgmental.

If—glory be!—the editor has read your release, and is warming up to explain, gently, why the release is (a) inappropriate or (b) poorly timed, maintain your cool. By doing so, you may have the opportunity to turn a negative into a positive. For example, you may point out to the editor that some other details of the story have suddenly made your release even more timely than the day it was sent. If the press release, for example, describes a book you have written, you might be able to let the editor know that your book has received good notices in the interim. Try to show the editor a new angle to a story. Many press releases have been picked up because of the quick thinking of press agents and businesspeople during a follow-up call.

The editor may compliment you on the release and then go on to talk about the timing being wrong. Fine. Make a mental note as to the right timing (or issue) and make sure that your next release is timed to the specifications of the magazine—perhaps a holiday issue or special issue.

If the editor is undecided about your release, it is often best simply to assure him that you're happy to answer any questions or provide additional information. Always have a few ideas or facts at your fingertips when you call, because one of them may set the editor thinking about a new angle for the future. Let the editor know that you'll be happy to research any question he may have about your release, and that you'd be happy to send over more material—by messenger, if need be.

Remember that follow-up calls are a great opportunity to sharpen your promotional talents. If you can find out why a particular release was not accepted, you can begin to home in on the best media for your releases, as well as focus even more sharply on which media have specific issues or features most apt for your service or product. Timing and knowledge of the media are your tools for successful placement.

• Chapter 8 •

SPEAK UP FOR YOURSELF—AND YOUR BUSINESS

There are times when you need help in promoting your own business and there are other times when *you* are your own best spokesperson. Recently, corporate presidents and chief executive officers have taken to the airwaves to promote their own products. Lee Iacocca talks about Chrysler, Orville Redenbacher talks about his popcorn, and the wife of the largest Cadillac distributor in the United States has become a household name in New York City.

But what if you can't afford to pay to be the star of your own TV commercial or radio spot? Perhaps you've never looked into the possibilities of free publicity via articles in magazines, speeches to associations and clubs, and community relations. There are, literally, millions of dollars in free publicity that go a-begging each day in the United States. There are thousands of opportunities to give talks, write articles, go on the radio, and tap local resources. Many people don't know about them because they don't take the time to look for them.

Radio and TV: The Not-So-Impossible Dream

Tonight, all across America, hundreds of authors will be guests on radio and TV shows. Will they be there because they are famous people with best-selling books? No, they'll be there because public relations people—or the authors themselves—contacted the program directors at the radio and TV stations and *asked* to be on the shows.

Radio and TV shows face an overwhelming problem: They must fill up hour after hour of air time. And although their staffs may be adept at conceiving of program ideas, they depend heavily on outsiders to suggest segments and to fill up the remaining time. Even a show as popular as *The Tonight Show* leans heavily on publicity people to supply them with guest stars, ideas for segments, and topics for discussion. The publicity people are, naturally, eager to help out. They know how valuable it is to have a client seen by nine million viewers. They know that an author who holds his book up to the camera will, in one second, create a demand for that book which can result in crowded bookstores the following morning.

If authors can get themselves on local shows, news shows, and even network programs, perhaps you can get on radio and TV too. If you have a product or service (or some type of clever, humorous, or timely "gimmick") that is unique or indicative of some trend or fad, you might qualify for a few minutes of local air time. First, you need an idea.

Certain ideas are a "natural"; they reach out to thousands of people because they are universal, entertaining, and timely. The recent boom in the erotic-apparel industry has given rise to dozens of TV stories about these garments and how they are sold, usually by women, in the home. The story has media appeal, and, as a thank-you for suggesting the story (and sometimes even providing videotape coverage of the event) the show's host may not be averse to mentioning the brand name of the products shown. He may even interview the head of the company, who can then sprinkle in some choice remarks about her products and her business while commenting on the industry at large. It's done every day. The local show gets a story and the enterprising entrepreneur gains exposure for her products.

What can you do to attract media attention to your product or service? First, you can become media-minded. Take notes when you watch the local news, talk shows, and magazine-format shows. How often are products mentioned? In what context? Who gets interviewed? How often is the interview tied in with an upcoming event or book or film?

It will soon become apparent which segments were inspired

by newsworthy events and which were inspired by newsworthy promotions. Newsworthy promotions will ultimately mention a product, service, or company in a favorable light.

People love fantasy, and it would be easy to get TV exposure for a "sexy" service business, such as one that provides breakfast in bed (complete with personal maid, butler, caviar, Dom Pérignon, smoked salmon, and a dozen roses). If you offered this service, a press release or letter sent to assignment editors, program directors, or producers at local TV shows might be enough to get attention.

Naturally, the less intriguing or innovative your product or service, the more difficult it is to get it noticed by the media. It may be that you consider your product or service too mundane to rate TV coverage. Fine. Ask yourself, "How can I make it less mundane?" Think of ideas that might appeal to the media's thirst for the special, the unusual, the romantic, the refreshing. Suppose you owned a flower shop. And suppose the local baseball team had a superstar with a hitting streak. You might wish to create a promotion focusing on the hitting streak—perhaps sending the star's wife a rose for each day the streak lasts. Then let the press know about your civic- and sports-minded gesture. You can almost bet that the promotion will be covered. Don't be surprised if the station sends a camera crew to cover the delivery of the roses.

You can also try to appeal to the public's need for useful information: This type of imaginative thinking can be applied to almost any business, product or service. The promotion need not be obvious, noisy, or gauche; it should be well timed, clever, and low-key.

Radio: The Listening Audience

There are hundreds of radio talk shows across America.* Many of the shows have half-hour, hour, and even all-night formats, and many originate in towns of fewer than 20,000

---

* For the names, addresses, and program directors of radio talk shows, consult *Broadcasting Yearbook*.

people. These shows are constantly on the lookout for new interviewees, new ideas, and new approaches to old ideas. A "pitch" letter sent to the program director of each talk-show program—even if the letter is only a personally signed form letter—should bring some response for any interesting idea.

Recently, the enterprising young publisher of a small newsletter in the sweepstakes field decided that he wanted to gain radio exposure for his newsletter. In order not to seem to be tooting his own horn, he asked a friend who was in public relations to help him write a pitch letter aimed at radio producers throughout the country.

Since the letter did what it was supposed to do—attract attention—we're reprinting it, in slightly altered fashion, in its entirety:

Dear Program Director:

A house in the country, a new Jaguar, a 60-foot yacht—are these the things that dreams are made of? Yes, but some people are doing more than dreaming.

Millions of people compete for these and thousands of other prizes by entering sweepstakes and contests. And they're not just casual entrants either. With 14% inflation and $1.30-a-gallon gas, men and women are approaching giveaways with newfound respect and with a sense of purpose worthy of a Wall Street investor.

The tremendous demand for sweepstake and contest information—as well as tips—has given rise to a publication aimed solely at sweepstakes and contest fans.

John Jones, publisher of WIN NEWSLETTER, recently described the founding of his newsletter in this way: "I've always loved contests. Because I've won thousands of dollars in prizes, people were always asking for my advice. Last year, I decided to make my avocation into a vocation. I started WIN NEWSLETTER."

John Jones has spent many years perfecting techniques for cashing in on contests and sweepstakes. He has literally dozens of wonderful stories and hints for would-be contest winners.

Speak Up for Yourself—and Your Business • 99

John is 31 years old, and works by day as an investment banker. He is extremely articulate and is quite enthusiastic whenever he displays his contest and sweepstakes savvy. He's at ease on the radio, whether he's answering questions from the host or listeners. He'll be delighted to share his expertise with your audience at your convenience.

We're sure that John would make an excellent guest for a telephone interview—with or without phone-in questions. If you'd like to talk to John in person, just give me a call or drop me a line and we'll be in touch with you.

Sincerely,

Fred Ryan, President
Ryan Public Relations Co., Inc.

The letter worked. During the next four months, the publisher was a guest on nearly forty radio call-in shows. On some shows, he was on the air for five minutes; on others, he was on the air for as long as two hours! During that time he chatted with the host, took calls from listeners, and gently tried to weave his own publication's name into the conversation. The shows yielded more than 500 inquiries for a tip sheet suggesting how listeners could improve their chances of winning sweepstakes and contests. The names that were acquired from this free offer became a mailing list of highly qualified prospects for the newsletter itself. In fact, more than half the people on the list eventually became subscribers.

Let's assume *your* letter gets results, and program directors ask you to be on their call-in radio shows. Here's how to handle it in a way that will get you some free publicity:

1. **Help construct and plan your own interview.**

    Very often, talk-show hosts have little time to study the subject you are presenting. Although they are professionals, they can use your help in selecting some areas of interest within the field under discussion. Don't be shy about asking the person who interviews you to ask questions about a particularly noteworthy aspect of your subject. Obviously, these areas can't be self-serving. No radio-show host will permit you to go on the air and give what amounts to a free commercial for your business. However, if you're clever, you can construct pointed questions that emphasize areas of interest that will lead naturally to a discussion of what you are doing.

We know of a particularly assertive retail merchant who was given the opportunity to appear on a local radio show. The merchant took the time and trouble to write a list of sample questions that she could handle easily. Many of the questions were indirect lead-ins to topics that would allow her to mention her experience in a variety of areas.

As it turned out, the show's host arrived late and hadn't prepared to conduct the interview. The host was delighted when the merchant presented the list of possible questions (it was done in a way that did not seem intimidating or threatening to the host—e.g., "Here are a few questions you may wish to use, since they touch upon interesting aspects of what I do"). Because of the questions, the merchant, who had been scheduled for a ten-minute segment, got half an hour of air time. And because of the subtlety of her "sample questions," she was able to show her products and her business off to best advantage. It was as if she had had a job interview and knew what questions the interviewer was going to ask—she was able to relax, and to concentrate on planning her "spontaneous" responses.

2. **Set up a time and a date for the interview.**

Many call-in shows interview you while you are at home. The show is either taped for later broadcast, or it goes out "live" as you speak. The sweepstakes publisher scheduled times and dates for each radio show to call him at home. He made sure that he chose dates that assured him of privacy, quiet, and lots of time. Sometimes, because of time differences throughout the United States, mistakes are made and calls come in later than expected. Do not expect everything to work like clockwork. A time may be arranged and then reset for an hour later; a show that was supposed to last ten minutes might decide to keep you on for an hour.

3. Keep an eye on the clock.

Five minutes of "air time" is not quite the same as five minutes of regular time: it goes by quickly. Why? Because talk-show hosts are trained, like actors, to keep the pace lively. Unless you're forewarned, you may miss any available opportunities to say what you want to say. Therefore, you should be aware of the passage of time, decide on the points you wish to mention on the air, and try to bring the conversation back to those points. This need not be done abruptly or impolitely. It can be accomplished by just keeping the interview's purpose—and your own business purposes—in the front of your mind. And it takes a willingness to be assertive.

4. Thank the host.

An obvious but important point. Thank the host both immediately following the show and, later on, by letter. It leaves the door open for a return engagement. It also may, in some cases, persuade the host to mention you or your business again, even after the interview ends. There are lots of cases of an interviewee's gaining thousands of dollars in residual publicity because he made an impression on the talk show's host, and the host mentioned the product or person months after the segment was aired.

By-lined Articles: The Recognition Game

Even sophisticated peopel put halos around writers. Having an article printed—even if the article is poorly written and says little that is new—adds to the author's reputation as an authority in his field.

For the promotion-minded person, there are two basic types of articles that will help advance his promotional goals: by-lined articles about a facet of his business and articles that are written by a publication's staff reporters and editors.

An optometrist who sells an article titled "How to Choose Eyeglasses" to his local newspaper will usually receive a by-line ("By John Peterson") and an identification at the conclusion of his piece ("John Peterson is an Albany optometrist and the author of *The Eyes Have It!*"). The by-line and ID give Peterson exposure in the community, and label him an expert in eye care.

If John had decided not to write the piece but to suggest it as an idea, he'd still write or call an editor or reporter, but he would not ask to write the article himself. He might send a press release on the subject of eyes and leave it to the editor to choose a particular angle for the story. His goal might simply be to be mentioned in the article or interviewed by the writer who is assigned to work on the article.

The Query Letter

We have discussed how press releases are written, but have not yet mentioned either the type of letter that is used to sell a story to a magazine or newspaper or the type of letter that one writes to suggest an idea.

Free-lance writers and journalists refer to letters pitching article ideas as "query letters." The letters "inquire" about the editor's interest in a specific subject, event, or idea (see Fig. 8-1).

Whether you wish to sell an idea based on some facet of your business or merely to generate an "impartial" news story that could mention you or your business in passing, you should understand the elements of a query letter. In a way, the letter resembles the type of pitch letter sent to radio program directors.

The letter should contain material about the following: your specific idea, the approach to the subject, a sense of enthusiasm, details about your sources, word length, and due date.

The specific idea

A florist queried the *New York Times* about the idea of a flower shop for browsers. The shop was unique because it displayed its flowers in the open instead of behind the doors of a refrigerator. The idea resulted in a three-column story which showed the owners of the store, and even mentioned the store's address and business hours. Hard news? No, but

Dear _____

Almost everyone in business writes letters or memos, yet few people find any joy in putting pen to paper. Business writing, despite the influence of best-selling books such as Strictly Speaking and A Civil Tongue, remains mired in mediocrity. Poor writing costs American business tens of millions of dollars in lost productivity every year.

I'd like to suggest a 1,500-word piece titled "LETTER PERFECT: Six Ways to Give Your Letters Clarity, Conciseness and Clout." Using lively examples, this how-to article will help business and non-business travelers improve their writing and make the chore, if not a joy, at least less stressful.

As an executive recruiter, I'm aware that good writing skills are high on the list of criteria for top managerial positions. That's why I feel that most of your readers will find this article lively, informative, and relevant to their lives.

I can have the finished manuscript on your desk within two weeks. Would you care to have a look?

Sincerely,

Bridgford Hunt

P.S. By way of introduction, my articles have appeared in Mainliner, Pace, American Way, Advanced Management Journal and Iron Age.

Fig. 8-1 This query letter, written by the president of an executive search firm, is specific, crisp, and enthusiastic.

a clever idea for a brief story, and one which brought overwhelming reader response. Because the idea was good, and because it caught someone's eye, the owners received thousands of dollars in free publicity.

When a writer actually proposes writing the article himself, he is usually interested in establishing himself as an authority rather than just being mentioned in a reporter-written story.

For example, a career counselor might benefit from having a story written about her, but she might gain even more prestige if she herself wrote an article about some aspect of career counseling. In the by-lined article, the career counselor may be restricted from describing her own business or its location, but she has the advantage of being perceived as an impartial authority in the field. Ultimately, the ability to provide factual, reliable information will lead to business.

Naturally, there are some businesses that simply don't lend themselves to articles, and even if they did, an article would not result in tangible prestige or sales. Articles are effective promotional tools for businesses selling sophisticated products, products on which the more information given, the better the possibility for sales. However, a flower shop can be helped immensely by an article that "positions" it as different from its competitors.

There are many cooking instructors who publish articles with recipes. This type of recognition of one's creativity and versatility is a first step in the chain of events leading to people willing to sign up for cooking classes.

Finally, publishing articles and papers is a surefire way to gain prestige and acceptance in just about any technical field, from aerospace and automotive engineering to plastics and petroleum to textiles and communications. Technical prospects (engineers, scientists, and industrial managers) are often more receptive to a reprint of a technical publication than to sales brochures.

The approach

"Approach" is defined as your attitude or "slant" toward a subject. If you were writing about restaurants that literally "float" on bays and lakes throughout the United States, your approach might be the joys of physically being on the water while eating. The wrong approach would be to suggest a piece about *your* floating restaurant. In the same way, if you owned an all-night pharmacy, you might wish to generalize the subject by suggesting an article on all-night pharmacies in your city. You might elaborate on your idea by pointing out that it would cover well-established pharmacies which cater to people in emergency situations. It could include anecdotes about some of the emergencies that arise late at night.

Enthusiasm

There's a difference between enthusiasm and drum-beating. Your query letter should suggest your enthusiasm for writing about a subject that intrigues you, in the same way a scientific proposal will show signs of a scientist's eagerness to grapple with a scientific problem. Your enthusiasm should be for the universality, intrinsic interest, and value of your idea, not for its potential as a self-promotion.

Sources, Word Length, Due Date

The willingness to use sources, to go beyond your own experience, is the earmark of a professional. An editor expects you to go to the source of your story and not settle for secondhand or merely convenient information about it. As for word length, try to judge whether the article merits brevity (500 words) or extended treatment (more than 2,000 words). Let the magazine's format and past articles help you in deciding how lengthy a piece to suggest.

Finally, suggest a due date (if you are to write the piece yourself), telling the editor when he might reasonably expect to have the piece on his desk.

Need some ideas as to which magazines or newspapers to query? A stroll to the local newsstand may give you some ideas. Also, you may wish to check *Bacon's Publicity Checker* and *Writer's Market*. *Bacon's,* as we mentioned in Chapter 7, is the "bible" of public relations. It groups magazines by category and tells which are open to by-lined articles by nonstaffers. *Writer's Market* (Writer's Digest Books, 9933 Alliance Road, Cincinnati, OH 45242) is available at libraries as well as at most bookstores, and it describes approximately 5,000 publications, giving editorial requirements, subject matter, and addresses as well as other helpful details of each periodical's requirements for articles, artwork, and reviews.

One more thing: Keep trying! It takes a while to break into print. Writing a clear, well-organized article takes time and innumerable drafts. Your first efforts may go awry. Perhaps you can ask help from a friend who has editorial skills. Start small: Write a brief piece (for free) for a small magazine or newspaper. After all, a small, well-written article in a local newspaper may do more for your business than a lengthy piece in a magazine with a national audience. It depends on your business, the market you are trying to reach, and the location of both.

Speaking Up for Your Business

Some surveys have shown that people regard public speaking as slightly more frightening than flying . . . or even dying. We may all have memories of wobbly knees and stage fright from the time in high school when we were asked to give a speech in front of the class.

Speaking in front of a group requires skill and more than a drop of courage, yet we can reach unbelievable heights of eloquence when we are asked to speak about something we identify with—like our own business.

We've seen the most inarticulate people suddenly speak in torrents about the latest accomplishment of a five-month-old grandchild. Why? Because the subject captivates the speaker. And when the speaker is committed, enthusiastic, and concerned, audiences quickly warm up to the subject matter.

By arranging speaking engagements throughout the community—or country—you'll be able to enhance your business or your image. There are many opportunities. But first, think of your goals.

If an author wishes to speak at a meeting of his local MENSA society in order to tout his book and perhaps even sell copies, he may not accomplish both goals. He may motivate a few people to buy the book later on, but may not sell a single book at the meeting itself. Why? Because the program may be a prelude to an event or social activity, and not the focus of the evening. In other words, the speaker may only be a prelude to an evening of music and good fellowship. So, if his book is a somewhat somber tome, he may be catching his audience at the wrong time. If he simply wanted to get his name in the MENSA bulletin, gain some recognition, practice his speaking skills, and distribute his promotional materials, then he could be said to have met his goals.

An eminent psychologist once turned down the opportunity to appear on *The Tonight Show* because he found out that his segment was to be preceded by a circus act. The psychologist felt that the carnival atmosphere engendered by the circus act would be detrimental to the mood he wished to create when speaking about his theories.

In any free demonstration or speech, you must be able to identify your ultimate aims. If you are a politician, your goal is to meet voters, and it would be absurd to fill up your schedule with lecture dates at grammar schools. In the same way, you are searching for prospects or, at least, people who can tell prospects about yourself and your business. It is important to target your audiences with the same accuracy and meticulousness with which you choose an advertising medium.

Where Can You Speak?

Almost anywhere. Associations, clubs, religious organizations, civic organizations, charitable groups, chambers of commerce, community centers—any might be open to a program that would be both entertaining, informative, and relevant to its members.

You need not be a Winston Churchill, Erma Bombeck, or Orson Welles to succeed as a speaker. A florist can demonstrate the art of flower arranging; a karate instructor can demonstrate the art of self-defense; an art-gallery owner can give pointers on buying sculpture; a dentist can talk about saving money on major dental work.

Make a list of societies and neighborhood groups you belong to, adding the names of local clubs that might be attracted to what you have to say. The next step is to contact the program chairman and propose your program.

Don't expect to be paid for your efforts. Comparatively few speakers are paid. Of course, if you were being paid, you'd probably be restricted from mentioning your own business—no one likes paying for a commercial. As a speaker who is not being paid, you should ask yourself several questions:

1. *How many people will attend?* The more people, the more prospects. Make sure that if your speech has visual elements, they can be seen by everyone.

2. *What else is on the club's agenda?* As we mentioned, the event may be the incorrect forum for your product or service. You want to speak to people who want to hear what you have to say, not just people who happen to be members and are showing up merely to socialize with other members.

3. *Do you expect to take orders after the speech?* At some gatherings, it is perfectly acceptable for a speaker to hand out promotional information after a speech. However, many organizations feel this is too blatantly commercial, and will forbid you to hand out promotional material or even refer to your business directly. Find out how the program chairman of the organization you're interested in feels about your blending information with salesmanship.

4. *Remain factual.* Never take a swipe at the competition or indicate that only your product or service can answer people's needs. Good speakers try to remain factual, even when a person requests a comparison between the speaker's service and a competitor's. Try to be a spokesperson for your field, and, in that way, you rise above petty squabbles and are perceived as an authoritative source of information, not just another person with something to sell.

Community Relations

"This program has been presented through a grant by the Mobil Corporation. . . ."

Just as big business has learned the value of being a participant in the "community," so too small businesses should never miss an opportunity to create goodwill and public recognition as well as be better citizens.

If no man is an island, then certainly businesses are even more closely related to their surroundings. Businesses exist within the framework of a community, and simply cannot afford to ignore the political, social, and cultural changes that surround it. Business people who just curry favor with their suppliers and their biggest customers will soon find themselves isolated, and that can spell financial as well as social disaster.

Take the local store on the corner. Is it the type of place that announces, "No Children, No Bicycles, No Cones, and No Baby Carriages" on the door (thus setting up a feeling of intimidation), or is it the type of place that says "Hi!" to everyone who walks in, offers a cup of tea or a piece of candy, and provides Bach or the Beatles on the radio or stereo? Good community relations begin with having a good feeling about everyone who approaches our business, regardless of whether or not he becomes a customer. A person who regards the public in much the same way W. C. Fields regarded children and dogs just shouldn't be in a business that depends on face-to-face encounters.

On the other hand, a storeowner or other business person soon realizes that it is prudent and often enjoyable to participate in community activities.

Is it opportunism or Good Samaritanism? Only you can answer that. Only you can say whether you should buy an ad in the school yearbook or donate a product to a charity raffle or become a scout leader willingly. No one is suggesting that you should let your enthusiasm for community functions outstrip your enthusiasm for your own business, but you should understand that the best community relations come about when you do things for other people without expecting to be rewarded for your efforts.

Contributing to the United Way or to your local hospital's clothing drive may not catapult your business's name into the pages of your local newspaper, but it will make you feel good and it will earn you the respect of your neighbors. In the same way, working with a neighborhood group, becoming a block watcher, getting involved in helping the political candidate of your choice, or volunteering to man a booth at your church bazaar won't make you rich, but it will add richness to your life.

Realistically, it may have more tangible benefits, too. By banding together, business people can help improve their community, and the more neighbors, politicians, and civic leaders you know, the better. If you're trying to get a permit to open an outside café or trying to close down a nearby rowdy video-game parlor, your community relations may be as helpful to you as your business acumen.

Keeping your name in front of the public is another realistic benefit of community involvement. Whether you're sponsoring a local bowling or Little League team or donating samples of your product to a worthy cause, you're gaining exposure in the community. Theaters are in the habit of giving free tickets to disabled and disadvantaged people. While it is a noble gesture, it does help publicize shows, build a new audience for the theater, and fill up empty seats. In fact, one theater, the Trinity Theatre in Providence, has set such a fine record of community involvement that Marion Simon, the public relations director, was recently granted an honorary Doctorate of Public Service from Rhode Island College for her outstanding contribution to "one of Rhode Island's prime cultural assets . . . the Tony-winning Trinity Company."

So whether you consider yourself a "joiner" or not, you must remember that your business is not isolated and neither are you. Groups such as a chamber of commerce, a mayor's action committee, or a neighborhood association offer a network of contacts as well as a spirit of involvement. As long as you keep your business ambitions in tune with the community you are servicing, you won't run across a conflict that makes you sacrifice one commitment for the other.

Teaching: A Textbook Example of Publicity

We are living in an age of adult education, and with it has come an age in which teachers are offering their students "relevant" courses taught by people with "hands-on" experience in a variety of fields. With this trend toward adult education, it is not uncommon to find courses taught at vest-pocket colleges (informal adult-education centers) in subjects like interviewing, stress management, networking, meeting a lover, public speaking, and auditioning for commercials. In general, the teachers are poorly paid, but they do it for—you guessed it—the publicity.

For many teachers, the class provides an endless flow of qualified prospects. It's an ideal way for businesspeople to talk about what they do in front of a group of people who view the information as educational. The only thing to bear in mind is professionalism: never slight the competition, and never use your prestige as a teacher to blatantly solicit business instead of providing factual information. After the class has formally ended, you may wish to briefly mention your business or pass out a brochure or business card, but this "pitch" should be clearly segregated from class time.

Adult education, with its mass distribution of catalogs, flyers, and brochures, helps give visibility to those who are willing to suffer short pay. It can give you recognition in the community, and it can help direct people to you. For many entrepreneurs, adult education is the best low-cost promotion in their entire promotion campaign.

Chapter 9

ADVERTISING BY LETTER: DIRECT MAIL

What Is Direct Mail?

Direct mail is mail consisting of advertising matter, sent individually to large numbers of people. Some people refer to this type of mail as "junk mail," because so many solicitations for so many products are mailed each year that most hit the wastebasket within moments of being received.

And yet, advertisers persist. In fact, the use of direct mail is growing. That's because direct mail can work; it can be highly profitable, and it fits the growing American trend toward specialization of interests.

Advantages of Direct Mail

For many small and large businesses, direct mail is the preferred way of reaching customers. It offers great selectivity, since businesses can choose to send mail to people of a particular age, occupation, sex, special interest, marital status, or locale. There are mailing lists available that are remarkably specific, and the more accurately you pinpoint your potential customer, the better the chances that each of your pieces of mail will be read carefully.

Direct mail also gives you complete control over your schedules. You can mail whenever you choose, in whatever quantity your choose. And you can adjust your mailing schedule as you learn more about how many inquiries are being generated over a specified period of time.

Direct mail is perfect for small businesses because of its simplicity. You can create an effective direct-mail package with a typed, offset letter. Total cost? About $30 per 100, including postage, printing, paper, and envelopes.

If your business is slow, you can step up your direct-mail program. When things get busy, you can cut back. Once you've created the elements of a direct-mail program, you can keep them on hand and send them out on the spur of the moment whenever the time is right.

Another advantage of direct mail is that you control what you spend: Your costs are only at the mercy of rising postal rates. And, of course, it is your choice whether you wish to create a simple package like a typed, offset letter or one that is elaborate, such as several full-color brochures, and a reply envelope. If you wish, you can do limited runs of 1,000. Or even 100. This makes direct mail particularly attractive to new and expanding businesses with limited promotion budgets.

Finally, direct mail allows you to evaluate the success of your promotional program quickly. In general, you receive 70% of whatever responses you are going to get within two weeks, and 90% within four weeks. If your response rate is low, you may wish to change a particular element in your mailing or try another mailing list. Testing different forms of mailings is the only way to learn how your audience will respond to your business; almost everyone in direct mail advocates a program of never-ending testing—"test, test, and test again." With direct mail, you can create a separate mailing for each of your target markets, even if those markets are comparatively small.

Uses of Mailings

Direct mail has a number of specific uses in business. Perhaps its most common use is in mail-order selling. A number of products such as books, insurance, clothing, food, and magazines are sold by direct mail. Your prospects need not live in a rural setting to respond to a direct-mail offering of an unusual food or even a new book. Witness the success of the Fruit-of-the-Month Club and the Book-of-the-Month Club.

Many people enjoy shopping by mail (see Chapter 10 for more information on mail order).

Naturally, direct mail is also an important source of leads for your salespeople. It helps them eliminate cold canvassing for prospects. By generating real leads, direct mail helps salespeople make the most cost-effective use of their prospecting time.

Direct mail is a personal form of communication, and it is the appropriate form of communication for inviting people to see your place of business. Many direct-mail campaigns aim simply at getting people to see a new store or visit a brand-new business. The direct-mail campaign can center around an opening-day party, an exhibit, or any special event. In any case, it alerts people to a specific happening that may persuade them to think of you. An author autographing his new book, for example, is an event that can serve as the basis of a direct-mail letter aimed at bringing book buyers into the store.

There are other uses of direct mail, including:

- *Keep-in-touch mailings*. These "cordial contacts" serve to remind clients and contacts of your existence. Fig. 9-1 is an example of this type of letter. It was sent as an accompaniment to a recent reprint of a pertinent article.
- *Building mailing lists for future promotions*. Fig. 9-2 shows this type of letter. It was sent to people at corporations for the purpose of building an accurate mailing list of people in charge of corporate catering.
- *Image-building*. This type of letter keeps your name in front of your prospects.
- *Advertising*. This type of letter or package is used to get information out to a selected audience.

Elements of Direct Mail

From the moment your prospects pick up a piece of direct mail, they are the audience for an array of elements and effects that has taken days, weeks, or even months to create. Energy and talent have been put into that one piece of mail, despite the knowledge that ninety-eight out of every hun-

THE HUNT COMPANY
A Division of Hunt Management, Inc.

Are all executive search firms "headhunters"? No. At The Hunt Company, we realize that it doesn't matter how good a head you have if your heart isn't in your work.

This is especially true for those whose only affiliation with a particular company is that they sit on the board of directors. In "The Changing Role of Outside Directors", which recently appeared in _Enterprise_, I focused on the changing role of outside directors, people who must be as sensitive to the interests of consumers and environmentalists as they are to shareholders and employees. The best outside directors are those who aren't afraid to voice their opinions and do battle with corporate complacency.

By now you must know that at The Hunt Company, we're keyed into the top managerial talent in the United States. The only "heads" we hunt for are those attached to people who have talent, experience and the will to succeed. They're people who view the future with eagerness instead of anxiety, and who know that a little change is good for the corporate soul.

We hope that you'll think "Hunt" the next time you search for an outside director or for anyone with the type of head -- and heart -- well-run businesses demand.

274 Madison Avenue at 40th Street • New York, New York 10016 • (212) 889-2020

Fig. 9-1   This cover letter, used to transmit a recent article, helps reinforce the article's ideas as well as keep the author's name in front of his clients. In this case, the letter writer is also the author of the article.

116 • HOW TO PROMOTE YOUR OWN BUSINESS

Catering with an Italian accent

Why choose a caterer out of habit when we can send you food that's out of this world?

Now you have an opportunity to discover for yourself what the food writers of *The New York Times, The Wall Street Journal, The News* and *The Post* have been writing about.

In Italian, Abbondanza means "abundance." And we offer an abundance of entrées, cheeses, breads, salads, meats, desserts and drinks for any occasion.

Whether you're interested in box lunches or sumptuous sit-down meals, we're ready with more than 100 different specialties.

All of our dishes are prepared in our own kitchen. You're welcome to drop in at any time, sample our array of specialties and even talk to our chef. We're sending along our brochure which describes our catering services. Of course, words are no substitute for tasting our food.

Please take a moment to fill out the enclosed card so that we may arrange a visit for you to experience Abbondanza first-hand.

Abbondanza

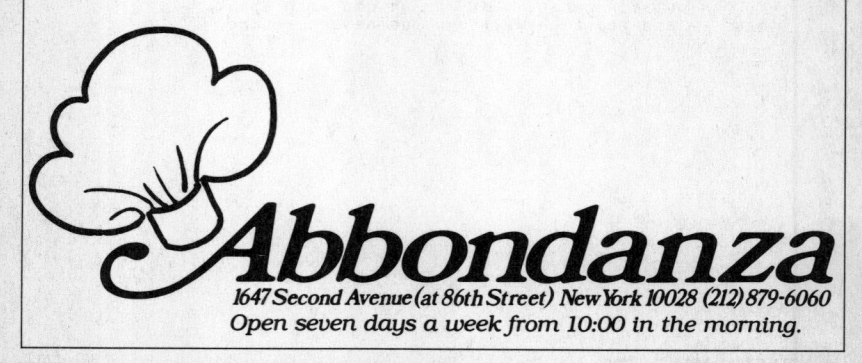

1647 Second Avenue (at 86th Street) New York 10028 (212) 879-6060
Open seven days a week from 10:00 in the morning.

Fig. 9-2 Sent to food-service managers as well as office managers, this cover letter helped Abbondanza introduce itself to the potentially lucrative corporate catering market, and also helped Abbondanza build a mailing list for future promotions.

dred people who receive it will throw it away, in a split second, without even a backward glance.

As we have stated, the elements of a direct-mail package will depend upon your business and your budget. You may send a simple sales letter or you may send an array of colorful literature. Here are some of the elements that are most common to direct mail:

Envelope

Naturally, every piece of direct mail needs an envelope (except for self-mailer brochures or flyers). Direct-mail professionals like to begin the sales process by putting an arresting message right on the envelope. One such message is "Stop!" (in the shape of a stop sign). The rest of the message may be "Don't throw this away unless you want to lose a chance at making millions!" Since the envelope is the first thing a reader sees, direct-mail professionals feel that the crucial moment is the instant that the reader first looks at the envelope. That's when the sale must begin. For small businesses, however, printing envelopes with specific sales messages can become rather expensive.

Letter

Solicitation letters are an art. If they are well written, they can persuade thousands of customers to purchase goods and services. No wonder leading professional direct-mail writers can earn as much as $7,500 from creating a single direct-mail letter!

Letters are integral to direct mail and are also considered sales literature. They lead the reader to take action, and direct his attention to other elements in the mailing. The letter, sometimes spiced with testimonials or factual claims, conveys a sense of the personal relationship between prospect and seller. The letter must awaken a need within each reader if it is to move many people to read it and respond to it.

Fig. 9-3 shows a letter that generated a 7% response and $15,000 in business in just six months. Fig. 9-4 shows a letter that effectively distinguishes one writing consultant from his competitors. This letter led to assignments from a half-dozen

118 • HOW TO PROMOTE YOUR OWN BUSINESS

An effective business writing program will save your organization time and money.
Here's how to find the right one.

1. **An effective writing program defines your writing problems before training begins.**
   The first step in improving writing is to identify the specific problems that need to be solved. Ask a consultant how he plans to uncover stylistic, organizational, and job-related writing problems <u>prior</u> to training.

2. **Choose an authority.**
   Your managers will listen closely to consultants who have achieved recognition in their field. Ask a consultant, "What have you written lately? Any articles or books on writing?" There is no substitute for publication.

3. **Business writing experience is important.**
   In addition to having written letters, memos, reports, and proposals, a business writing consultant should also have written successful sales, marketing, or promotional literature aimed at consumers or clients.

4. **Look for versatility as well as experience.**
   Select a consultant who has designed and implemented writing programs for top organizations in both the public and private sector.

5. **Pay for imagination, not image.**
   The person who conducts your writing program is half the program. You should be paying for time, talent, and expertise—not paneled walls, four-color brochures, or other frills.

If these ideas make good sense to you, call or write us. We make even better sense in person.

Gary Blake

Gary Blake, Ph.D.
Director

THE COMMUNICATION WORKSHOP

207 East 85th Street
New York 10028
(212) 794-1144

Fig. 9-4 Aimed at training directors, this letter takes a low-key approach. It attempts to make logical suggestions rather than sales points, hoping that the sense of the suggestions will sell itself.

Advertising by Letter: Direct Mail • 119

Fig. 9-3 This letter, mailed with brochures to prospects in advertising and public relations, led to a 7% response and about $15,000 in business in six months.

Bob Bly
Copywriter/Consultant

How an Engineer and Former Ad Manager Can Help You Write Better Ads and Brochures.

For many ad agency people, industrial advertising is a difficult chore. It's detailed work, and highly technical. To write the copy, you need someone with the technical know-how of an engineer and the communications skills of a copywriter.

That's where I can help.

As a freelance industrial copywriter who is also a graduate engineer, I know how to write clear, jargon-free, technically sound copy. You'll like my writing samples—ads, brochures, catalogs, direct mail, PR, and AV. And you'll like having a writer on call who works only when you need him—by the hour, by the day, or by the project.

Here are my qualifications:

I have an engineering background (BS, chemical engineering, University of Rochester). I started out writing brochures and AV scripts for the Westinghouse Defense Center. After I left Westinghouse, I became advertising manager for Koch Engineering, a manufacturer of chemical process equipment.

In my freelance work, I've handled projects in a wide variety of industries including computers, construction, chemical equipment, electronics, telecommunications, and many other areas. My articles on business communication have appeared in Industrial Marketing, Writer's Digest, Chemical Engineering, and Audio-Visual Directions. And, I'm the author of two books: Technical Writing: Structure, Standards, and Style (McGraw Hill) and the forthcoming How to Promote Your Own Business (New American Library).

Now, I'd like to help *you* create ads, brochures, and other promotions. Call me when your creative team is overloaded, or when the project is highly technical.

If it sounds like I can be of service, please complete and mail the enclosed postcard.

Sincerely,

Bob Bly

major corporations planning to institute a business-writing program. It has also led to very profitable repeat business.

Brochures

Brochures give detailed descriptive information about products and services. Their format is conducive to gaining product knowledge quickly, concisely, and with a minimum of formality. Not every direct-mail package contains a brochure, but many do. While a letter can be tailored to a specific person, or group of people, a brochure or flyer conveys a more general—and more timeless—type of information about your business.

Reply envelope, postcard, coupon, or order form

A reply element is a major element of almost every direct-mail package. A return postcard helps you gather information on prospects, gain feedback, and build a mailing list, just as an order form or coupon allows readers to purchase a product. A reply enclosure persuades the prospect to take action now.

Tips on Writing Direct Mail That Pulls

Everyone—or so it seems—has had a say on what makes direct mail successful or unsuccessful. If anyone had a foolproof formula for getting people to respond, they would have, by now, found a way to bottle it, sell it, and become rich enough to retire to the French Riviera.

Still, there are a few bits of advice that seem to us to be useful. Keep in mind that probably you are the person who knows your customer best, so don't ever be afraid to go against the "experts" or against supposedly "time-tested" theories.

One advertising professional says there are three rules in direct mail: Make it short, make it clear, and make it count. Yet, as we've mentioned, short copy may not always be adequate for describing high-priced or sophisticated products or services.

Most people agree that your direct-mail piece must quickly

show the reader the *benefits* of what you are selling, and that your mailing piece should reflect the personality of your business. It's generally a good idea to put your product's chief benefit right in the first paragraph of your brochure or letter.

Many professionals agree that you need to back up your statements with proof. It may be a testimonial from a famous person, or from someone known in your field. Ads or direct mail promoting new books lean heavily on "blurbs" praising the book, especially blurbs from people who have solid reputations and are well known.

There are other tips that may work for you, such as indenting paragraphs or enclosing a postage-free business reply card. Reply cards stimulate a greater response than order forms that require the consumer to affix postage.

Perhaps the greatest cliché of direct mail is the "Act NOW!" closing of the letter or brochure. Subscriptions for magazines and other types of direct mail in which a check is being elicited try to provoke action by promising you a "premium" or gift for sending your check quickly. These premiums are often the deciding factors in making the sale. If you can purchase a book, calendar, or novelty at low cost, you may be able to offer it to your prospects as an incentive to buy what you are selling. But be careful: Most premiums seem "cheap" to sophisticated readers, and most people are wise to the gimmick of offering a low-priced premium as an inducement.

Like all other promotions, direct mail works best when your product has relevance to a person's life, when it is something that he considers vital. Good copy, handsome packaging, carefully timed mailing, and pretty graphics all help, but nothing makes up for the persuasion that goes into convincing people that your product is going to enrich their lives.

Selecting Mailing Lists

Some people are good prospects for your business, yet many are not. That simple fact is the cornerstone of the mailing-list business.

At some point, many businesses come to the stage at which

they require expansion. Mailing lists help you reach prospects efficiently. Of course, you can begin by creating your own mailing list, simply keeping records of present customers as well as anyone who may have inquired about a particular product or service. Don't miss the opportunity to add a name to your own mailing list. You can never tell when you will want to send that person information about a new product or service.

Compiling your own list is not necessarily difficult. Stores, galleries, and boutiques sometimes keep "guest books" prominently displayed so that browsers can sign their names and addresses. This appeal to one's ego is a subtle way of collecting names for future mailings. Other businesses simply check their sales slips or credit-card receipts when they want to pull together a mailing list of recent customers. Responses to advertisements and PR provide other valuable names of prospects or past customers.

At some point, however, you may need outside help in identifying new prospects for your business. There are a number of sources of potential prospects. The following are the most common:

The telephone book

Don't ignore the obvious. The Yellow Pages of your phone directory lists businesses by category. If you are marketing a product or service to a particular industry (or if you wish to identify certain companies by location) the Yellow Pages is valuable . . . and free.

Subscription lists

Magazines have become more specialized over the past decade, and their lists of subscribers are usually highly focused. You may wish to try to identify a particular magazine that is read by people who might also be good prospects for your business. Then, contact the magazine and ask to rent its mailing list (lists are rarely "sold"; they are "rented" for one-time use). Sometimes a magazine's subscription list will be valuable simply because the magazine is read by affluent people and your product appeals to that market. If you sell products to the teenage market, one of the teen magazines might provide a valuable list for your business.

Club and service organization lists

Using the same logic, you may wish to buy or rent the membership list of a club or service organization whose members are prospects for whatever you are selling. The membership list of the Society for Technical Communication, for example, would have great potential value to a publisher of a book on technical writing. A cooking-utensil maker would certainly see the value of buying a mailing list of the students of a gourmet cooking school. In the same way, professional-organization and trade-association directories can be valuable to a business. Some people join organizations for the sole purpose of receiving the group's membership directory.

Newspaper listings and town-hall records.

To people who sell products to newlyweds, the newspaper's wedding announcements are a perennial source of prospects. Similarly, you are welcome to go to the county clerk, town hall, or state motor vehicle department and find out public information about land ownership or car registration—a boon to businesses trying to reach those people.

Mailing-list brokers

The renting of mailing lists is a large, sophisticated industry, and list brokers (people who compile and rent mailing lists) have become known for the reliability, type, and number of lists they rent.

Business and consumer lists are culled from phone books, credit organizations, newspapers, magazines, directories, trade-show registrants, people in the news, and buyers of products and services.

These lists can be compiled and sold by industrial classification (SIC*), company size (number of employees, sales

---

* Standard Industrial Classifications are code numbers used to define different industries for advertising and marketing purposes.

volume, net worth), home vs. branch office, city size, geography (state, metro, city, 3- or 5-digit zip), and job title. With the advances in computer technology, mailing lists can be merged or divided in such a way as to provide astoundingly specific sublists. If you want to reach apparel executives who are 30–35 years old and who live in the suburbs of northern New Jersey (and who smoke Pall Malls), somewhere there's probably a list broker with just such a list!

Many small list compilers supply segments such as insurance, banking, churches, schools, and professionals by discipline. For example, all physicians at office addresses are available from the American Medical Association.

Although you can find the names of mailing-list brokers in the Yellow Pages, you should also "think lists" whenever you hear of a magazine, association, club, or newspaper that serves your market. All may be sources of prospect lists.

To determine the quality of any list, determine what percentage of the names you are buying will truly be good prospects. How many have the right title, fall within the right age group, or live within the vicinity you can most easily serve? No list will ever have 100% of the precise types of people you want to reach, but the best lists are those that most closely match the demographics of your business. Good lists are accurate (correct addresses, correct titles), up-to-date (corrections are made frequently), and well targeted to contain a high percentage of the type of people you've determined to be your best prospects.

If you're selling computers, your prospect may not be the data-processing manager. There may not even be such a title in a prospective organization. It could be the president in a small company, the vice-president of data processing, the administrative VP, the director of management information systems (MIS), the treasurer, the controller, the operations manager, or the general purchasing agent.

So, as you thumb through mailing-list catalogs, list the basic Standard Industrial Classification (SIC) categories that could use your item based on the research you've done. A business catalog offers you a choice of hundreds of such categories.

It is only by shopping extensively and making innumerable comparisons that you can choose between lists, all of which may contain drawbacks. Some lists will include people who are not really qualified prospects, others will take in too wide a geographic sweep, others will take in too wide an economic or age grouping. Finding good lists is a result of learning precisely whom you wish to reach, finding out what is available and at what price, and then making your decision based upon which list will yield the most qualified prospects for the least money.

And speaking of money, renting mailing lists will cost $50–$100 per 1,000 names. Most lists are available printed on labels, making them convenient for pasting directly on envelopes. Since list brokers want you to use the list only once, labels inhibit you from making a permanent record of the names. Names are available on either pressure-sensitive labels (labels that peel off by hand, and can be affixed to envelopes) or "cheshire" labels, which can be affixed automatically by machine.

Other list sources include *Direct Mail List Rates and Data* (Direct Mail Lists Rate and Data, 5201 Old Orchard Road, Skokie, IL 60076), the "Standard Rate and Data" of mailing lists. It contains about 25,000 indexed lists. Also, the Direct Mail Marketing Association (6 East 43rd St., New York, NY 10017) has information on list sources.

Keeping Your Own Lists

If you rely on list brokers, they will maintain the lists and you may rent them when necessary. If you compile and maintain your own lists—lists drawn from advertising, publicity and direct-mail-generated sales leads—you take the responsibility for updating them, keeping them accurate, and making the addition and deletion of names a simple procedure.

Both Xerox and Avery put out 8½-by-11-inch sheets designed to keep the names and addresses on your mailing lists. These sheets, known as "label matrices," are available at many business supply stores and stationery stores. Each matrix is divided into 33 equal rectangles; guidelines are drawn in nonreproducing blue ink. By typing directly onto the matrices, you can keep a permanent mailing list, ready, at any time, to be photocopied directly onto pressure-sensitive labels. The matrices are easy to store, prepare, and change.

Doing the Mailing

Sending the direct-mail package presents almost as many challenges and decisions as creating it. Should you send all the packages at once, or stagger them? Should you send them bulk mail? First class? Third class? Does your mailing have the required postage for its class and weight? How do you create a business reply card? Do you need a permit for a business reply card?

Many of the answers to these questions can be found at your local post office. Generalities won't help, so the best we can do is to refer you to post-office publications that may.

Publication No. 113, for example, tells you every regulation pertaining to first-class, third-class, and fourth-class bulk mailings. This publication defines the eligibility requirements for mail sent via each class.

Bulk mail

Your direct-mail package may be forwarded via third class, first class, or airmail. Detailed information on these classifications of mail and the postage rates applicable for each are given in the Postage Manual and in Post Office Publication No. 3, titled "Domestic Postage Rates and Fees."

Third-class bulk mail costs substantially less than regular third-class mail, first-class mail, or airmail. For this reason, most direct mail is forwarded via third-class bulk mail.

In order to qualify for the third-class rate, the contents of the mailing must be printed—not handwritten or typewritten. Third-class mail is subject to inspection by the post office. Check your local post office for conditions under which third-class mail may be forwarded at bulk rate.

The bulk-mail permit

A bulk-mail permit can be obtained at your local post office on completion of the appropriate form and payment of an annual bulk-mail fee. The permit is valid only at the post office at which it is issued and is good for the calendar year of issue. The mailer must pay the annual bulk-mail fee each calendar year before he sends out his first bulk mailings for the year.

Reply envelopes

Reply envelopes make it easy for customers to place an order. It saves them the addressing of an envelope and having to search for a stamp.

The reply envelope may be a regular self-addressed envelope with or without postage affixed, or it may be a business reply envelope which can be returned by the recipient to the mailer without affixing postage.

The most convenient and cost-effective type of reply envelope is the business reply envelope. Not only does it save a search for stamps, but it also saves the mailer postage because he pays only for those envelopes that are returned—presumably with the names of prospects or with the orders themselves.

In order to use business reply envelopes, the mailer must first obtain a permit from the post office. Application must be filed at the post office to which the envelopes will be returned. The permit is annual and costs under $50. The business reply envelope must have the mailer's permit imprint and the phrases "Business Reply Mail," "Postage Is Not Necessary if Mailed Within the United States," and "Postage Will Be Paid by" followed by the return address printed on the face of the card. Postage on returned envelopes is payable to the mailman on delivery of the envelopes.

For further details on business reply envelopes, take a look at the Postal Manual or Post Office Publication No. 13, titled "Mailing Permits." The latter may be obtained from your local post office.

Direct-Response Postcards

A direct-response postcard is not an element of a direct-mail package; it is a special type of direct mail (Fig. 9-5). Typically, a trade journal will offer advertisers three or four postcard mailings a year. For $600–$1,200, your company's postcard can be included in a packet of cards (usually wrapped in plastic) sent to all of the magazine's subscribers.

Direct-response postcards are a low-cost alternative to space advertising. Their only mission in life is to generate sales or leads. A typical card contains reply-card information on one side. The other side contains a simple advertising message and invites the reader to fill in the card and drop it in the mail to receive a brochure, catalog, or other offering.

Response rates vary, usually hovering at about 0.5% to 1%. Not bad, considering that the cost is usually less than that of running an ad. A 0.5% response rate to 50,000 people still yields 250 inquiries. They'll come directly to you, and most will have a name and address. If the card costs $900, that's about $3.60 per sales lead.

Cards have generated excellent response for companies as diverse as a window-blinds manufacturer and a maker of specialized machine parts. Color and frequency are not factors in success.

Here are some tips on getting the most out of response postcards.

- *Don't run a card unless you are able to handle the response*. Whether you turn leads over to a sales force or handle them yourself, you must be ready to answer many responses quickly. There's nothing colder than a dead sales lead.
- *Be selective*. You have only 3 by 5 inches of space, and about a third of that is space where prospects can fill out their name, title, address, and phone number. If your product or service has seven or eight key benefits, you may have to settle for mentioning only the two most important ones.
- *Don't be cute*. There's no room to make connections between odd headlines and the product itself. Keep the ideas simple.

Advertising by Letter: Direct Mail • 129

Is stress robbing your company of productivity?

Teach your people to manage stress with

The Stress Mess

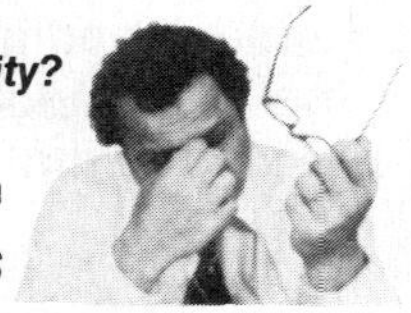

a valuable training film that
- Teaches how to reduce and manage stress.
- Reveals many common signs of stress.
- Explains important time management techniques.

Color, 24½ minutes – Order #C316G

☐ 2-Day Preview (16mm only) ....$ 50.00*
☐ 5-Day Rental $100.00*
☐ 5-Year Lease or Purchase $565.00*
☐ 16mm ☐ Video   ☐ Send me more information!

*Shipping and handling additional. Prices subject to change without notice.

Name _____ Position _____

Organization _____

Dept. _____ Phone _____

Address _____

City _____ State ____ Zip ____

Signature _____

Barr Films
P.O. Box 5667
Pasadena, California 91107
(213) 793-6153

Fig. 9-5 This direct-response postcard is typical in its brief, self-contained sales message.

TAP 9/82

BUSINESS REPLY CARD
FIRST CLASS PERMIT NO. 2285 PASADENA, CA

POSTAGE WILL BE PAID BY ADDRESSEE

Barr Films
3490 E. Foothill Boulevard
P.O. Box 5667
Pasadena, CA 91107

NO POSTAGE
NECESSARY
IF MAILED
IN THE
UNITED STATES

- *Line art is often preferable to photos.* When photos are reduced to small size, they often lose quality. The subtle distinctions blur and the photo looks "muddy." On the other hand, line art can usually be reduced without losing too much quality or impact.
- *Keep the card as clean-looking as possible.* White space adds to a postcard's "clean" look. Don't try to fill every available inch of the card.
- *And, most important, offer something:* a brochure, a demonstration, a free sample. Cards are an inquiry medium, and all efforts should be directed toward that one objective.

Measuring the Response

Mr. Mutsakis sends 1,000 direct-mail packages to prospects and receives twenty return postcards. Mr. Birch also sends 1,000 packages and gets three return postcards. Did either campaign "succeed"? It's impossible to say unless we know how much each program cost to create, how many strong leads were developed, or how many sales were made, and the profit per sale.

It is one thing to design a direct-mail program that yields response, and quite another to design one that gets people to send checks. To measure your success, you must first set goals, set a budget, and set up reasonable expectations for converting leads into sales.

Naturally, if your direct-mail program cost $1,000 to launch and any one sale would gross $100, you need to make at least ten sales to meet your expenses. And you've not added to the equation the "cost" of your time or the energy you've spent on the program.

Measuring a response, of course, is more than bookkeeping —counting inquiries, true leads, and sales. Anyone who can add can count return postcards or telephone calls. Anyone can be trained to calculate the costs of the mailing program and decide whether the effort was worthwhile. You should concern yourself with a broad look at the effect of direct mail on your business.

Direct mail has publicity value. It lets your prospects know that you exist. There is no telling when a prospect might pull your direct-mail piece out of a file and give you a call. Therefore, never assume that a direct-mail campaign is dead if it doesn't yield immediate results.

Direct mail should also be weighed against the cost of other advertising. Since direct mail is easier to pinpoint than advertising, you may want to try it for its experimental value alone.

If you believe that your direct mail has yielded a *low* response rate (1.4% is a figure often mentioned as an *average* response rate), or if you find that the people who respond are not, on the whole, people who can make the decision to buy your product, you may wish to find a better list of prospects or change one of the elements in your package.

Through marketing research, Procter & Gamble discovered that when a product is put on eye level in a store (instead of foot level), sales increase by as much as 200%! Same product, same price, different position on the shelves. Similar benefits might be gained by changing a headline or a reply postcard or even the color of an envelope in your direct-mail package.

• Chapter 10 •

SELLING BY LETTER: MAIL ORDER

Mail Order: A $100 Billion Market

In Chapter 9, we talked about direct mail—a kind of "advertising by letter." In this chapter, we'll see how products can actually be bought and sold through the mail—something called mail order. Since the two terms *direct mail* and *mail order* are often confused, we'll start with some definitions.

Like television commercials, catalogs, and coupons, direct mail is a type of promotion, a mass communication used to inform prospects about your products and services.

Mail order, on the other hand, is a type of *selling*. As the name implies, mail order is the offering of a product through the mail. In mail order, there is no personal selling involved. The promotion, purchasing, and delivery are conducted entirely through the mail.

In some cases, direct-mail sales letters or catalogs serve as the promotional vehicle for advertising mail-order products. But newspaper ads, magazine ads, free publicity, and TV commercials are also used to move mail-order merchandise.

The mail-order market is *tremendous:* Nearly $100 billion worth of mail-order merchandise is sold each year. And it's a growing market: Mail-order sales are increasing twice as fast as sales through stores.

For some small businesses, mail-order sales may supplement wholesaling, retailing, and other selling techniques. Other entrepreneurs may find it cost-effective to start *mail-order* businesses—companies in which 100% of the business is conducted by mail. This chapter will tell you how to select and sell mail-order products, and how to measure the results of your mail-order promotions.

What Sells by Mail?

Not everything is appropriate for sale by mail. A lawnmower is too large, a bottle of soda pop too easily purchased at the corner store, a legal service too important and expensive to buy without meeting the lawyer face-to-face.

Why do people buy through the mail? Convenience, for one thing. People use mail order to buy what is not readily available at the local department store or town shopping mall. Privacy is a second incentive for using mail order; mail is an easy way of purchasing items you'd be embarrassed to buy in public: a seductive negligee, a lotion to prevent baldness, or an especially racy romance novel. Sometimes, mail-order houses offer items you can't get in *any* store, such as unusual collectibles or odd-size shoes. And finally, shopping through an L. L. Bean or Neiman-Marcus mail-order catalog is just plain *fun*.

According to the *Mail Order Industry Annual Report,* published by the Maxwell Scroge Company, *insurance* is the leading mail-order product, with sales of mail-order insurance policies hitting $4 billion in 1980. The other leading mail-order product categories include general merchandising, home furnishings, housewares, gifts, magazine subscriptions, books, ready-to-wear clothing, collectibles, sporting goods, crafts, foods, and records and tapes.

In addition, we looked over our "junk mail" this month and found offerings for a variety of other products, including appliances, home decorations, health and beauty aids, business stationery, auto accessories, toys, pet products, lawn and garden items, cigars, cigarette holders, needlecraft kits, costume jewelry, watches, radios, and home-study courses.

How to Select Mail-Order Merchandise

It's a relatively simple matter to determine whether your own products are suitable for mail-order sales. Selecting mail-order merchandise is like playing the game "Twenty Questions." And here are the twenty questions to ask:

1. *Can you buy it in a store?* If buyers can find the product on the store shelves, there's no need for them to send for it by mail.

2. *Do people want it?* Products with broad appeal stand a better chance for success. Make sure the potential market is large enough.

3. *Will it appeal to well-defined segments of the market?* With your limited small-business budget, you can't possibly advertise to every man, woman, and child in the United States. Make sure the product appeals to specific market segments so you can target your promotions.

4. *Does it have sales appeal?* Mail-order advertisements for unique and interesting products stand a better chance of being noticed (and acted upon) than advertisements for dull, mundane ones.

5. *What's the competition like?* The marketplace can't bear too many similar products. Make sure your product is just a little bit different, a little bit better, than the competition's.

6. *Is it too big?* What size and weight is the product? Can it be shipped economically? A small business may not have the capital or the facilities to handle large mail-order merchandise.

7. *Will it survive shipping?* Fragile and perishable products do not make good mail-order merchandise.

8. *Can I make a good profit on it?* To sell profitably, the price should be at least twice, and probably four or five times, your cost. Can you make this markup and still sell at a price your prospects will pay?

9. *Are sales seasonal?* With some items, such as Christmas cards, swimwear, and back-to-school supplies, sales are seasonal. Most mail-order marketers prefer items that will sell well all year round.

10. *Can I count on repeat sales?* Repeat sales are the backbone of the mail-order industry. Is yours a one-shot product, or will the customer need a refill or replacement later on? High-potency vitamins are a classic example of a mail-order product that can pull replacement orders again and again.

11. *Does it work?* Consumers today are wary indeed of

products that don't live up to their promise—especially in mail order, where they never get to meet the salesperson face-to-face. Mail-order products should live up to any claims made in the advertisements. Beware of baldness lotions, instant weight-loss programs, pills that claim to increase sexual potency, and other "miracle" products. All too often, they spell s-c-a-m to the buyer.

12. *Is it simple enough?* Products that must be assembled, installed, or operated should come with a set of clear, easy-to-follow instructions. Nothing infuriates mail-order customers more than products that turn out to be too complicated to use.

13. *Is it a good product?* Is this something you yourself would buy? Or is it substandard? Mail order is not the place to unload junk merchandise.

14. *Is it interesting?* Does descriptive copy about the product make you yawn or make you smile? Pick products with unusual selling features that, if highlighted in an ad or catalog description, will make for compelling reading.

15. *Does it look good?* Mail-order buyers are at a severe disadvantage—they can't actually see or touch the merchandise until after they've purchased it. Products that can be illustrated or photographed in an interesting fashion will stand out in an ad or catalog and catch the buyer's attention.

16. *Can one or two models satisfy all customers?* If too many different sizes and colors of a single product are required, inventory can become a problem.

17. *Does it tie in with your other mail-order items?* When a group of similar items appeal to the same market, they can be promoted together at far less cost than a single item.

18. *Have similar items succeeded in the past?* Does the success of similar products indicate that this one will succeed? Or does the track record say that this product won't sell? Mail-order marketers are a close-knit community, and the competition will often be glad to chat with you about successes and failures.

19. *Does the product fill a void in the marketplace?* Is there a crying need for the product that has, until now, gone largely unfulfilled? Select products because there's a demand for them—and not solely because you like them.

136 • HOW TO PROMOTE YOUR OWN BUSINESS

20. *Can you handle it?* Is mail order worth the time and trouble? Or are you content with your normal methods of selling the product?

How to Promote Mail-Order Merchandise

With mail order, no salesman calls, no store opens its doors. The promotion does all the selling. Traditionally, mail-order marketers use the following types of promotions:

Direct-mail letters

You see this one at least three or four times a month. It's the long-winded, chummy letter from the company president asking you to join the Book-of-the-Month Club, subscribe to *Business Week,* apply for the American Express Card, or take out a life insurance policy.

To you it's junk mail, but to the mail-order people these solicitation letters mean big business, and they'll pay professional copywriters $2,000, $4,000, and even $7,500 for a well-written letter that will bring in orders.

At these prices, you might want to take a crack at writing the direct-mail letter yourself. Here are a few hints to help you write a better letter:

- Make it long. For some strange reason, a two-page letter pulls better than a one-page letter. And a four-pager does better than two pages!
- But don't pad it with clever copy and fancy phrases. You want a letter crammed with reason-why-they-should-buy copy. A letter that sells from the first word—to the last.
- Use indentations, underlining, and capital letters for added emphasis. Letters with indented paragraphs pull twice as well as letters without them. Note how the Thompson Cigar Company uses these techniques in its sales letter (Fig. 10-1).

Fig. 10-1 (opposite page) Direct-mail solicitation letter from the Thompson Cigar Company.

Thompson Cigar Company

    Promise me one thing.

    Before you light up your first cigar from the box of 50 I want to send you to sample free -- promise me you'll <u>examine</u> it carefully.

    In particular, I want you to feel the smooth texture of its exquisite brown wrapper. And smell the rich aroma of its expertly cured tobaccos.

    Unless I miss my guess, you will realize immediately that you are scrutnizing no ordinary cigar.

    Indeed, it is quite possible that you have <u>never</u> seen -- much less smoked -- a cigar such as <u>this</u> in your life. Why? Because the seeds from which its tobaccos were grown once flourished in the sun-drenched fields of Pinar del Rio -- perhaps the finest tobacco-growing region of all Cuba.

    Yes, I said <u>Cuba</u>.

    You see, the cigars I want to send you are all genuine <u>Cuban seed leaf cigars</u> -- blended and crafted in the old Cuban way from tobaccos whose seeds were literally smuggled out of Cuba from under Castro's beard! To discover the incredible story of these magnificent cigars -- <u>and to receive a box of 50 to sample free</u> -- please read on . . .

Dear Fellow Cigar Lover:

    With this letter -- and with your O.K. on the enclosed card -- I'm going to break the great, ironclad "law" of cigar-smoking. You know:

        <u>"You gotta buy 'em BEFORE you smoke 'em!"</u>

  <u>Not</u> with this remarkable invitation from the Thompson Cigar Company.

    If you'll send me the enclosed Reservation Card as soon as possible (before my supplies run out), I'll send you one of my "Victory Sampler" boxes of 50 superb Cuban seed leaf cigars -- a tempting selection of Panetela Extras, Corona Chicos, Juniors and Plazas. Each cigar is factory-fresh and ready to smoke -- direct from our temperature and humidity controlled humidor.

    Now, here's how we break that "law" . . .

- Be personal. Note the use of the personal pronouns *me, you, your,* and *I* in the cigar letter. Talk to the reader—as one human being talks to another.
- Be friendly. Win the reader's confidence.
- Use short sentences.
- Write in a relaxed, conversational style. This is the secret of all successful mail-order letter writing. Read your writing aloud; your ear will help eliminate half of your errors.
- Ask for the order—today. Not tomorrow.

Direct-mail catalogs

While letters are used to sell a single item, catalogs offer many different products and are a favorite promotional tool of mail-order houses. For more information on catalogs, see Chapter 11, "No Fear of Flyers—and Other Sales Literature."

Newspaper and magazine advertisements

Print advertisements are another way to sell single mail-order items. Mail-order advertisements are the most difficult to write, since no salesperson can step in and explain the ad or answer the consumer's questions. A good mail-order ad tells what the product is, shows a photograph or illustration of the product, highlights the key features, explains the benefits the reader will derive from the product, and includes testimonials to the product's superior performance.

In newspapers, mail-order ads can be seen anywhere, in any section. Some magazines, however, have special sections for advertising mail-order products.

Free publicity

The mail-order sections of magazines often run free publicity items on new products. To obtain this free publicity, send the editor a press release (see Chapter 7) and photograph of the product. Some editors will ask to see a product sample before they decide whether it's worthy of mention in their publication.

Television and radio commercials

Recently, television (and less frequently, radio) has been used to advertise a wide range of mail-order items—everything from record collections and kitchenware to exercise machines and costume jewelry. These commercials usually end with a request to "send check or money order" or to call a convenient toll-free number and place an order COD or with your credit card.

Fifteen Tips for Effective Mail-Order Promotions

It doesn't matter whether you're writing a letter, catalog, ad, or commercial—these fifteen tips will help make *any* mail-order promotion get better results. Each tip is designed to get prospects to send you a check or order. (Remember, the goal of mail order is immediate sales, not long-term image-building.)

1. Offer a premium.

A premium is a bonus. It's a gift you give the prospect just for sending in his order promptly. A supplier of mail-order vitamins offers a free booklet on diet and nutrition with each purchase. The Literary Guild, a book club, used to offer a free tote bag to each new member.

Often, mail-order promotions close the sale by offering the reader just one more reason why he should buy, just one more added incentive for writing out that check. A thoughtfully selected premium, one with real value to your prospects, can be that added incentive.

2. Give first-time buyers a low introductory price.

Welcome prospects to the ranks of customers by giving them a break on their first order.

3. Make charter offers.

In a charter offer, your ad or letter lets prospects know that the product is being offered for the very first time, and that they are among the carefully selected list of people chosen to receive this special offer. In a sense, charter offers appeal to a person's ego by saying, "You can be the first on the block." And really, that's the whole secret behind any successful advertising—to make people feel good about buying your products.

4. Use temporary price reductions.

This tactic urges prospects to send in the order immediately, because, after a brief period of time, the price will go up or the supply will be depleted. Most mail-order shoppers respond to a promotion as soon as they see it; few people hold on to them to make a later purchasing decision. So, there is every reason to add incentives for sending in the order *now*.

5. Offer special discounts to repeat customers.

Here's how a sales letter from the ACME Office Supply Company uses discounts to reward its steady customers:

> Dear Mr. Banner:
>
> Thank you for trusting ACME to fill your office equipment and supply needs during the past year.
>
> It's the steady business from valued customers like you that has made us the nation's leading direct-mail office supply distributor.
>
> And, Mr. Banner, I believe that one good turn deserves another. That's why we're offering you a 50% DISCOUNT on your next order of business cards, letterhead, or envelopes!

Price breaks and special offers for repeat customers help make them *feel* special and build loyalty to your company.

6. Guarantee the offer.

Because of its "sight-unseen" nature, there's a certain risk to ordering products by mail. Mail-order shoppers live in fear of receiving shoddy merchandise, not getting the right merchandise, or not getting any merchandise at all.

Put your customers at ease. Guarantee the quality of the product. And promise a speedy refund if they're not satisfied. Here's how the sales letter from Thompson Cigar puts the buyer's fears to rest:

> When your sampler arrives, put my cigars to your own test:
>
>> Examine them with a critical eye. Smoke several of each of the four shapes. Then decide. If you are not completely delighted, return the bill unpaid, along with the remainder of the box. You'll owe me not a cent.

With this paragraph in the sales letter, the customer can't lose. (In fact, one of the favorite phrases of mail-order copywriters is "You can't lose!")

7. **Include testimonials.**

McDonald's, the *New York Daily News,* and *Reader's Digest* all promote their sweepstakes with commercials showing big-money winners talking about their newly won wealth. Nothing sells like a satisfied customer, and testimonials add believability to all promotions—including mail order.

8. **Leave adequate space on the coupon.**

Few things are as infuriating or as difficult as trying to write your name, address, city, state, zip code, and phone number on a horizontal line that's only half an inch long. Coupons and reply cards should contain adequate space for filling in this information. Make it easy, not difficult, for prospects to respond to your mail-order promotions.

9. **Use an actual object in the mailing.**

Today's consumers and businesspeople are bombarded every month by dozens of unwanted direct-mail solicitations. By including an actual object in the mailing—a penny, a postage stamp, a product sample—you can make your promotion stand out from the crowd. And breaking through the clutter, getting noticed, is the first and most vital step in making the sale.

10. Make a personal promise.

Most people do not trust corporations, and so a mail-order offer should come from an individual, not a faceless corporate entity. Make the copy as personal as possible. And above all, assure the reader that a real live human being will take the responsibility for making sure the order is processed promptly and correctly, and filled with quality merchandise. Examples of this personal style of writing are given below in the column at right; note how much more encouraging it is than the corporate we-are-not-responsible tone in the column at left.

Corporatese: No-One-Responsible-Here	Personal: We're-Here-to-Help-You
Your current situation with regards to marketing, accounting, and management will be analyzed carefully and expertly. Based on the results, you will receive a written recommendation on which system of hardware and software is optimum for the application.	We'll take a look at how you run your business, and then furnish a clear, concise report on what computer system would best meet your needs.
Unfortunately, the deadline for this offer cannot be extended.	Much as I'd like to, I can't extend the deadline.
The assorted cheeses will be shipped in a humidity-proof container.	I'll send your selection of cheeses in a special package designed to keep the food fresh and delicious.

11. Add a touch of drama to the copy.

Mail-order customers like to think they're getting something a little bit out of the ordinary for their money . . . something you can't buy at the local department store. Adding a dash of drama to your copy reinforces this feeling and gives

Selling by Letter: Mail Order • 143

your prospect more pleasure in his purchase. Here's how the Thompson Cigar Company added excitement and intrigue to a box of cigars:

> A Cuban tobacco farmer, sympathetic to American cigar lovers, managed to smuggle 12 pounds of the finest Pinar del Rio seed out of the country—in the diplomatic pouch of an ambassador stationed in Havana. The precious contraband was now in our hands!

Be careful not to overdo it when using this approach. There's an awfully thin line separating the credible from the cornball.

12. But don't be absurd.

Mail-order copywriters know that to sell, they have to tell prospects the whole story about their products: how they're made, where they come from, why they're the best on the market.

By all means, describe your product in detail. Add flourish and fancy to the package. But don't let your descriptive prose go overboard.

13. Make the package foolproof.

Avoid, whenever possible, using order forms that force prospects to calculate sales tax and handling charges. Include a self-addressed business reply card or envelope. Explain the exact terms of the offer as clearly as possible. And make sure the offer itself is simple to follow. Orders won't come through if the mail-order package is needlessly complex.

14. Call for action.

Mail-order promotions always ask for a check—or at least an order. Here are some closing lines from recent solicitation letters:

To avoid disappointment, better send in your order today, using the enclosed postage-paid envelope.

*   *   *

Surely it would be a shame to let this opportunity slip by. So send in the token to receive the next three issues on trial.

*   *   *

Why wait when you can begin enjoying the privileges of membership now?

15. Get feedback.

Test your offer. Your mailing package. Your advertisements. Your mailing lists. Keep track of which promotions bring in the most orders. And which ones flop. As with all promotions, measure the results.

Measuring the Results of Mail-Order Promotion

David Ogilvy, founder of Ogilvy and Mather, one of the world's largest advertising agencies, points out that it's fairly easy to gauge the results of mail-order advertisements.

"Either the reader clips the coupon, or he doesn't," writes Ogilvy in his book, *Confessions of an Advertising Man*. "A few days after his advertisement appears, the mail-order writer knows whether it is profitable or not."

And that's the beauty of mail order—the cost of the promotion can be weighed directly against the profit from the orders it brings in. The results aren't influenced by outside factors such as in-store displays, shelf position, service, sales meetings, and business lunches. As Ogilvy says, the mail-order ad pays for itself . . . or it doesn't.

How soon can you expect the orders to start rolling in? Well, for a mail-order ad in a daily newspaper, you'll get about 70% of your orders within the first week, and the rest within two months.

By comparison, an ad in a weekly magazine or Sunday newspaper will pull only 40% of the orders in the first week, 65% by the second, and 80% after a month has passed. Surprisingly, orders may still come in for several months after the ad has run.

With an advertisement in a monthly magazine, orders roll in even more slowly—which shouldn't come as much of a shock, since a monthly periodical is kept around longer than a daily or weekly publication. If you advertise a mail-order product in a monthly magazine, expect 10% of your orders within the first week, 22% within the second, 50% after a month has passed, 75% after two months, and the remainder within half a year.

Direct-mail letters generate 35% of their orders in the first week, 50% in two weeks, 71% in a month, and 90% in two months. The remainder will trickle in over the next four months or so.

How many orders can you expect the letter to pull? The average direct-mail letter persuades between 1% and 2% of the prospects who receive it to send in orders. Therefore, if you mail 10,000 letters, expect between 100 and 200 orders.

Like most mail-order entrepreneurs, you'll probably experiment, varying the copy and layout of your ads and letters to see what works best. The problem then becomes: How can you tell which ad or letter a given order came from? The solution: *Key the address.*

By keying the address, you're inserting a code that lets you know a prospect is writing in response to a particular promotion. For example, advertisement A for your mail-order T-shirts may ask readers to send their orders to "Tease Shirts, Inc., Dept. 101-A, Fair Lawn, NJ," while a second advertisement, ad B, directs inquiries to "Tease Shirts, Inc., Dept. 101-*B*." This way, you can see how many inquiries the A ad pulls and how many the B ad pulls. Compare the two, and select the version of the ad which yields the best results.

• Chapter 11 •

NO FEAR OF FLYERS—AND OTHER SALES LITERATURE

Why You Need Sales Literature

A housewife walks into her local deli and says, "I'm having a party next week for fifty people—do you have a catering menu?"

A businessman calls a word-processing service with which he's unfamiliar and asks, "Do you have any literature you can send me about your company?"

A consultant visiting a major insurance company is asked for his business card, brochure, and a list of his clients.

We live in a world of documentation, of paper, of establishing "credibility." A friendly smile and the appearance of competence aren't enough. We like to feel that we are doing business with people who are established in business, in the same way we prefer a name brand over Brand X. Of course, no amount of fancy brochures, business cards, streamlined logos, well-crafted sales letters, or colorful catalogs will guarantee that a job will be done well or that a product won't stop working five minutes after it has been purchased. Still, sales literature does go a long way toward setting a professional business tone, one that adds a sense of credibility and stability to our enterprises.

It isn't surprising to find that some of the best-established businesses have the most uniform and attractive sales literature. A certain sureness of tone and style comes with practice. For example, one of the finest old inns in the United States, the Publick House in Sturbridge, Mass., has a folder in each guest room containing no less than twelve brochures

—each dealing with a service or element of the inn's features. The brochures contain the Publick House logo, and each is characterized by a similarity of tone and a warm-spirited, low-key approach.

The Publick House has been in business for 200 years. Not every business has had the opportunity to hone its image for that period of time. Yet almost every business requires some form of sales literature to help keep products and services in the customer's mind, to distinguish itself from the competition, and to answer a prospect's basic questions about who, what, and where you are. Sales literature has a variety of specific uses, among them:

"Leave-behind"

Long after the details of your eloquent sales presentation have been forgotten, a brochure, flyer, or catalog that has been "left behind" continues to keep the sales message alive in your customer's mind. Sales literature recapitulates the highlights of your business as well as the usual information about address, telephone, and business hours. If a leave-behind is well executed, it gives you a second chance at a sale, and serves as a permanent reminder whenever it is viewed.

A response to inquiries

Not every prospect comes to you with money in hand. Many people respond to ads to get more information, and that information is a necessary step toward making the sale. A person answering a telephone-directory advertisement for a local airport limousine service may have several questions on his mind before actually placing an order for a limo. Some people answer ads because they anticipate needs far into the future. For these people, a ready-made brochure or flyer saves you the time of creating an individual response to each inquiry. If you are competing with a service that does not have sales literature, you put yourself in a preferred position to make the sale when the prospect is ready to place an order. After all, your literature will be on hand. A flyer with your phone number on it saves the prospect the need to start his research all over again.

Mailer

Flexibility is the key to sales literature for the small business. After all, a brochure or flyer that is presentable as a leave-behind may also have to serve as a mailer to new prospects. That's one reason why brochures are created to be as timeless as possible. The moment you start specifying prices or other transitory details, you date the piece, and are then put into the awkward position of having to explain the price increases to everyone who has the old brochure.

Naturally, there are times when naming a price will be proper (for example, when you're selling a low-cost service or a service or product whose price is not due to change for a long time). When you create a piece of sales literature to be mailed, you do have to consider several things that did not matter with leave-behinds. You'll have to consider the weight of the mailer (if it exceeds one ounce, the postage will increase) and you'll have to consider whether it is better to send the piece as a self-mailer (designed to be sent through the mail without an envelope) or in an envelope. If the brochure is of an unusual size, then you'll need envelopes to match, and they may well have to be custom-made.

Display in a store

Almost every supermarket or other type of food store has sales literature on the counter. The literature reminds customers of various sales, and sometimes provides recipes that, conveniently, make use of items in plentiful supply in the store. Almost every enterprise can use some type of sales literature within a store. A bookstore, for example, may post the current best-seller list, thus transforming that list into a piece of sales literature. Of course, a travel agency is the essence of a business surrounded on all sides by sales literature—a permanent display of multicolored travel brochures and flyers. So many new brochures come in through the mail every day that it would take a full-time employee in every travel agency just to keep the brochures current.

No Fear of Flyers—and Other Sales Literature • 149

Sales support

Salespeople rely on literature to give the full story of each of their products or services. No *Encyclopedia Britannica* salesperson lugs the whole encyclopedia around with him, nor is an Avon lady likely to carry every conceivable eye shade, mascara, or nail polish. Catalogs, product sheets, and brochures help educate salespeople and help them make presentations. At the end of these presentations, these sales pieces may be used as "leave-behinds."

Types of Sales Literature

Even though terms such as *flyer, brochure,* and *catalog* are probably quite familiar to you, let's take a moment to define these pieces of sales literature, and possibly even expand our concept of each.

Flyers

Flyers—also spelled "fliers"—are small handbills. They are perhaps the simplest form of sales literature, unless you consider business cards a form of sales literature. Flyers can be as primitive as a handwritten message on a piece of note paper or as elaborate as a four-color, expensively illustrated announcement. Generally, a flyer is relatively inexpensive to produce and easy to distribute. It can be a one-page menu for a Chinese restaurant, or a rack-size—about 4-by-9-inch—slip of paper with your name, logo, a few lines of copy, and, if you're not easy to find, a simple map or directions to guide readers to your place of business.

In tourist areas, rack-size flyers for every circus, zoo, theme park, restaurant, furniture store, inn, museum, and hotel proliferate. In urban areas, flyers for a variety of businesses and services cluster around places and events that attract crowds: photocopy stores, supermarkets, outdoor concerts, and street fairs.

Since flyers are usually mass-produced and mass-distributed, many will not find their way to qualified prospects. However, since flyers are relatively inexpensive (5,000 8½-

by-11-inch flyers, typeset, and offset, could cost as little as 3 cents each), there's a comfortable margin for waste.

Brochures

"Brochure" is a difficult word to define, but most dictionaries consider it a synonym for "pamphlet." Generally, a brochure is a free piece of sales literature that has more than one page. Typically, it is folded, dividing a sheet of paper into several "panels." Brochures have a look of permanence or at least semipermanence; they are usually designed and typeset. A brochure need not be fancy, but it does present a "face" to the world, and its style and tone epitomize the unchanging aspects of your business in a more comprehensive way than any flyer could.

Brochures come in all shapes and sizes. One company that specializes in reducing the width of neckties created two small brochures, one which tells readers the fine points of tying neckties, and the other a cleverly illustrated, more sales-oriented brochure titled "How to Take Care of the Ties You Treasure." Both brochures contain an abundance of information, but the second brochure discusses prices and guides the reader to the details of the service being offered.

While many of the descriptive details of a brochure could also apply to flyers, they are more often associated with brochures: captioned photographs, layout created by a designer, identification of products and prices, typeset copy, at least one "fold" that serves to separate sections of the brochure.

While flyers can be produced inexpensively, it should be clear that even a relatively simple brochure can cost hundreds of dollars to produce. A brochure requires copy that has a "timeless" quality to it, and may require graphics and design that, once created, will serve as the epitome of the very best elements of your business.

A flyer, with its "here today, gone tomorrow" feel to it, need not involve elaborate copywriting or design, but a brochure that may describe your business to prospects and customers for years to come, and that may reach prospects by mail as well as by hand, requires thoughtfulness about everything—down to how much postage it will cost to mail, and whether it should be a self-mailer.

Circulars

Circulars are intended for mass distribution, and usually detail the prices and product information of a particular retail business. A supermarket may print a circular containing that week's food prices and specials. Even though the circular may be printed as a tabloid or as a flyer it is still considered a "circular," because it is intended for wide circulation.

A photographic supply store might also find a circular beneficial, especially if it has different types of films or printing services available at different prices on a regular basis. A drugstore also may use circulars to alert customers to specials on certain cosmetics, drugs, or sundries.

Catalogs

Catalogs have always held a mystique for Americans. In their pictures, we have seen glimpses of a new, sleek way of life, a fashionable, elegant, forever-young grouping of people, places and things.

Whether it meant gathering around a crackling fire and seeing Sears Roebuck's image of next spring's garden tools and home accessories, or peering at Neiman-Marcus's status-laden offerings, catalog reading has never really gone out of vogue. Pick up almost any magazine and you'll see dozens of ads ending in the familiar words "Send for our free catalog." Of course, some of the fancier catalogs, replete with full-color photographs of watches, rugs, and jewelry, are no longer free.

Catalogs are lists of offerings, usually labeling each piece of merchandise, illustrating it, and attaching a price to it. Catalogs make the best sense for businesses that have numerous lines of products: a clothing manufacturer, a large jeweler or department store, a cosmetics manufacturer, a boutique. They are usually expensive to produce, and are justified only when you expect to distribute them to thousands of prospects who request them.

Some of the most famous catalogs are those of L. L. Bean,

Sears, Bloomingdale's, Brooks Brothers, and Neiman-Marcus.

A catalog is generally larger than a brochure. In fact, it resembles an extensive booklet. It presents your products to either the public or to business clients or both.

Bill stuffers

Bill stuffers are a type of literature included with invoices, monthly statements, and other routine correspondence. Because they enjoy a "free ride" in the same envelope carrying bills, they give companies like Consolidated Edison of New York, American Express, and a variety of telephone companies the opportunity to sell new services or merchandise. These bill stuffers sometimes simply serve to reinforce sales messages or to pass along useful information. Their size, typically, is 9 by 3 inches or 6 by 3 inches, depending upon the size of envelope you plan to use.

Other types of sales literature

There are a variety of types of sales literature. *Case histories* briefly describe product success stories; *price sheets* give the latest price information on available services or products; *product data sheets,* like press-release fact sheets, boil down the essentials of particular products. *Business cards* may be the most common type of sales literature. They sell you as well as your business.

Eleven Tips for Creating Better Brochures

Now that you're familiar with the various types of sales literature, here are some tips on making your brochures more effective:

1. Make sure the cover tells your story.

The front panel or page of your brochure is the first thing that your customer sees. That cover should communicate the basics of what you are selling. This need not be an elaborate explanation of what you are offering, but simply a statement of what you do. A barber shop has a barber's pole, a doctor may have a sign on his door identifying him as an "M.D." Similarly, a brochure or catalog or flyer should state *your* business. It can be terse (e.g., "career counseling," "publicity," or "oil paintings") but it should be there.

A catalog may also use a brief description on the cover (e.g., "Gourmet Cookware," "Books for Direct Marketers"), for without such an identification, the prospect may lose interest immediately, and never open the catalog to see what is inside.

2. Let the quality of the sales piece suit its purpose and audience.

Although sales pieces should always look neat and clean, they need not always be printed on fine paper stock or illustrated with photographs. These decisions depend on the nature of your business and of your audience.

A slick catalog may well be needed to sell fancy gift-items, but a slim, serviceable black-and-white catalog may be all that is required to sell any of a number of special-interest books. Why? Because some catalogs are selling status and glamour in addition to the product, while other catalogs replace style with practical, much-needed products: tools, equipment, utensils. That's not to say that style doesn't matter. One of the most beautiful brochures we've ever seen is the one for the newly revived Orient Express. This fully illustrated piece is handsomely produced and colorful, and it exquisitely captures the elegance and mystery of this fabled train. There would be no way to sell this luxurious trip without permitting readers to enter into a fantasy world, and fantasy is often expensive and time-consuming to create.

3. Acquaint the reader with your service or product.

One of the purposes of sales literature is to make common ground with prospects—telling them who you are and what you have to offer. A cover may communicate this information, but you may need to spend a few lines of copy describing specifically what you do. You may also wish to use your brochure to set forth a description of your company's purpose. What distinguishes your company? What are the principles upon which it has been built? Most of the rest of the brochure details, in restrained, factual language, what you can do for your customer. The brochure's style must take its lead from your business and the industry of which you are a part.

4. Don't promise what you can't deliver.

Without lying and without exaggerating, you can produce a brochure that is impressive. If you're a one-person business, you can create a brochure that gives the impression that you're a medium-size business. But don't lie. Keep your brochure defensible. Don't list clients you don't have or products you know you can't deliver.

5. Make benefits meaningful to customers.

A charming inn sells coziness, and its brochure might emphasize features such as fireplaces, sleigh rides, hospitality, and hot mulled cider. These features translate into customer benefits such as comfort, warmth, and a chance to get away from urban pressures. Put yourself in the reader's position. Does he need a car to get to town? If you're five minutes from town, let the customer know it. That way, he can develop a trip in his mind that does not require using a car. An indoor pool? That's going to appeal to those people who want to feel that they'll have some exercise to rid them of the extra calories that the hot mulled cider will add!

6. Keep a uniform look in all of your literature.

Not everyone can afford to furnish a living room or bedroom all at once: Therefore, people are often forced to settle for a more random, catch-as-catch-can decor—at least until they can afford to complete the room. With sales literature, the advantage of maintaining a similar graphic look to all literature is not just the uniformity, but the cumulative effect thereby produced. By seeing the same logo, the same typeface, the same paper stock, and even the same packaging, customers come to develop a Pavlov-like response to your product or service even before they see the name of your company. Think, for example, of the pride and uniform look that attaches itself to particular brands of ice cream, chocolate-chip cookies, and perfumes.

7. Always put informative captions on photographs.

Research indicates that photos capture our interest, so that we're likely to look at a photo in a brochure before—and even *in lieu of*—reading the copy. Since people are drawn to photos, they read captions. Therefore, make sure your captions are informative and highlight the benefits of what you are selling. In other words, don't just *identify* the photo as one of a tennis court or pool; *tell* the reader about the benefits of each facility.

8. Let the copy run as long as necessary.

While brevity is usually a plus, there are times when readers exhibit a preference for lengthy copy. You should be concise, but you should also include all of the important information. When you're selling an expensive product or service, like a condominium or car, you may have to write lengthy copy to be comprehensive and persuasive.

9. Don't rush!

Creating excellent sales literature sometimes takes hours of meticulous detail work. It involves checking and rechecking the work of copywriters, designers, and printers. It means deciding whether to use photos, which photos to use, and when reshooting a photo may be required. A good phrase, a fine photo, the right paper stock, the appropriate typeface—they may be worth the wait. So, before you start compromising on troublesome elements of the piece, ask yourself: "How can I make the piece even better?" Remember, you'll be living with the sales literature for a long, long time, so be a perfectionist about everything—from how the headlines and subheads read to the texture of the paper stock and how the color of the ink will look when it touches that paper.

10. Make your brochure worth keeping.

If your brochure tells people something they don't know or something that they feel is practical, they may want to keep it around. Try to find ways to make your brochure the kind of piece that people will want to keep. Whether your brochure gives tips on tying ties or your calendar helps people keep track of holidays, try to make the piece *valuable* to your customer. A brochure that tells people ways to tie a necktie, or of the services of a travel agent, or tips on improving the chances of winning sweepstakes, may be kept simply because it provides factual information which, in the reader's mind, might come in handy someday.

11. Tell the reader what to do next.

A brochure should not leave the reader hanging. Generally, it should lead the reader to take action. In most cases, a catalog, flyer, brochure, or sales letter will request an order. They provide everything necessary for completing the sale. A brochure might contain a coupon for the reader to use in responding, although this might not be proper form for a brochure that aims at simply describing a company or service. The final line of many sales brochures asks the reader to write, to call, to send for more information, to fill out a coupon, to enclose a check—direct action. Brochures and catalogs cannot be vague about how the sale will be consummated. Generally speaking, sales literature should spell out exactly what the reader has to do to obtain the product or service.

• Chapter 12 •

ADVERTISING IN PRINT: NEWSPAPERS, MAGAZINES, DIRECTORIES, AND THE GREAT OUTDOORS

Newspapers: The Number-One Advertising Medium

Despite what we may read about the decline of literacy in an era of cable TV, personal computers, and home video games, newspaper advertising remains the number-one medium for promoting products and services: In 1981, American business invested an estimated $17.4 billion to run advertisements in newspapers—more than was spent on radio and TV advertising *combined.*

Newspapers have long been the backbone of retail promotion. Typically, retailers run what is called "price and where-to-buy" advertising—simple display ads that emphasize the price of a featured item of merchandise, and then direct local consumers to a nearby retail outlet to make the purchase. The effectiveness of the ad is easily measured by keeping a tally of the next few days' sales.

In addition to retailers, newspaper ads are used by restaurants, nightclubs, beauty salons, home-improvement contractors, and many other types of businesses. Small businesses prefer to advertise in newspapers because newspapers provide an intensive local coverage that's rarely available in magazines or TV. Newspapers get *read*—by almost seven out of every ten consumers in the United States. Daily newspapers allow advertisers to time ad campaigns to the specific day of a particular sale, opening, or other event. And finally, newspapers give advertisers the flexibility to quickly and inexpensively change ad layout, size, and position.

Running a Newspaper Ad

Okay. Let's assume you want to do some newspaper advertising, but don't know how to go about it. We think we can guess your questions:

How can I write an ad that will get noticed?

The first thing your ad must do is get the reader's attention. And getting attention is the job of the headline.

Because the most important goal of newspaper advertising is usually immediate sales rather than long-term brand recognition or image-building, the headlines are pithy and direct. Nothing fancy here—just a short statement of the sale. As an example, take a look at these headlines from a recent issue of the New York *Daily News:*

> BE ENERGY WISE! MAKE FUEL-SAVING IMPROVEMENTS (American Window System)
>
> DIAMOND SALE (Lader & Weisberg Inc. Diamond Importers and Cutters)
>
> BIG SALE! (Kaye Wholesalers)
>
> AS SEEN ON TV/QUALITY COVERS/WHY PAY MORE FOR SLIPCOVERS!!! (Quality Covers)
>
> WHY ARE PEOPLE FLOCKING TO OUR SAME-DAY DENTURE SERVICE? WORD OF MOUTH. (The Denture Center)

The old standbys—headlines like SALE!, SAVE, GRAND OPENING, 50% OFF, and FOR A LIMITED TIME ONLY—are used again and again for one simple reason: *They work.*

What other information should I include in the ad?

First, the basics: Your store locations. Phone number. Dates of the sale. Store hours. Credit cards accepted. Product descriptions. Prices. Etc.

Then, go beyond the nuts-and-bolts information to tell readers the *benefits* they will derive from buying the product. Again, reread Chapter 5 for a refresher course on how to write copy that sells.

Should I include a photo of the product in the ad?

Photos can make ads more appealing to the readers. But beware: the quality of photo reproductions in newspapers is notoriously poor. If the photo contains a great deal of detail, or if it must be greatly reduced in size to fit the ad, you're better off with some simple line art or no visual at all.

How many words will fit in my small display ad?

The number of words you can fit into a given space depends upon the size of the lettering; the larger the *type size* (see Chapter 6), the fewer words the ad can hold. Listed below are type sizes and the maximum number of words of each size that can fit in a 1-inch-square display ad:*

5-point type—69 words

6-point type—47 words

7-point type—38 words

8-point type—32 words

9-point type—28 words

10-point type—21 words

11-point type—17 words

12-point type—14 words

14-point type—11 words

How do I put together a newspaper ad?

The newspaper's advertising department will help you create the layout and mechanical for your ad. Some newspapers

---

* Ted Schwarz, *The Successful Promoter* (Chicago: Contemporary Books, 1976), p. 102.

will charge a small fee; more often the service is given to advertisers free of charge. Although the newspaper's advertising department may make suggestions on headlines and copy, it is not an advertising agency, and *you* are responsible for writing the ad.

As for illustrating the ad, the newspaper may be able to supply simple clip-book art. But you will have to provide any product shots or other photographs.

How is newspaper space sold to advertisers?

Newspaper space is sold in units called "column-inches." A column-inch is 1 column wide by 1 inch deep. A "3 col. × 6 in." ad is 3 columns wide by 6 inches deep—a total of 18 column-inches.

Some newspapers charge by what is known as a "line rate." For example, a "2 col. × 70 line" ad takes up 2 columns in width and is 70 lines deep. An inch is equal to 14 lines, so you can easily convert line rates to column-inches.

How do I choose which newspapers to advertise in?

You can quickly and easily evaluate which newspapers are best by using the "cost per thousand" or "CPM" formula. When you buy an ad, CPM tells you how much money it costs to reach 1,000 of the newspaper's readers.

CPM is equal to the cost of the advertising space divided by the newspaper's total circulation in thousands. Thus, the CPM of a $100 ad in a paper with a circulation of 40,000 would be

$$\text{CPM} = \frac{\text{cost of the ad}}{\text{circulation in thousands}} = \frac{\$100}{40} = \$2.50$$

That is, you spend $2.50 to have your ad seen by 1,000 people. The lower the CPM, the more cost-effective the newspaper as an advertising medium.

Any other criteria to consider besides CPM?

Sure. A CPM only compares the *cost* of reaching a newspaper's readers. But you also care what *kind* of readers you reach. For example, if you are selling a mail-order book on tax loopholes for the well-to-do, you'd be better off advertising in the *Wall Street Journal* than the *National Enquirer*, regardless of what the CPM is. Remember, a promotion must be targeted to the *right people*—not just the right *number* of people.

I'm running a small display ad. Where on the page is the best place to put it?

Right-hand pages are better than left-hand pages; top of the page is better than bottom of the page; and the outside column is better than an inside column. Thus, the best position for your ad is the upper right-hand corner of a right-hand page.

However, a choice spot like this is what's called a "preferred position," and if you want it, you'll pay a premium. Otherwise, you'll be given a "run-of-page" position, which means the ad will appear wherever there's room for it.

In addition, it helps if your ad is positioned next to some editorial matter—in other words, next to an article. Ads completely surrounded by other ads are, in advertising lingo, "buried." And buried ads are like buried treasure: hard to find and unlikely to pay off.

What about running in a special section of the paper, such as sports or the society page? Any advantage in this?

Yes—depending on the product being advertised. A bookstore could benefit greatly from running its ad in the book-review section. And a marriage counselor might choose to place her ad next to "Dear Abby." Usually, requesting placement in a special section will result in the higher "preferred-position" rate. But the results are often well worth it.

Does it pay to run the ad more than once?

Not only does it pay, but it is *vital* to the ad's success. Research has shown time and time again that most readers can't be moved to action with a single ad. Readers forget ads. Repetition helps them remember.

So repeat your ad—every day, every other day, every week, every two weeks, every month. But, of course, don't repeat ads that fail. Instead find out why the ad failed, and replace it with one that will work for you.

Am I better off running a few large ads or many smaller ones?

Size helps get attention, but *repetition* is the key to success. So, schedule many repeat ads and run them as large as your budget will permit. In general, it is better to run fifty 10-inch ads than it is to run ten 50-inch ads. An exception to this is advertisements for especially newsworthy events, such as the grand opening of a store or the introduction of a new business to the community. These ads should be as large as possible—a full page if you can afford it.

What about running an ad in a pennysaver?

"Pennysavers" or "shoppers" are newspapers that are distributed free through blanket coverage of most households in a neighborhood or community. Pennysavers contain mostly advertising material and exist mainly as an advertising medium. Some are considered "junk mail"; others may be well read. It really depends on the individual publication serving your area. Many neighborhood retailers and small service businesses have gotten good results from pennysaver advertising.

Magazines: The Medium for On-Target Advertising

Magazine and newspaper ads often *look* pretty much the same. But in many other respects, the two are not at all alike.

To begin with, newspapers are read by the general public, not specific groups of people. Magazines, on the other hand, are written for specialized audiences. There are women's magazines and men's magazines. Magazines for parents and magazines for singles. Technical magazines and travel magazines. Whatever group you're selling to, you can be sure there's a magazine published just for them. Magazines deliver a loyal special-interest audience, while newspapers give advertisers a consumer-oriented readership.

Newspapers have a highly local flavor. Magazine readers are more spread out. Some magazines do have regional editions covering the East Coast, West Coast, South, and Midwest. And many metropolitan areas such as New York, Philadelphia, and Dallas are served by city magazines. But if you want to reach the people in a small town or a particular neighborhood of the city, newspapers, not magazines, are the tool to use.

Magazines generally have a longer life than newspapers. A daily newspaper may go out with the next morning's trash. But ads in monthly magazines have been known to pull inquiries *six months* after the date of publication. Magazine ads get their message across and build an audience over a prolonged period of time.

Because of the specialized readership and longevity of each issue, magazine advertising can accomplish different objectives than newspaper advertising. Newspapers, as we've said, generate next-day sales. Magazine advertising has a more far-reaching effect. It can support the sales force. Open doors. Build a company's image and reputation over the long term. Build brand recognition. Change your image. Keep your name in front of your customers—in effect, keeping them sold on you, your company, and your products.

This is not to say that magazine advertising does not generate valuable sales leads. On the contrary, small magazine display and classified ads can pull dozens of inquiries. And experience shows that at the very least, one of every three of these inquiries is a response from someone actively in the market for the type of product being advertised.

Like newspapers, magazines are a good media buy because they are read. Research shows that 89 percent of the adults in this country are avid magazine readers who read an average of eight different magazines each month. For small businesses such as restaurants, entertainments, specialty shops, and mail-order companies, magazine advertising can provide a good return on investment.

Anatomy of a Magazine Ad

Print advertising can serve two basic functions: generating inquiries, leads, and sales; and building buyer awareness and recognition. Newspaper advertising accomplishes the former; magazine ads concentrate on the latter.

While newspapers are eager to help you produce your ad, most magazines prefer to receive your ad in "camera-ready" form, meaning the layout and mechanical are prepared by the advertiser or his agency. A camera-ready mechanical can be sent directly to the printer for reproduction in the magazine.

What will it cost to produce your own ad? According to *Adweek* magazine, production costs for a full-page black-and-white ad run about $2,800 and for a full-color ad about $7,700. But more realistically, if you work with a free-lance graphic artist or print shop, you can produce an effective black-and-white magazine ad for as little as $150 or so.

Magazine ads are generally more sophisticated than newspaper ads in layout and copy. Rather than motivate a consumer to come to a store, they try to convince qualified prospects that a company and its products are superior to the competition.

Magazine ads will often omit price information altogether, and instead work to present, in an interesting and compelling fashion, information that will tell the reader how buying the product advertised can improve his or her life—what the *Harvard Business Review* calls "the shock of personal recognition."

A good magazine ad's headline reaches out to prospects the same way a catchy book title reaches out to bookbuyers. When Writer's Digest Books titled a book on free-lance writing *How You Can Make $20,000 a Year Writing (No Matter Where You Live),* the publisher knew that the title would strike a responsive chord in struggling free-lance writers—the primary market for the book. In the same way, a magazine ad with the headline "Cut Your Summer Electric Bills in Half!" immediately arouses the interest of consumers faced with skyrocketing utility bills and sweltering homes or apartments.

Unlike newspapers, magazines have a reproduction quality

that is quite high, and magazine ads can use more sophisticated photos, illustrations, and other graphics. Most magazines also offer full-color reproduction. While color ads have a 40% higher readership than black-and-white, the cost of producing and running them is usually beyond the budgets of most small businesses.

Display advertising space in magazines is sold in fractions of pages, and not by column-inch or line rates. The most popular units are two-page spreads, one page, half page, two-thirds page, one-third page, quarter-page, and sixth-page. Smaller units are available. For a monthly magazine, you have to reserve space at least one month before the publication date of the issue in which your ad will appear.

Positioning of a magazine ad is not as crucial a factor as it is for newspapers. However, if you're running full-page ads, the cover positions (inside front, inside back, and back) are "preferred positions," and with good reason—they get 31% higher readership than "run-of-book" ads. (In advertising lingo, magazines are known as "books.")

For small businesses with bigger budgets, a full-page ad is the best buy. The price is not necessarily prohibitive; a full-page ad in some highly specialized trade journals can cost less than a small fractional-page ad in a major newspaper. Surprisingly, a two-page spread is generally *not* a good investment: Two pages cost twice as much as a single page, but deliver only a third more impact.

Selecting the Magazine

CPM—cost per thousand—is a useful technique for buying newspaper space, where you're evaluating several local papers that claim to reach the same audience, more or less. CPM can be a consideration in selecting magazines, too. But it's less important, since magazines deliver special markets, not general consumers. So, even if *Law and Order* and *Lawn and Garden* did, by some strange coincidence, have identical CPMs, they would in no way be comparable or competitive advertising media—one deals with felonies, the other with fertilizers!

Need to know more about a magazine? Consult *Standard Rate and Data*. For each publication it provides the address of the local advertising sales office, plus all sorts of useful information including circulation, rates, mechanical requirements, closing dates (the closing date is the last day you can reserve advertising space in a given issue), discounts for frequency (each insertion becomes less expensive the more times you run the ad), and a description of the magazine's editorial thrust.

Standard Rate and Data is indexed by category, e.g., magazines for funeral directors, magazines for horse enthusiasts, magazines for hospital administrators, etc. Make a list of the publications in your area of interest. Contact each, and ask for a sample issue and a *media kit*.

The media kit is a package containing detailed information on a particular magazine's readership. By studying this information, you can learn what percentage of a magazine's total readers are potential customers for your business . . . and what percentage are what advertising people call "wasted circulation" (nonprospects). Naturally, you will want to advertise in the magazines that give you the most qualified prospects at the lowest CPM.

The Yellow Pages and Other Directories

There's a *big* difference between directory ads versus newspaper and magazine ads, and the difference is this:

People reading newspapers and magazines are reading articles for information or entertainment, and they tend to pass over the ads. (The average person reads only *four ads* in a magazine.) Therefore, to be effective, a newspaper or magazine ad must forcefully grab the reader's attention through a novel, interesting presentation—a fascinating photo, a distinctive layout, a compelling headline.

But when people turn to a directory, they are prime prospects, *ready to buy and looking for suppliers*. They do not have to be persuaded to buy: they merely have to be persuaded to buy *from you*. As a result, directory advertising is appropriate for nearly every type of small business—manufacturers, retailers, service businesses, and even wholesalers.

According to the Thomas Publishing Company, publishers of *Thomas Register,* a leading industrial-products directory, the surest way to get your directory ad to generate inquiries is to have the biggest ad on the page. The largest ad generates 40 times the response of an ordinary name-and-phone-number listing. And *any* ad is better than no ad—just printing your company name in boldface type will double the response you'd get from a regular listing.

Obviously, it's best to have your ad at the front of your section of the directory, since readers generally start with the A's and end with the Z's. Normally, you won't have much control over this. But if directory advertising is your primary source of new business, you might seriously consider choosing a company name beginning with A just to get your ad up front.

Another time-tested gambit is to list everything you sell or do in your directory ad. One New Jersey insurance agent begins his Yellow Pages ad with the direct headline "INSURANCE" and goes on to list the more than thirty different types of items he insures, reasoning that if he is the only agent to list snowmobiles in his advertisement, then anyone turning to the Yellow Pages with a snowmobile to insure will be hooked by the ad. As a result, his small (2-column-by-2½-inch) display ad generates one or two telephone inquiries on just about *every business day of the year.*

Almost every small business can benefit from an ad in the Yellow Pages. Directory advertising is another story. In some industries, a directory ad is a "must." In others, the standard directories are not often used by customers, and advertisers would be better off putting their money in trade-magazine advertising or direct mail. When you have to decide whether it is worth advertising in a given trade or professional directory, consider these four points:

1. *Completeness.* Does the directory contain enough real information to be useful to buyers? Or is it just one big advertising supplement?

2. *Ease of use.* Is the directory well organized, indexed,

and cross-referenced? Are manufacturers listed by geography, company, *and* product category?

3. *Reputation.* How long has the directory been around? Is it well respected and well used? Check to see if you find it on your customers' desks. Is it considered the leading directory in its industry? Or is it a Johnny-come-lately?

4. *Circulation.* How many people does it reach? Does this circulation include the majority of your potential customers?

Outdoor Advertising: Billboards

If you run a hotel, restaurant, gift shop, recreational facility, or other business buried in a remote area bypassed by the major highways, billboards can guide travelers to your door.

To passing motorists, your billboard remains in view for about five seconds—barely enough time to read a single sentence. Therefore, don't fill your billboard with lengthy copy. Just make sure your name and a capsule description of your business ("diner," "children's zoo," "miniature golf") are visible at a glance. And don't forget to include directions ("Take exit 17 ½-mile ahead and turn right").

Standard billboards are 14 feet high by 48 or 25 feet wide. Billboard graphics should be simple: strong, pure colors; realistic artwork or photography. Legibility is the truest test of a billboard design.

Aside from directing prospects to places off the beaten path, billboards can do little else to tell people about your products or services because of the limited number of words their messages contain. Therefore, for most small businesses in urban and suburban locations, billboards are not an effective promotion.

To find out more about billboard advertising, write to the National Outdoor Advertising Bureau, 711 Third Avenue, New York, NY 10017.

Transit Advertising

Don't look down your nose at writing ads for buses, subways, and commuter trains. If such leading literary lights as F. Scott Fitzgerald and Ogden Nash wrote transit ads, then you can, too.

Actually, for small businesses located in metropolitan areas, transit ads can ensure that your prospects see your message. "Interior" ads—those posters plastered on the insides of buses and trains—are especially effective because they have a captive audience: The ads stay in front of the passengers for as long as they're riding in the vehicle. The average transit rider spends 22 minutes inside the vehicle on each ride and takes 24 rides a month. So chances are your transit ad will be well read. Again . . . and again . . . and again.

But few riders will give up a seat on a crowded bus to walk across the aisle and read an ad on aluminum siding. Keep the copy short so the type will be large enough to be easily read from the opposite side of the vehicle.

Simplicity is also a virtue in transit advertising. As we've mentioned, readers seldom remember advertisements. And the rider can't take a transit ad with him, unlike a newspaper or magazine ad that he can clip and save. (At least not if there's a transit cop around!) Therefore, your message should be short and sweet. Include the name of your business, a brief description of what it is you're selling, and your address and phone number in large, legible lettering.

To increase inquiries, we recommend the use of "Take-ones" in your transit advertising. "Take-ones" are the reply cards you see attached to some transit ads and point-of-purchase displays. The ad copy urges the reader to send for a free brochure or other literature using one of the reply cards. On the card, which is usually postage-paid and addressed to the advertiser, the reader can fill in his name, address, phone number, and request. "Take-ones" are so-named because they often bear the headline "FREE: TAKE ONE!"—urging transit riders to do just that.

The standard interior transit ad unit is 11 inches high by 28 inches wide. But you can't rent a single ad on one vehicle: Transit advertising space is sold on a number of vehicles for a set period of time. You might, for example, pay anywhere from $4,000 to $8,000 a month for a standard unit on 2,200 buses. For the rates in your area, contact the local transit advertising company or sales organization.

Other Print Media

Consider church bulletins, newsletters, company magazines, club and association bulletins, programs, playbills, school papers, and community bulletin boards when planning your print-advertising campaign. Small publications may be diverse, limited in circulation, and difficult to evaluate, but they offer one crucial advantage to small businesses, and that's low cost. Try out some of these media options and see what they do for you. Don't be afraid to experiment; after all, the price is right.

Cooperative Advertising

Cooperative (co-op) advertising is a kind of cost-sharing promotion between a manufacturer and a retailer. Here's how it works:

The retailer agrees to advertise the manufacturer's product (a product that the retailer sells). In return, the manufacturer pays for all or part of the cost of running the ad. The manufacturer may also help the retailer create the ad, or may provide the retailer with ad "mats" or "slicks"—finished, ready-to-run ads with a space for the retailer to insert his name and store location.

Co-op programs often give the retailer free advertising. In return, the manufacturer is spared the time and trouble of executing advertising programs on the local level, since the retailer is scheduling and placing the ads.

Each year, $6 billion in co-op funds is available from manufacturers. Co-op advertising is an excellent way for small retailers to stretch their ad budgets, and you might inquire of manufacturers to see what co-op funds they will make available to you. Be sure to find out how funds are allocated, and what the method of reimbursement is.

Although co-op advertising is traditionally a manufacturer/retailer promotion, other types of businesses are now taking advantage of it. For example, several consumer and industrial trade associations are making co-op funds and promotional materials available to the manufacturing companies that compose their membership.

• Chapter 13 •

BROADCAST ADVERTISING: RADIO AND TV

Radio

Suddenly, radio is "in" again. From tiny transistors to sophisticated Sony Walkmans to huge "boom boxes," radios are everywhere—the streets and the subways, the beach and the park, the bedroom and the bathroom. And where radio goes, advertisers follow.

All fads aside, radio has always made it easy for broadcasters and their sponsors to reach the masses. Today, 99% of all households and 95% of all automobiles have radios. More than 7,800 AM and FM stations broadcast music, news, sports, and talk shows daily to some 458 million radios across the country. People *listen* to radio—the average man or woman has his or her radio turned on about 3½ hours a day. And 88% of these listeners say they are listening to radio as much as or more than they always have.

Although radio doesn't dominate our lives the way television does, as an advertising medium it has two major advantages over the tube. One is comparatively low cost; the other is *selectivity*.

How Radio Reaches Listeners

In order to compete with television, radio stations became specialized in their programming, reaching out to certain select audiences. There are many different types of radio stations: easy listening, religious, Top 40, news, talk, sports, country and western, jazz, hard rock, "middle-of-the-road," Hispanic, black, soft rock, oldies, classical, disco. Each type of station reaches a specific segment of the market—and this is what the stations sell to their advertisers. As a result, radio advertising is extremely effective for businesses catering to specific groups: teenagers, commuters, housewives, college students.

For example, research shows that teenagers are the audience for Top 40 and disco rock-and-roll stations. But the big-band stations, featuring the music of Benny Goodman, Glenn Miller, Count Basie, and Harry James, attract a more mature crowd—60% of their listeners are between 45 and 64 years old.

A recent study by Robert E. Balon and Associates reveals that the listener's *mood* is a crucial factor in what station he or she selects. As one would expect, people in their mid 20s to early 30s prefer news, weather, and soft music when they get up to go to work in the early hours of the morning. But coming home after a hard day's labor, they like to hear mostly music—shows featuring familiar oldies, with little talk in between. Teenagers and young adults like to hear a fast-talking DJ like Don Imus or Dan Ingram early in the morning; after school or work they prefer straight rock.

Naturally, you want your radio spots to reach the right audience at the right time. Here, then, are a few helpful hints on buying radio time.

First, make sure you buy time on the right type of station. As we've mentioned, radio stations are narrowly targeted to specific audiences—primarily on the basis of age, and sometimes by race, ethnic background, and income, too. Find out which stations in your area appeal to your particular market. If you own a sporting goods store, for example, you may wish to sponsor a sports show. If your theater is pushing tickets to a highbrow play, the classical-music stations would be the place to advertise.

To find out if a local station reaches *your* market, call the station's advertising sales department and explain what you're selling and who you're selling it to. If the station's listeners don't match your target market, the sales department may recommend another station.

If, however, the station represents a potential advertising vehicle for your product, ask the station to send you a *media kit*. This package is similar to the kit you'd get from a magazine and contains the following items:

• A coverage map that indicates the geographic area the station reaches. Some powerful stations broadcast to people too far away to be potential customers for your business; other stations broadcast signals that are too weak to cover your area adequately.

• Market-research reports that show how well the station competes with other stations in the area when it comes to attracting listeners.

• Descriptions of the DJs and their shows. In some areas, certain DJs can become minor celebrities, and as a result, more people listen closely to their shows.

• A list of other businesses in the area that have advertised on the station.

• A rate card that tells you the cost of buying air time. Rates vary with the time of the broadcast (morning, afternoon, early evening, late night) because the size of the audience varies with the time of day.

Radio delivers its largest audience during "drive time"—the times when listeners are driving to work (6:00 to 10:00 A.M.) and from work (3:00 to 6:00 P.M.). Naturally, drive time is the most costly time—radio's equivalent to television's "prime time." The least expensive radio spots run from midnight to 5:00 A.M. During this "graveyard" time, few people besides insomniacs and the third shift at the factory are tuned in to their sets.

Rates vary with time, number of commercials, and type of station. Prices for a 60-second spot to air once a week range from $5 in some rural areas to $400 for drive time in a metropolitan area. Sixty-second spots are by far the most popular, but 30-second and 10-second chunks of time are also available. Radio stations will offer "bonus" spots free to advertisers who buy a number of spots at one time. In addition to spot buying, advertisers can elect to buy sponsorship of certain program segments such as the weather, sports, news, or the traffic report. As a sponsor, your name and product will be plugged by on-air personalities at certain points during the broadcast.

Thousands of small businesses have successfully promoted themselves through radio advertisements; these include auto dealers, accountants, banks, boutiques, bars, clubs, lounges, restaurants, theaters, health clubs, and hairdressers, to name a few. If you wish to join them, ask the advertising sales departments of your local radio stations for help in planning your radio advertising. They can set up a schedule and budget, help you plan advertising strategy, recommend an ad agency to produce the commercial, and even help with the writing of the commercial. Best of all, this free service comes with the price of the air time.

Depending on the nature of your business, the radio salespeople may recommend drive-time spots, late-night commercials, sponsorship of program segments, or a combination of several alternatives. Naturally, as with newspaper and magazine radio advertising, you want to reach the greatest number of *qualified* prospects at the lowest possible cost per thousand.

Eight Tips for Writing Radio Commercials

Two major advantages of radio are its short lead time and its minimal production costs. While television spots have to be performed in a studio, recorded on film or videotape, and sent to the station to be aired, a radio commercial can be written, handed to the announcer in script form, and read live on the air—all in the same day.

Some companies do hire advertising agencies to produce more elaborate radio spots using professional narrators, actors, singers, musicians, and sound effects. But for most small businesses, a well-written "live" commercial—one read by the announcer from a script—can get the word out . . . and eliminate production costs altogether. Often, the radio station's advertising sales department can help you write the script.

Chapter 5 presents many helpful hints on how to write effective advertising copy—but it deals mainly with *print* promotions. Broadcast advertising is a little different from magazines, newspapers, and direct mail. Here are eight additional copy tips specifically designed to help you write better radio commercials:

1. **Make it sound the way people talk.**

Radio, after all, involves talking and listening, not reading and writing. By controlling the volume, tone, and inflection of his or her voice, the radio announcer can emphasize certain points, and communicate in ways a printed page cannot. A natural, conversational style in radio helps keep listeners interested; awkward or stiff monologue sounds false and turns them off.

2. **Repeat the product name and the store name.**

Ever since Pavlov rang a dinner bell for his hungry dog, we've known that repetition aids the memory. To get listeners to remember your product or your store, repeat the name. We recently heard a 30-second radio spot repeat the advertiser's name *eight times!*

3. **Use short words and short sentences.**

Two reasons for this. First, although grammarians hate to admit it, people do *talk* this way. They use short sentences. Sentence fragments. And sentences beginning with the conjunctions *and, or,* and *but.*

Secondly, short words and sentences are easier to understand and remember. Listeners cannot grasp long, convoluted arguments and complex terms.

4. **Supply the visual.**

The major disadvantage of radio versus newspapers, magazines, and television is that *radio has no pictures*. It is a medium of words and sound. The listener's imagination supplies the visual based on what the ear takes in.

So, if it's important that the listener know what your product looks like, you must describe it in the copy. For example, in a radio spot advertising a line of home-baked pies that are packaged in red aluminum foil, end the commercial with a line like: "So, ask for the pie in the bright-red wrapper at your favorite supermarket or grocery store today."

5. Use sound effects.

A lifeguard's whistle, children laughing, the tinkling of the bell on an ice cream truck—these are the sounds that can add warmth, drama, and believability to radio advertising. Promoting stock-car races at the local speedway? Your commercial should include the roar of engines revving up for the big race. Selling mufflers? Let listeners compare the sound of an auto before and after the new muffler is installed.

One important note: Adding sound effects to your spot means you will have to pre-record your commercial . . . and that, in turn, adds considerably to the cost of your radio advertising.

6. Identify with the listener's situation.

In print advertising, you can use hundreds of words plus photos and diagrams to explain the benefits of your product in great detail. In radio and television, you have only 10, 30, or at the most 60 seconds of time to hook the listener's interest and explain your selling proposition. Radio and television are better for eliciting an emotional rather than a logical response from consumers. One way to make this a positive response is to create a situation that empathizes with the listener's own life, to get the listener to say, "Oh yes, that's me." The well-known radio-comedy team of Dick and Bert uses humor to accomplish this in the opening of a spot they wrote for Weil Olds auto dealers:

> SHEILA: Sam, you are ready for any pushy car salesman they've got here.
>
> SAM: But I'm still practicing my answers.
>
> SHEILA: Okay, okay. When the car salesman first comes up you say what?
>
> SAM: *I'm just looking!*

178 • HOW TO PROMOTE YOUR OWN BUSINESS

SHEILA: Okay, and when he comes around a second time you say what?

SAM: *I haven't made my mind up yet!*

SHEILA: And when he comes up to you a third time you say what?

SAM: *Beat it, buster, before I break your nose!*

SHEILA: Ooo, you're going to be perfect.

SAM: (laughs) Okay!

SHEILA: Ooo, this time no salesperson's gonna talk you into the first car you see. You'll see . . .*

7. Ask for the order.

Don't forget to mention your phone number or address. Most stations will also allow listeners to write to you, the advertiser, care of the station, and you can mention this, too —just in case listeners forget to jot down your number.

8. Experiment.

"Don't be afraid to experiment," says Burt Manning, vice-chairman of J. Walter Thompson, one of the world's largest advertising agencies. "Radio's lower production costs are an invitation to do that. And if you make a mistake, you'll know about it fast, and you can fix it." †

Try a variety of different approaches in your radio scripts —drama, dialogue, humor, warmth, hard sell. Run the spots that do work; rewrite the ones that don't.

• • •

In one sense, radio is the *easiest* advertising medium to succeed in. Readers will turn the page on a dull or boring ad. TV watchers use commercial breaks to run to the refrigerator. But according to a recent study on radio audience listening habits, only 4% of radio listeners change the station when

---

* © 1981 The DOCSI Corporation.
† From *Advertising Age,* Sept. 13, 1982, p. M-10.

they don't like the commercial.* So practically any commercial you write and broadcast will be heard. The trick is to get people to listen—remember—and act.

Television

These days it seems as if the president of every company, big *and* small, is starring in his own TV commercial. Lee Iacocca pitches for Chrysler; Frank Purdue, a tough man, extolls the virtue of his tender chickens; Tom Carvel articulates the benefits of giving Carvel ice cream cakes as Father's Day gifts.

Armand Schaubroek, musician and entrepreneur, achieved status as a minor celebrity in Rochester, N.Y., by starring in self-produced TV commercials for his House of Guitars music and record store. While most advertising textbooks poohpooh the practice, Schaubroek feels that being your own TV spokesperson can help bring in business because "it gives the customer something to look for when he comes to the store." Schaubroek's home-grown 15-second TV spots helped to transform the House of Guitars from a basement operation into Rochester's largest musical outlet, a thriving business grossing upward of $5 million a year.†

Small wonder that the House of Guitars and thousands of other small businesses put their advertising dollars in television. TV is undeniably the dominant form of mass communication in the United States today: 98 out of every 100 homes have television, and the average adult watches TV for $6\frac{1}{2}$ *hours every day*. Radio and print simply do not have the impact or the mass appeal of television. And that's why TV advertising appeals to record stores, auto dealers, vocational training institutes, mail-order marketers, restaurants, and other businesses trying to reach a broad audience of general consumers.

---

* The study applies to listeners of *car* radios only.
† Andrew Helfer, "A Lot of People Would Like to See Armand Schaubroek—Dead. An Interview," University of Rochester *Campus Times,* February 1, 1978, pp. 6–7.

Television advertising is expensive, and small businesses cannot compete with national advertisers and their Madison Avenue ad agencies in terms of either coverage or quality. To run a single 60-second spot on certain national prime-time programs can cost more than $10,000—a sum that exceeds the entire year's advertising budget for many small companies. And production costs for the commercial can run anywhere from $40,000 to $100,000 if you hire an agency to produce the spot.

David Ogilvy laments that television is "an infernally difficult medium to use." That's certainly true—especially when you can't afford the services of an advertising agency or professional director to guide you in the use of storyboards, answer prints, voice-over tracks, mixing, dubbing, transferring, and other technicalities. Certainly, we advise you to get professional guidance if you can afford it. But, realizing that, like Armand Schaubroek, you may have to do it yourself, we offer the following five tips on producing television commercials:

1. *Read a good book on the subject.* We recommend Hooper White's *How to Produce an Effective TV Commercial,* available from Crain Books, 740 N. Rush St., Chicago, IL 60611.

2. *Demonstrate the product.* Television is a visual medium. Take advantage of it by showing how the product works. If the product doesn't lend itself to demonstration, at least feature it prominently in the picture. Show off the product, its function and its packaging so your viewers will remember it.

3. *Make it lively.* Use action, dialogue, testimonials, and drama to make your commercial interesting to watch. Television programs provide viewers with pure entertainment, and they expect as much from the commercials.

4. *Make it memorable.* The average consumer sees thousands of commercials each month. Make yours memorable so that it sticks out from the crowd. Do not fret if viewers say they do not *like* your commercial; research shows that there is no correlation between people's *liking* commercials and their being *sold* by them.

5. *Repeat the product name and the selling proposition.* Broadcast advertisements come and go quickly—in 60 sec-

onds or less. Help consumers remember your message by repeating it at least twice.

When to Use Television

Radio, like magazines, delivers narrowly targeted audiences. Television is more like newspapers, in that it reaches a broad consumer-oriented audience.

Print can accommodate detail; television cannot. For one thing, there's not enough time in a commercial spot for a lengthy explanation of a product's features and benefits; for another, a television can't handle complex visuals such as tables of prices, long lists of retail outlets, and complicated graphs. As a result, television is good for advertising simple products and services that the average consumer can buy: hamburgers, soap, records, chickens, clothing, rugs, automobiles, soft drinks. Highly technical products and services which require a great deal of explanation generally do not lend themselves to promotion through TV commercials. And television has too broad an audience to be useful as a tool for industrial or business-to-business selling.

When you buy television time, you should understand how the television advertising salespeople price the spots. Generally, air-time price varies with audience: The more people watching, the more expensive the spot. Shows are rated according to "gross rating points" (GRP) and "shares." GRPs measure the percentage of all the television sets that a show can reach in a given market area. A share is the percentage of these sets actually in use and tuned to the program. Therefore, a show of "rating 1, share 16" reaches 1% of the homes in an area . . . but only 16% of the families living in these homes actually watch the broadcast.

Standard commercial lengths are 10, 30, and 60 seconds; many local stations also offer 15- and 20-second spots. Ask the advertising sales department of your local station for a schedule of programs including information on share, rating points, market penetration, cost per thousand, and other data to help you make a buying decision.

One way to save money in television advertising is to buy

what is known as "preemptible time." As the name implies, a commercial scheduled during a preemptible slot can indeed be preempted if another advertiser wants to pay the full rate for the spot. In exchange for giving up the certainty that your commercial will run at the appointed hour, preemptible time will be sold to you at a greatly reduced rate.

How long should a commercial run? Most experts agree that a commercial should stay on the air until it doesn't sell anymore. For some spots, this has turned out to be years . . . and sometimes *decades.*

Finally, in answer to your question "What about cable TV?" we reply, "It sounds good—but it's too early to tell for sure." Despite the thousands of articles written on the cable industry, cable stations are just beginning to provide advertisers with the hard numbers (market penetration, cost per thousand, share, rating, and so forth) they need to evaluate cable as an advertising medium. Cable is a local, fragmented medium, and one that does not easily lend itself to sweeping generalizations.

One thing we *can* say with certainty is that big business is beginning to invest in cable; during the first three months of 1982, more than $31 million was spent on cable TV advertising over four major cable systems (CNN, ESPN, USA, and WTBS). Whether this advertising is effective remains to be seen.

Nonbroadcast Commercials

Next time you're standing in front of a store with TV sets displayed in the window, observe the people who pass by. Inevitably, some will stop to watch the television for minutes on end—*even though they can't hear the sound!*

Go to the neighborhood bar when the ballgame is on the tube. Count how many of the people seated at the bar have their heads turned to the set—again, even though they can't hear the sound.

Novelist Jerzy Kosinski tells of a classroom experiment in which a teacher, lecturing to a class, set up a television monitor on the other side of the room; the monitor showed the teacher speaking. Even though there was a live teacher present, *the students watched the television image!**

If these experiments prove anything, it is that people become mesmerized in front of a TV screen. They're lulled by it, hypnotized by it, captured by it. As a businessperson, why not take advantage of the fact that a film or videotape doesn't have to be broadcast over network TV in order to grab the viewers' attention and get them to watch?

There are many nonbroadcast uses for commercials and films. One manufacturer of designer jeans produces 10-minute spots that run in department stores on movie projectors and videotape monitors. Many industrial manufacturers make films about their equipment and use the films as tools for sales, recruitment, employee communications, public relations, and trade-show displays. An automatic slide show set up in a kiosk at the local airport can make your hotel's advertising stand out from the rest. The list goes on and on, and the message is clear: Even if your film or tape is never aired over regular television channels, it can still sell effectively as an on-location promotion or audiovisual support for the sales force.

Now, about the cost. Hiring a professional director or audiovisual production company to produce nonbroadcast videotapes will cost between $400 and $600 per minute of finished footage; to produce a 10-minute show would cost $4,000 to $6,000. Film is even more expensive: about $1,000 to $1,500 per minute of finished footage.

However, these hefty fees include cameramen, lighting assistants, scriptwriting, actors, and professional editing. Suppose you just want to get the company president to sum up the annual report on a short video program. You can hire a videotaping service to hold the camera in front of him for about $50 to $75 an hour. These taping services don't *produce* shows the way AV production houses and ad agencies do;

---

* Harlan Ellison, *Strange Wine* (New York: Warner Books, 1978), pp. 24–25.

they merely rent you a camera and a technician to squeeze the trigger by the hour. (Mostly, their services are used by people who want a videotape record of a wedding, bar mitzvah, birthday party, or other special event.) For some simple presentations, this may be all you need.

• Chapter 14 •

MAYBE YOU SHOULD BE A PUBLISHER: NEWSLETTERS

What Is a Newsletter?

Newsletters are printed sheets, pamphlets, or small newspapers that contain news or information of interest to a particular group. Generally, they are mailed to a regular list of paying or nonpaying subscribers and are published on a regular basis—daily, weekly, monthly, or quarterly.

In recent years, newsletters have become a popular form of communication, primarily because they are concise, easy to read, focused, and, from a publisher's point of view, inexpensive to start and to produce.

Types of Newsletters

There are a variety of styles of newsletters, but they are usually one of three basic types:

Company newsletters exist to inform people about the activities of others in the organization. These newsletters are usually distributed free to members of the organization. A corporation, hotel, apartment house, or charitable institution may put out such a newsletter to communicate its activities to its own members as well as to have a vehicle for stating policy, reminding people of upcoming events, or noting changes in the organization's structure or functions. It may contain community announcements, regular columns, photos, and features.

An *industry newsletter* is generally sold, at a profit, to people within a particular industry. People buy the newsletter because they want to be well informed about a particular subject. Financial newsletters such as the *Kiplinger Letter* or the *Ruff Report* appeal to people who require fast-breaking information about investments. A newsletter such as *Platt's Oilgram* commands a high price because it gives readers in the petroleum industry vital information about that industry's happenings.

The third type of newsletter—and the one that most concerns us in this chapter—is the *free newsletter* that is distributed by a business as a "soft-sell" self-promotion. A retail store may decide to put out a free newsletter, distributing it either through the mail or at the store itself. In it, customers and browsers may find a blend of tips, hints, and new ideas relating to the products or services offered by the store. An art gallery's newsletter may give helpful advice on framing watercolors or choosing sculpture. But the letter is primarily a promotional vehicle for the store. By blending objective information with articles relating to items that may be purchased at the store, people are inclined to save the newsletter, read it at their leisure, and learn more about your offerings.

For example, The Party Place, a highly successful party-goods store in Stamford, Conn., puts out a newsletter (Fig. 14-1) that alerts its customers to seasonal party items and new ideas for celebrating holidays. It also offers creative ideas for planning successful parties. The blend of specific, useful information about parties and information about the latest party goods never fails to bring about a surge in business soon after the letter has been distributed.

TIMES TO CELEBRATE

Mother's Day May 9
Memorial Day May 31
Father's Day June 20
Graduations May–June

TIMES TO CELEBRATE

Showers April–September
Weddings April–October
Cookouts-Picnics-Swim
Parties May–September

Dear Friends and Party-Lovers,

If you've seen our new Spring windows, you know pastels are high on our excitement list this season. All those luscious ice cream shades in gift wrap, tableware and stationery and not a calorie in them!

Inside, The Party Place is even more brimming than usual (and you know we can brim) with super gifts for the special days coming up ... Mother's Day, Father's Day, Graduation, Bat and Bar Mitzvahs and Confirmation.

Maybe You Should Be a Publisher: Newsletters • 187

We have desk accessories blooming with soft rose tulips on a blue background and Oriental prints by Caspari covering photo albums, pad holders and picture frames. For a handsome tailored look, there are blotters and accessories in navy or grey suede, while hearts and rainbows are hands down favorite with the younger set. Rainbows continue to star (if that's possible) on diaries, address books, scrapbooks and new memo pad and pen sets in clear boxes... a wonderful birthday gift or party favor.

Strawberries, not pastel, but luscious, are on paper plates, napkins and notes by Gordon Fraser, as well as the whole kitchencaboodle by C. R. Gibson: recipe books, memo pads and coupon holders. And for the male saver, how about a coupon holder with Chef Kliban Cat on it?

On the off chance you do not know we personalize stationery and napkins right on the premises, we are again offering free personalizing on any box of stationery or 50 pack of napkins you buy. This includes the fabric covered catchall boxes filled with notes or letters, Matagiri's handmade Indian paper, Mary McFadden and the full range of soft colored Crane sheets, notes and correspondence cards.

We also have a super selection of personalized stationery, social and business, printed by other good people: Crane, Ten Bamboo Studio, Consortium, Buening, Hampton, Lallie, James Aridas, to name a few. Hurry in if you want delivery in time for graduation.

April means showers, wedding, that is, and we have all the fixings... matching paper tableware with foldout centerpieces, parasols, garlands, favors in the new lavender and pink shades. We also rent a wishing well and shower umbrellas. You can call to reserve. Personalized toasting glasses, albums and bridal files are popular shower gifts. Allow at least two weeks for delivery on these.

Spring and Summer is wedding time for some, parties for all! Here are just a few of the newest of new things at The Party Place:

...A sturdy wicker buffet caddy... Fill it with napkins and cutlery and carry to the table or to a friend's house as a great hostess gift.

...Chinese food containers... three sizes... in a brightly colored floral design. Use for picnics, gifts or favors. The same petit fleur is on tissue paper, gift bags and totes.

...The Smurfs... paper napkins, plates, cups, tablecovers, balloons...

...Garfield... all of the above plus stickers, memo pads, shoelaces...

...Asparagus and tomatoes to burn... candles for your summer tables and garden torches to light your guests' way...

...Pam Marker's Museum Collection... unbelievable reproductions on dinner, dessert plates and three size napkins. English rose... a new solid color in plates, cups, napkins joins the family of 15 other solid colors we carry.

Postage being what it is, we'll have to temper our enthusiasm and let you make your own discoveries. But one more thing. If you see a store floating through the air some Saturday, it will be The Party Place aloft with helium-filled balloons: silver, gold or rainbow hearts, stars, Smurfs and Smurfettes, etc. etc. We do so many balloon bouquets sometimes we get an inflated picture of ourselves.

Fig. 14-1 This informal newsletter is circulated by The Party Place, a party-goods store in Stamford, Conn. It's a chatty blend of product information, party ideas, and tips on successful party planning.

Newsletters carry with them the aura of objectivity, and they are helpful to small businesses that welcome the role of industry spokesman. Newsletters are ideal ways of saying "Hello, again!" to prospects who are not as yet ready to make a purchase. They also identify you as an expert in your field, or at least someone willing to take the time and trouble to communicate ideas as well as sales literature throughout the marketplace.

How to Decide If a Newsletter Is Right for You

For most businesses, a newsletter is simply too unwieldy, inappropriate, or sophisticated to be worthwhile. Imagine a garage, barbershop, delicatessen, or drugstore putting out a newsletter. Even if the newsletter is free, who will want to read it? A bar owner who puts up a sign saying, "HAPPY HOUR—5-7 P.M." is communicating with his customer better than any newsletter ever could.

However, a fancy gift shop, like the party-supplies store, might help spur business with a newsletter. An art gallery certainly could profit from communicating with its customers via newsletter, especially if the newsletter is targeted to those people who have signed a "guest book" at a previous art exhibition at the gallery.

Your business may be right for a newsletter if you have an identifiable audience in need of specific information, and if you have the time, inclination, and resources to provide that information on a regular basis.

How to Publish a Newsletter

1. Identify your audience.

Some businesses know just where to find their customers —by looking at the addresses on sales slips, by going to mailing lists, or by inventive methods such as guest books. If you can identify the people with whom you'd like to communicate, make a record of their names and addresses. You can either type each name on a "master" sheet (and then reproduce the names on pressure-sensitive mailing labels) or, if you have a word processor, simply store the names, thus automating the process for repeat mailings.

2. Decide on a format.

Most newsletter formats are simple. All that's needed is a clear layout, a title and date, and headlines to introduce the stories. There is no set form. The simplest newsletters are typewritten and offset; they are often no more than two sides of a single 8½-by-11-inch piece of paper.

The newsletter's "look" should match its intended audience. Typewritten newsletters are fine when the information presented is vital. But sometimes, image may be as important as the information itself. If your business is concerned with image, it may pay to make your newsletter graphically distinctive, and to spend money reproducing the information on fine paper. In any case, let a designer lay out your first issue and help you to choose typefaces and paper stock.

3. Keep your purpose in mind.

Ask yourself, "What is the compelling reason to read my newsletter?" List the benefits of your newsletter, translating those benefits into practical actions that will be *vital* to your readers' lives. If you deal in coins, stamps, antiques, or fine art, a newsletter may provide a handy way of staying in touch with infrequent customers. By telling them of trends, sales, and news events, you are reinforcing your image as an expert in the field and putting your name in front of them on a regular basis.

4. Are there additional prospects for your newsletter?

If your newsletter deals with gourmet food, maybe it would be of interest to cooking schools and the food industry as well as to the gourmet who visits your store. A store that sells decorative paperweights may be surprised to find that coin buyers, antique buyers, and Americana enthusiasts would also like to read about paperweights.

5. What makes your newsletter special?

If your newsletter is competing with others, it must have a distinctive angle. Ideally, a newsletter offers inside information, news that would be hard to find elsewhere. Perhaps your method of distribution is unique. Or the frequency with which you publish. Or perhaps it's your method of offering discounts.

How to Write a Newsletter That Will Be Read

Newsletters help people answer problems and meet their needs. Most of our needs are basic—to live, to be healthy, to be loved, to be secure, to be well informed, and to be ahead of the crowd. The following case history tells briefly about an entrepreneur who met the specific needs of a special group of people by appealing to their profit motive.

A Long Island lawyer wanted to start a newsletter that would bring in income and also stimulate new business for his law practice. He came up with an idea based on a need that was going unfulfilled.

He saw opportunities for profit in mortgage-foreclosure purchases. The problem, he reasoned, was that the average person had difficulty uncovering these sales. Foreclosure sales are rarely well publicized; legal notices are printed in obscure local newspapers. And most notices don't provide basic information needed for making a purchasing decision, such as the types of properties involved or the amount of default on each property.

The lawyer met this challenge by publishing a newsletter which gave weekly notices of foreclosure sales of real estate located in the New York City metropolitan area. His newsletter was pitched to real estate brokers as "the only authoritative source of useful foreclosure information available." It would provide a way for people to screen hundreds of properties without ever leaving their offices.

He sent out a solicitation letter in which he described his newsletter as giving the "basic information an investor requires before further investigating a property." He sent it to real estate dealers in the area.

His newsletter met a need: the growing market for moderately priced "distressed" conventional properties. He used the "testimonial" technique when his letter noted that "all the popular how-to-get-rich-through-real-estate books advise purchase of property at foreclosure sales.'' He was offering people an opportunity to acquire property at bargain prices, property which might later be sold at a significant profit.

The foreclosure newsletter is an example of a well-thought-out, highly specific idea that can be marketed to a defined readership. In this case, the newsletter functions as a stimulus to the lawyer's business as well as a money-making proposition on its own. The rationale for this newsletter shows the type of specific thinking and targeting that all successful newsletter ideas require.

Tie-ins with the Newsletter

One of the ways in which a newsletter can support itself or bring in additional revenue is through the promotion of products and services that tie in with the newsletter's main thrust. A dating service that circulates a newsletter about where singles meet may wish to advertise for mail-order sale a new book about being single. (Or the newsletter can sell advertising space to advertisers promoting related products or services.) Since the book will be of interest to the same people who wish to read about singles spots, it makes a natural tie-in, complementing the newsletter as well as other promotions (e.g., singles weekends, dances, etc.) which may also appear in the newsletter.

Almost every business that lends itself to a newsletter has a variety of other products or services that could easily be tied in to the newsletter. The most common tie-in promotions are those involving books, clothing, vacations, novelties, records, and insurance.

A stamp dealer who circulates a newsletter may sell a wide range of tie-ins, including stamp catalogs, stamp albums, stamp books, magnifying glasses, and, of course, the stamps themselves.

How Newsletters Fail

Failure to be timely, failure to be accurate, failure to find an audience, failure to be objective, and failure to be news—

these are a few critical problems that doom newsletters. Even if the newsletter has a pleasing package (format, graphics, paper stock), as well as timely, informative copy, a built-in audience, a reasonable price, and good promotion, there are no guarantees that it will succeed.

To succeed, you need to have a realistic idea of exactly how many people will want to read the newsletter and of how many of these people are potential customers for your business. For more information about making a go of newsletters, contact the *Newsletter on Newsletters*, 44 West Market Street, Rhinebeck, NY 12572.

Case History: An Art Gallery Newsletter

A small New York City art gallery specializing in Oriental art decided to promote itself by putting out a two-page newsletter. The gallery owner did not want to be committed to publishing the newsletter on a regular basis, so each issue was undated.

The newsletter was printed in a lavender ink on a beige paper stock. The name of the newsletter was handsomely lettered and designed. The newsletter made no pretense at objectivity, since each issue was signed by the gallery owner, a person who spent part of the newsletter describing art treasures he had accumulated while touring the Orient. Included in the newsletter were several photographs clearly illustrating several unusual pieces.

The articles were a mixture of information and "invitation": information about Oriental art, correct ways of framing art, etc., and a subtle invitation to visit the gallery to view new arrivals.

The newsletter continues to be distributed free to interior designers and other regular customers.

The newsletter (Fig. 14-2) is easy to produce, informative, and yet keyed totally to the particular art gallery that publishes it. People enjoy reading it because it is well-written, colorful, and brief. It provides the gallery owner with a handy reason to contact interior designers—who are the gallery's prime market—and yet does not commit the publisher to a

Buddha sits on a stepped, waisted throne in contrast to the Thai and Indian Buddha who sits on a single or a double lotus throne.

Towards the end of the 18th century a more naturalistic style of Buddha, the Mandalay developed. The eyes of the Mandalay Buddha have a Mongoloid slant and the large mouth is set in a Mona Lisa smile. The fingers and toes are occasionally of unequal length. Instead of thin clothing, the Buddha's robes are set in thick folds, suggestive of Chinese drapery. Whether of metal, stone, lacquer or wood, the predominant style of Burmese Buddha figure is the Mandalay Style.

Constant in the tradition of Buddha sculpture is the sense of serenity which eminates from the sculpture. This sense of all-pervading calm may explain the attraction of the Buddha sculpture for homes throughout the world.

Rare Finds
Ancient Holy Book

We found a beautiful, rare Holy Book in Burma. The books' two wooden covers enclose 16 pages of palm leaf decorated with lac and gold. The Burmese calligraphy is black lac on a cinnabar-colored ground. This is in striking contrast with the very fine gold work decorations. Each page is 6 inches by 24 inches. Properly framed, this 18th century rarity would be a highly decorative piece for the focal point of a room. The total book would make a smashing large piece on the wall.

Antique Screens

We were fortunate to acquire an extraordinary pair of antique Japanese screens. Painted in sumi, go-fun, colors and gold leaf on paper, these beautiful screens illustrate scenes from the Tales of Genji. They are composed of six panels each 67½ inches by 24 inches, for a pair of screens that is 12 feet wide. These museum quality screens can grace the finest home.

Exhibiting Art
Mounting Sculpture

Just as good framing compliments and protects a painting, good mounting enhances and protects a piece of sculpture. The design considerations of framing and mounting are similiar: Where will the piece be displayed? What is its size? What is its color and texture? The answers to these questions help determine the base on which the sculpture is mounted.

Sculpture - whether six feet or six inches - is usually mounted on a base or plinth. Whether the plinth is wood, stone, metal, or acrylic, the choice is governed by the size, material and color of the object. Often, the sculpture is not attached directly to the plinth but is wired in place. The sculpture with its plinth may now be placed on a table or on its own pedestal to bring the object to a convenient and safe viewing position.

A playful paper may be suspended in the air for an effective display. In one technique, an acrylic rod would be attached to the artwork - perhaps a puppet - and anchored to an appropriate base. The result, a floating sculpture.

Objects in relief are sometimes most effectively displayed when hung on a wall. They make a firmer statement when they are appropriately mounted. A mask could be mounted on a complimentary backing of linen, wood, mirror or other suitable material. The whole could then be hung on the wall. If more protection were needed for a fragile or valuable piece, or if design considerations required it, the object with its backing could then be placed in a clear box and hung.

Pre-Columbian terra cottas, contemporary American sculpture, African masks, etc. all benefit from appropriate mounting. Ed Waldman's framing department would be glad to advise or assist you with your mounting and framing needs.

Recent Arrivals
From Northern Thailand

We just received a six-piece teak orchestra from Northern Thailand. The musicians are seated and 20 inches high. They are hand carved and painted and decorated with gold leaf. In the same shipment is an orchestra of six standing musicians, 36 inches high. These 12 pieces represent a full year's work for one of Thailand's most talented artists, whom we discovered on our annual buying trip to Southeast Asia. Used singly or as a group, these musicians can make a dramatic statement in any room.

Around Town

The *Japan Society* features "Treasures of Asian Art from the Idemitsu Collection" from Jan. 28 through March 14. This exhibit includes Japanese and Asian paintings, pottery, bronzes, calligraphy and lacquer ware from one of Japan's great private collections.

The *American Museum of Natural History* just published a glorious book featuring treasures from the museum's vast collections of Asian Art. "Asia: Traditions and Treasures" by Walter A. Fairservis, Jr. presents the delicate ivories of Japan, the translucent jades of China, the wrought brasses of India, the terrifying demons of Tibet and much, much more!

Thai Musician

Fig. 14-2 This graphically sophisticated newsletter mirrors the artistic taste of its creator, an art gallery owner. It blends tips on displaying art with a roundup of personal notes about the gallery's recent acquisitions.

regular publishing schedule, high printing and production costs, or the need to keep increasing circulation. The newsletter accomplishes its purpose: to remind customers of the continued interest in serving their needs.

• Chapter 15 •

ON WITH THE SHOW: TRADE SHOWS AND EXPOSITIONS

Trade Shows: A $7 Billion Industry

Every year, industry spends more than $7 billion to exhibit its wares at trade shows and expositions throughout the country. There are more than 9,000 shows each year, so you can be sure there's a show specializing in whatever it is you do; there are shows for everything from chemicals to construction, from farm equipment to pharmaceuticals, from textiles to telecommunications.

At first glance, it seems as if exhibiting at trade shows is too expensive for a small company. And there's some truth to that—at least where the major national shows are concerned. For example, when you consider the cost of travel, lodging, shipping, space, and materials, a manufacturer in Wichita could easily spend $10,000 on a 10-foot booth at the Computer Sales Exposition in New York City. Obviously, continent-hopping is beyond the budgets of most small businesses. (And it makes little sense for a Kansas-based firm to exhibit in New York, unless the company is large enough to distribute nationwide.)

But there are alternatives. Regional shows. "Table-top" shows. County fairs. State fairs. Public shows. Chamber of commerce exhibitions. And thousands of other small, local shows that make sense for small business.

The questions are: Where do you find out about these shows? And how do you pick the ones that are right for you?

Selecting Trade Shows

Choosing the right trade show is like selecting advertising media or publicity outlets. You pick the places that let you reach the most prospects at the lowest possible cost.

Begin with a comprehensive listing of local and national shows. One such listing is *Exhibit Schedule,* published by *Successful Meetings* magazine, 1422 Chestnut Street, Philadelphia, PA 19102. Another is *Trade Show Convention Guide,* available from Budd Publications, Box 7, New York, NY 10004. Trade journals and business publications will include monthly listings of shows and conferences in your particular industry. And your local convention and exhibit bureau can give you the latest information on fairs and expos in your city or town.

From these listings, you'll glean perhaps a dozen or so shows—shows you might exhibit in because they're local, or because they are applicable to your type of business.

Write to the management of each of these shows, and ask for a prospectus or other literature. You'll want to know how many people are expected to attend the show, how many have attended past shows, where these people come from, what industries they represent, what job titles they hold. In short, are they the type of people that want, need, and can afford to buy your products?

Are your competitors exhibiting? That's one sure sign that the show may be worth attending.

Is the show a new one, or is it well established? Select shows that have proved their worth. Too many fly-by-night expos spring up one year and are gone the next. And the companies that invest in them are usually thousands of dollars poorer for their efforts.

What to Show at a Show

Assuming you do sign up for one or more of these shows, what will you display there? And why?

The most compelling reason for your company to partici-

On with the Show: Trade Shows and Expositions • 197

pate in a trade show is to introduce a new product to the marketplace. According to studies by the Trade Show Bureau, 50% of the people attending any given show are there to see new products and services. So if you've invented the better mousetrap, motor, or metal detector, a trade show may be the place to show it off. But if you're selling the same old thing, avoid trade shows and try some other promotion, such as a trade ad or direct-mail campaign.

The best way to get people to notice your new product? Demonstrate it. To your prospects, seeing new products in action is the main reason for going to shows. Live action is the one thing that separates a show from print promotions.

At the show, attendees can see your product. Touch it. Feel it. Smell it. Compare it with the competitor—whose booth may be right next to your own.

Prospects can't discuss product features with an advertisement; printed pages don't speak when they're spoken to. But at the show, buyers see whether your orange-juice machine really *can* squeeze 5 gallons an hour. Or whether it filters out the pulp. And if they want to know what kind of price break they can get if they buy juicers in bulk, they can get a straight answer from a real live salesperson—right then and there.

Unfortunately, straightforward demonstrations can produce more yawns than inquiries, since most products and equipment are—let's face it—just plain boring. (Ever hear of someone flying 300 miles to see a sump pump in action?)

If your product is nuts-and-bolts, make the demonstration a little less mundane by adding a touch of flair to the display. For example, a defense contractor was exhibiting helicopters at an Air Force show. In the middle of the display area was the hull of a chopper that had been struck point-blank by an enemy missile. Its windshield was cracked, its armor plating buckled by the impact . . . but that was all. The helicopter had survived the attack. And so, a huge sign taped to the windshield told us, did its two pilots. A most impressive display, combining drama with convincing product demonstration.

You don't have to be selling weapons to set up an interesting, unusual product demonstration that will bring the crowds swarming to your booth. One small manufacturer of scuba equipment built a huge Plexiglas "fishtank" for his booth. The tank was about 8 feet high and 6 feet wide, and inside it swam a bikini-clad beauty who stayed underwater all day, aided by—you guessed it—the exhibitor's marvelous scuba gear. Cost of the tank? About $800—less than a third the cost of placing a full-page ad in a trade journal. The results? A booth jam-packed with prospects; a demonstration that was the hit of the show.

Want to get people to take a look at your orange-juice squeezer? Offer a glass of fresh-squeezed OJ to everybody who stops by to take a peek. Are passersby passing by your display of home video games? Get them to stop and take notice by challenging them to beat the highest score on Pac-Man or Space Invaders—and by giving free game cartridges to the top ten players. Selling a minicomputer that works like magic? Have a professional magician on hand to demonstrate its features in a magical way.

As with any promotion, the first step in successful trade shows is getting the prospect's attention. Product demonstrations, giveaways, contests, and entertainment are four attention-grabbers that will pull people from the aisle into your booth. And that's where the selling starts.

Successful Trade-Show Selling

Retailers may take orders at the show, but the bulk of trade-show exhibitors—manufacturers—don't. Instead, they use shows to introduce new products or new applications of old products. They use shows to make contacts. Build prospect lists. Be seen by decision-makers. Talk to customers. And distribute sales literature.

Trade shows are an unusual hybrid of advertising and personal selling. Advertising, because you pay for a space (in the case of a show, it's an actual space on the floor). And personal selling, because once the display attracts the prospect to the booth, the salesperson has to do the rest.

So . . . although this is a book on promotion, not salesmanship, we're going to take a brief look at personal selling as it applies to the trade show.

To begin with, picture this scene: The prospect, attracted by the flashing lights, bells, whistles, and sirens of your product demonstration, walks toward the booth. You say, "May I help you?" The prospect's reply? A hastily muttered "No thank you" followed by a quick exit away from your booth.

"May I help you?"—the standard department-store lead-in—is the worst way to introduce yourself. If the prospect isn't intimately familiar with what you're selling—and chances are, he's not*—he'll feel threatened by this challenge. It will scare him off.

Instead, draw the prospect into conversation by asking a friendly, nonthreatening question about business. A general question. If you're selling globe valves to petroleum engineers, don't say, "Are you thinking of buying our model X-100 valve?" Ask: "Do you specify valves in your work?" A "no" answer means you're not talking with a qualified prospect; a "yes" tells you to keep the conversation going. Then find out the prospect's problem. And show him how your product can solve it. Get chummy—glance at the prospect's badge or ID tag so you can address him by name. Be personal. Friendly. And helpful. But not pushy.

A cardinal rule of trade-show selling: Stay on your feet. People will not disturb you if you're resting your rear in a chair—in other words, you can't sell if you're seated. So stand. If you need a rest, have someone take your place while you walk around the exhibit hall or stop at the snack bar. But no napping in the booth, please.

Another cardinal rule of trade-show selling: Don't gab with friends and fellow employees when you're manning the booth. Strangers will not interrupt a conversation between friends; instead, they will pass you by and stop at a display where the sales help isn't so occupied. Need to chat with the boss or your assistant for a few minutes? Find a nice quiet corner *outside* of the display area.

---

* According to the Trade Show Bureau, four out of five show attendees will not have known of your company or product prior to visiting your booth.

A question we get asked frequently is: "Should we hand out our brochure to everyone who asks for it?" Well, there are pros and cons to this practice. The *pro* of having literature on hand is that you can quickly satisfy a prospect's hunger for more information. And the brochure serves as a permanent reminder of his visit to your booth. On the *con* side, sales literature is costly to produce, and handing out a fancy four-color brochure to thousands of people, regardless of whether they're serious sales prospects, can be an expensive proposition.

The alternative—not having literature at the show—also has its pros and cons. Without a large supply of brochures, you will have to take down the names and addresses of the people who request information in order to mail the literature at a later date. (Many shows issue each attendee a plastic show card much like a credit card. When the attendee hands you the card, you use a special imprinter, also supplied by show management, to instantly record the sales lead on pre-printed forms.) This technique can work to your advantage, allowing you to build a list of prospects who have expressed interest in your product. A negative is that you've now got to mail thousands of brochures, where before, literature was there for the taking. Also, this system delays getting the brochure into the buyer's hands—and that could hurt sales if the buyers are in a hurry.

Here's our solution: Keep a small sampling of your literature on a table or in a display rack in open view for everyone to see. If a prospect wants a brochure, take down the information and mail it later—*if,* in your judgment, the prospect means business. If you think the person's just collecting brochures, then you can note this on the lead form or his business card, and mail the literature or not, as you choose. Behind the display or under the table, you'll have a surplus supply of several hundred brochures on hand. These are to be distributed to hot prospects who are really serious about your product and want to get down to business right away. With a little practice, you'll be able to tell the buyers from the brochure collectors without a second glance.

Finally, a few more tips to improve your trade show selling:

On with the Show: Trade Shows and Expositions • 201

1. Develop a schedule for manning the booth.

Even Supersalesperson will get tired, cranky, and bored after eight hours of standing in a 10-by-10-foot display filled with file cabinets or fishing poles. Let your salespeople man the booth in two-hour or four-hour rotation shifts, so prospects are always greeted by a salesperson who's relatively fresh and lively.

Naturally, the busier the traffic (flow of people through your booth), the more booth personnel you'll need. Plan the booth duty roster accordingly.

Experience teaches us that shows are busy during the middle days, and slower during their start and finish. As an example of this, take a look at the attendance figures for the 1981 Exposition of Chemical Industries:

day one—4,341 attendees
day two—5,417 attendees
day three—6,016 attendees
day four—2,850 attendees

2. Reduce prices on products sold at the show.

The opportunity to pick up merchandise at reduced cost gives prospects a reward for having taken the time and trouble to visit your display.

3. Use preshow promotion to build booth traffic.

Use advertising, publicity, and direct mail to get prospects to come to the show. For a nominal cost, show management will provide artwork, stickers, mail stuffers, and invitations you can use in your own promotions; this material can easily and inexpensively be imprinted with your company logo and the number of your booth. Include an imprinted show invitation with invoices, literature mailings, personal letters, and other day-to-day correspondence. And don't forget to mention the show in your ads.

Trade Shows vs. Expos: Some Definitions

We've been using the terms *trade show, exposition,* and *fair* interchangeably in this discussion. But they're really not the same thing, and we need to clarify our terms before we go any further.

By strict definition, a *trade show* is limited in attendance to those who meet certain qualifications by virtue of their occupation or industry. Some major national trade shows include the Farm Progress Show, the National Restaurant Show, the Association of Operating Room Nurses Congress, and the National Computer Conference.

An *exposition,* on the other hand, is open to the general public. Anyone can go, provided he is willing to pay the price of admission (usually less than $10). The two types of expositions are outdoor state and county *fairs,* which focus on agriculture, and *public shows,* which include garden shows, automobile shows, boat shows, and other hobby-related shows.

At trade shows, the audience is more select. If you sell products to highly specific markets—engineers, doctors, chemical plants, restaurant owners—concentrate your exhibit efforts on trade shows. However, for small businesses whose prospects are bound by geography and not by profession or industry, the best bet is local expos.

Producing the Display

If you look around at any show, you'll see that most exhibitors have some kind of display in their booths. This display can be as simple as a few photo blowups hung on a curtain, or as complex as a custom-made exhibit constructed out of 26d, plastic, or metal and equipped with overhead signs, rear-projection screens, illuminated photo displays, animated graphics, movable walls, Plexiglas™ product-display cases, and removable graphic panels.

Cost increases with complexity, and anything more involved than the simplest portable display is far beyond what

90% of small businesses can afford. But simple does *not* necessarily mean cheap or ineffective, and a practical working display can be had for under $2,000.

To begin with, you need to purchase a basic exhibit system—the self-standing structure that will contain the product photos, copy, and other graphics of your display. You will probably want a *portable display*—that is, a display that can fold up into an oversized suitcase or other container and be carried by *one person*. If you can't carry it, you'll have to ship it, and with freight, drayage, labor, storage, and insurance costs what they are today, shipping will eat up your budget in no time flat. So avoid it. Get a display you can lug around in the back of your station wagon or company van. If you exhibit in out-of-state shows, be sure the display can be carried on a plane as ordinary luggage.

Purchase a portable display that is easy to carry, easy to pack, and can be set up and dismantled quickly and with a minimum of time and trouble. See a demonstration before you buy. If a trained salesperson can't set up his company's display in the showroom, you can bet that *you'll* have trouble, too.

Avoid displays made of wood; they're heavy and easily damaged. Prefer lighter, more durable displays made of extruded plastic or a lightweight metal, such as aluminum.

When it comes to trade-show graphics, we have just three rules: Keep it simple, keep it big, keep it bold. Grab people's attention with bright colorful photo blowups and bold color graphics. Incorporate your company name and logo into the graphics—and make the logo *big*. Headlines should be short, pithy, and large enough to read from the aisle without eyestrain.

Don't cram your graphic panels with every available piece of technical information about your product. The type will be too small to read, and the customer won't spend enough time in your booth to get through it all. (According to Trade Show Bureau research, the average trade-show attendee spends only *3 minutes* at any given booth.) Besides, the purpose of a trade-show display is to attract customers to the booth, not do the whole selling job. If people want more detailed information, hand them a brochure.

Consult a professional trade-show-exhibit designer if you can, and see what materials and techniques are available. For example, product samples and graphic panels can be easily mounted on the display structure using Velcro, a kind of fabric tape that allows you to "hook" solid objects together. Transparent Plexiglas™ panels can be used to cover and protect pictures and graphics that could otherwise be damaged in handling. Carpet and cloth are frequently used on graphic panels to give displays a warm "homey" look and feel. Go to some trade shows. Take a look at what works. And what doesn't.

For additional information on the design of trade-show displays, write Exhibit Designers and Producers Association, 521 Fifth Avenue, New York, NY 10017.

A Checklist for Exhibit Managers

Much of handling trade-show exhibits can only be learned by doing. It's a trial-and-error business, and one where mistakes are inevitable.

There are *so* many little niggling details that must be attended to when you're in charge of your company's trade-show display. Did we order the right color carpet? Are there enough ashtrays? *Any* ashtrays? How can we fit our 12-foot-high display in an exhibit hall with a 10-foot-high ceiling? Can show management provide us with the right kind of electricity to run our imported electric motor—which is designed for Japanese outlets?

Are there enough brochures in stock to cover us for the show, or must we print more? Who's going to come in to man the booth on Saturday? Do we have up-to-date releases and photos for the press? Can we get our computer through the door of the exhibit hall? The list goes on. And on.

Slip-ups, goofs, lost shipments, and other problems are standard fare for even the most seasoned trade-show pros; there are just more tasks involved than any one person can keep an eye on all the time. To help you get through this ordeal, we've compiled a checklist of things to do that should help you plan effectively and cut down on errors. Trade shows do require much advanced planning, and you should look over this checklist at least three months before the opening of the show.

Here, then, are the things to do before you go to the show:
- Visit the show hall, if possible. Check out the display area for space limitations, plumbing and electrical supplies, and overall appearance.
- Set a budget for the show. Include exhibit construction, shipping, drayage, storage, plumbing, carpenters, electrical, labor, furniture and carpet rental, printing, models, product demonstration, travel, food, lodging, and the cost of the space.
- Look over the show regulations carefully. Don't base your display around a demonstration of your firecrackers only to find out on opening day that loud noises are forbidden in the exhibit hall.
- If you can't carry it with you, work out the details of shipping and storage for your display, literature, and products.
- Build shipping crates for exhibit material. Be sure the crates are marked so they can be identified at a glance. Crates are often misplaced at shows, and painting your crates with odd colors or distinctive markings can help make finding them easier.
- Order any special services you'll need for the booth—electricity, running water, drainage, compressed air, lighting, or signs. Also order carpets, furniture, and any labor you may need.
- Check your inventory of sales literature and product samples. Do you have enough, or will more have to be ordered?
- Work out a booth duty roster. Obtain badges or entrance passes for booth personnel, other employees, and your customers.
- Plan publicity, direct mail, and advertising to support the trade-show effort.
- Order premiums you'll be giving away at the show.
- Order invitations, stickers, logos, and other promotional material from show management.
- Make hotel and travel reservations.

206 • HOW TO PROMOTE YOUR OWN BUSINESS

Fig. 15-1 A 20-foot trade-show display unit for Argon Medical Corp. (exhibit designed and built by Contempo Design Inc., Northbrook, Ill.).

- Construct your display. If you already have a display, take it out of the case and inspect it. Are the graphics up-to-date and reflective of what you're selling at this particular show? Also check for damage and make any necessary repairs.
- Hire models, magicians, demonstrators, and any outside talent you need.
- Set up a system to handle inquiries and literature distribution at the booth.
- Check all details with show management and outside vendors, including freight handlers, printers, van lines, and hotels.

• Chapter 16 •

A MISCELLANY OF PROMOTIONS

This is our "odds-and-ends" chapter—a miscellany of promotions that don't fit in under any of the broad topics we've discussed in previous chapters. Chapter 16 will cover four topics in brief: sales promotions, business gifts, store displays, and personal selling.

Sales Promotion

As the name implies, sales promotions are programs used for promoting the sale of a product. Most often, these promotions are devised by the manufacturers of nationwide brand-name products and carried out in conjunction with local retailers. Sometimes, however, small retailers and service businesses create and execute their own sales promotions without the help of larger companies. In 1981, American marketers spent more than $58 billion on sales promotion. A few of the basic types of sales promotion are outlined below:

Cents-off packs

Cents-off packs consist of several of the same product bundled in a package with a label announcing a price-off discount for the quantity purchase. Cents-off packs are often used with soap and other health-and-beauty products.

Sampling

A sampling is an offering of a trial-size version of a product for the purpose of introducing it to the marketplace. Small samples can either be delivered free to the home or sold at a nominal cost in the stores. New powder and liquid detergents, toothpastes, and a variety of health-and-beauty products are often launched this way.

Coupons

There are two kinds of coupons. *Manufacturer's coupons* are distributed by the manufacturers of various consumer products. Consumers receive discounts on these products by redeeming the coupons at the retailer's cash register. Coupons are used in print advertisements, newspaper inserts, circulars, and other promotions. More than 100 billion manufacturer's coupons are distributed each year for a wide variety of products including cigarettes, coffee, pet food, cereal, fruit juice, bathroom tissues, and many others.

Retailers receive two benefits from manufacturer's coupons: an increase in sales of the product because of distribution of the coupon, and a small handling fee paid by the manufacturer to the retailer for each coupon redeemed.

Handling coupons takes a great deal of paperwork, and many small retailers find that the handling fee doesn't justify the time and trouble. These retailers often elect the second kind of coupon, where the *retailer creates his own cents-off coupons,* to be distributed through local advertising or circulars. A coupon can generate sales for any business in which price is a key consideration to buyers, and drugstores, groceries, supermarkets, opticians, and restaurants have all used their own coupon promotions with success.

Refunds

Refund deals require that the buyer mail in some sort of proof-of-purchase (usually a seal on the package or a receipt from the store) in order to receive a refund by mail from the manufacturer. Refunds generally carry a higher dollar value than coupons. Recently, the auto makers began offering $100 (and even $1,000) refunds on the purchase of new cars. (Detroit calls this kind of refund a "rebate.") The typical slogan for a refund deal goes something like "Buy three, get one free!"

Contests and sweepstakes

These generate excitement and sales by offering consumers a chance to win prizes. By definition, sweepstakes are games of luck (raffles, drawings, lotteries, etc.) and contests are games of skill. Because they require no special effort or intelligence to enter, sweepstakes are by far the more popular of the two.

Although the most publicized events are those sponsored by major manufacturers, sweepstakes and contests can work on a local level, too; a drawing for a color TV or stereo never fails to draw people to the stores. Sometimes the drawing can even tie in with the product being sold. For example, a tobacconist recently ran a small sweepstakes offering a year's free supply of tobacco to the winner—a prize that surely interested pipesmokers in the promotion and drew them to the store to fill in entry blanks.

Tie-in promotions

In a tie-in promotion, two or more products share an ad and a promotional hook such as a coupon or refund. Tie-ins work well when there is some logical relationship between the two products—hot dogs and mustard, milk and chocolate syrup, shoes and socks.

Point-of-purchase displays

These colorful cardboard constructions serve to hold and display a product while extolling its virtues with headlines, illustrations, graphics, and some short copy. A point-of-purchase (P-O-P) bookstore display for the horror novels of Stephen King bears a sign welcoming readers to "Stephen King *Terror*-Tory." The classic P-O-P display is the egg-shaped rack for L'eggs pantyhose and stockings.

While many national manufacturers supply retailers with ready-made P-O-P displays, stores may also choose to create their own display materials. This allows them to carry the theme of their own advertising and sales literature through to the point of sale, and adds continuity to the look of the store. The famous David's Cookies of New York has built its reputation on what are reputed to the world's best chocolate-chip cookies, and to sustain this image, David's logo appears everywhere at the point of sale: store windows, in-store signs, boxes, bags, and cookie tins.

Premiums

Premiums are gifts that serve as an incentive for buying a product. Classic examples of premiums include the prizes in Cracker Jacks, the toys that come in boxes of children's breakfast cereals, and the free sets of glasses gas stations used to give you when you filled up your tank.

Remember the barber who gave you a comic book after every haircut? Or the pediatrician who handed you a lollipop after a particularly painful mumps or measles shot? In a sense, these rewards were premiums—kind gifts that dried your tears and warmed your mom's heart to future visits to that barber or doctor. Other premiums are more blatant sales pitches—ball-point pens with the phone number of your insurance agent or accountant imprinted on them, or free bottle openers or corkscrews used as giveaways by the local supermarket or liquor store.

Ideally, the best premiums have some tie-in with the business's product or service. An example of this is when the New York Mets have "Bat Day" or "Cap Day" and give away a free baseball bat or Mets cap to every youngster who buys a ticket to the game that day.

• • •

In all cases, the best sales promotions are those that get their point across to consumers quickly and simply; shoppers do not have the time to digest complex promotional schemes.

Promotions should not be used alone, but should tie in with advertising, publicity, direct mail, and other sales efforts.

There are legal restrictions governing sweepstakes, contests, and similar promotions. You might check with a lawyer to make sure your plans comply with the law, which usually varies greatly from state to state. Or you can query the Promotion Marketing Association of America, 420 Lexington Avenue, New York, NY 10017, (212) 867-3990.

To learn more about sales promotion, we suggest you read *Sales Promotion Essentials* by Don E. Schultz and William A. Robinson (Crain Books, 740 N. Rush Street, Chicago, IL 60611).

Business Gifts

Giving business gifts is one of the best ways to get your customers and prospects to like you; after all, everyone enjoys getting presents.

Companies give gifts for a variety of reasons that all make good sense. Business gifts help develop new business. Build goodwill. Say "thank you" to loyal customers. And motivate employees. A recent survey showed that the majority of business people feel that giving gifts does indeed accomplish all of these goals.

Although half of all business gifts are Christmas gifts, a present is really appropriate at any time of the year. Some companies time their gift-giving to coincide with a customer's birthday, an employee's anniversary with the company, or some other special occasion. Other businesspeople think that gifts are more appreciated when they're least expected—sort of like Candid Camera.

In general, though, gift-givers agree that business customers should receive gifts they can use at the office, while gifts to consumers should have some application in the home. In this way, the gift remains in front of buyers when they are thinking of making a purchase.

There's a saying that goes, "It's the thought that counts," and this is surely the case as far as business gifts are concerned. Customers are more impressed with the fact that you remembered them than with the cost or size of your gift.

Still, different business situations call for different types of gifts. A 25-cent plastic keychain might be perfect for a locksmith's customers, but not for a $100,000-a-year corporate bigwig who might have been counting on a set of new golf clubs or trip to Bermuda.

Gift-giving requires a special kind of creativity that only mothers and lovers seem to possess. And so, to help the rest of you choose a gift that will please both your customers and your budget, we've compiled some suggestions on suitable business gifts. The lists below divide the various gift ideas by price category to make your shopping easier. You can buy these items from retailers, wholesale outlets, or specialty advertising distributors.

A SAMPLER OF BUSINESS GIFTS

50¢–$1	$1–$5	$5–$20
letter opener	Business card holder	Set of drinking glasses
balloon	Pen light	Tote bag
Yo-Yo™	Coffee mug	T-shirt
Frisbee™	Ashtray	Lucite paperweight
coaster	Playing card	Board game
corkscrew	Tape measure	Cigarette lighter
desk calendar	Plastic raincoat	Garment bag
sewing kit	Thermometer	Beach towel
poster	Pocket atlas	Necktie
	Mini-tool set	Windbreaker
	Wallet	Umbrella
	Luggage tag	Wall plaque
	Money clip	Desk diary
	Golf cap	Portfolio
	Pocket knife	Golf balls

$20–$100	Over $100
Pocket calculator	Cruise
Trophy	Furniture
Sportswear	Jewelry
Desk clock	Stereo equipment
Sculpture	Television
Fishing rod and reel	Camera
Desk accessory	Telescope
Golf clubs	
Blazer	
Gourmet food	

Depending on the customer and the type of gift, you may wish to have the item imprinted with your name, logo, phone number, and address. On a fun gift like Frisbees or T-shirts, the logo can be big and bold; on more personal presents—jewelry, a wallet, other luxury items—the imprint should be as small and unobtrusive as possible.

In-Store Displays

How the products look in the window and on the shelves is crucial to a retailer's success. Here are a few tips to help you create displays that sell more effectively.

Window displays

- Design the display around the space you have. Don't make it too crowded—or too empty.
- Keep it simple. Merchandise should be readily visible from afar.
- Display only what you have in stock. Exception: If you have remainders you want to get rid of, put them in the window, advertise them as remainders, and offer a big price break.
- Design the window display around a theme—music, sports, spy novels, Christmas scenes.
- Consider animated or even live demonstrations. One California bookstore specializing in fantasy literature had the well-known writer Harlan Ellison sit in the store window while he wrote some new short stories. Any customer purchasing $10 worth of books would get an autographed copy of one of the stories. This kind of creative window display always gets attention.

On the shelves

- Make sure the product name can be clearly seen by shoppers strolling down the aisle.
- Keep shelves at eye level, whenever possible. Studies have shown that raising a product from knee level to eye level will double its sales.

- Crowd the shelves. Research shows that three boxes of Brand X detergent placed end to end on a shelf will sell 50 percent more detergent than only two boxes.

Personal Selling

Chapter 15 touched lightly on personal selling as it applies to trade shows. As we mentioned then, this is a book on print and broadcast promotion, not salesmanship, and so a lengthy discussion of how to be a great salesperson is beyond its scope.

Still, we wanted to say *something* about how a flair for promotion can help the salesperson succeed at his or her task. And so we'd like to relate the following tale from George Lois's column in *Adweek* magazine:

> The most thrilling story of the marriage of expertise and style involved the art dealer Lord Duveen. Finally receiving an audience with J. P. Morgan, the most important collector of the day, the dandyish Duveen, with his cutaway, spats, top hat, cane and all, sashayed into the presence of Morgan in his luxurious mansion on Fifth Avenue. Without a civil greeting, Morgan pointed to three large vases on his marble floor and told Duveen that one was a 16th-century Ming masterpiece, and the other two exact copies that had cost him a fortune to have made.
>
> He asked Duveen to study the vases and tell him which were the copies and which was the invaluable original.
>
> Lord Duveen strutted up to the three vases, hardly glanced at them, raised his pearl-handled cane and, with two violent strokes, smashed two of them to smithereens.
>
> From that moment, every painting and art object that Morgan collected until the day he died he bought from the great English salesman.*

• • •

---

* George Lois, "Down Lois Lane: The Ethic of Mediocrity," *Adweek*, September 14, 1981, p. 25.

• Chapter 17 •

HOW TO MEASURE THE RESULTS OF YOUR PROMOTIONS

The Purpose of Promotion: Sales

Although it may be fine for an IBM or a GE to use part of its promotional efforts to build its image, small businesses need to get immediate sales. While big business has the luxury of creating a campaign that will pay off over the long term, you need to concentrate on the promotion's cost-effectiveness in the short term.

Your promotions, if all goes well, will result in tangible *sales*—you will transact business with some of the people who heard about your products or services via your promotions. Of course, not everyone who learns about your business or inquires about your business is ready to do business with you. A person may *inquire* about a product or service, and that inquiry may, on occasion, result in business. Sometimes a person inquires about a product or service only to discover that it was not what he had in mind. Perhaps it's too expensive. Any such response to a promotion may be termed an *inquiry*. However, a *sales lead* is someone who has inquired about your product or service and who seems to be in the market for it. Not every inquiry is a true lead.

In the case of a national doughnut chain that offers six doughnuts for $1, and makes the offer good for ten days ("just bring the coupon to the location nearest you"), every inquiry (person holding a coupon) will probably result in the sale of at least $1 worth of donuts.

In the same way, a restaurant offering a $6.95 lobster special on Friday nights may receive some inquiries ("Does that price include the salad bar?") as well as a number of customers. If the restaurant advertised four different specials on four different days of the week, one could easily determine which special tempted the most bargain-hunting diners.

A store advertising a one-day sale on video equipment may be able to measure the response to its advertising by determining the number of people who show up on the sale day and contrasting it with the number that show up at the store during a regular business day. A comparison of sales figures for both days will also help the manager determine whether his promotion yielded increased sales or just increased browsers.

What Kind of Results to Expect

A good response to your promotions is what you want. But just what does "good" mean? For some products (like a Rembrandt painting) one solid inquiry is all that is needed. For other businesses, a promotion must attract thousands of inquiries or else it must be deemed a failure.

A classified ad that costs $10 aims at making back the cost of the ad in addition to the cost of creating or selling the product or service being advertised. If you were selling your time, for example, at $100 an hour, you would start making a profit with your first sale. If, however, you were selling a product for $2, and it cost you $1 to manufacture, you'd have to sell ten just to make back the cost of the ad.

When you see the back page of a local newspaper filled with images of cowboys smoking a popular cigarette, you are looking at an ad that might be almost impossible to monitor, and one that may not be translatable into immediate sales.

Your expectations must be tempered by many things: potential readership of the magazine (or number of direct-mail pieces sent), competition, timing, the positioning of your ad or article. At best, only a few out of each hundred people exposed to the promotion will read it and react to it. There are just too many things fighting for attention each day.

Let's first consider your expectations toward advertising. When you advertise in a weekly magazine, you get approximately half of your inquiries by the end of the first week, more than three-quarters by the end of the second week, and, generally speaking, nearly all of the inquiries by the end of five weeks.

As for advertising in a monthly magazine, you can expect about half your inquiries after the first month, three-quarters at the end of two months, and just about all of the inquiries within three months following the ad's appearance.

Direct-mail results are measured in terms of leads and generated sales. The cost of the mailing package can be expressed in terms of cost per lead. If you spend $100 on your mailing and it has yielded only one lead, that lead has cost you $100. If you made one sale, the promotion cost you $100 for that sale. If you are selling a product or service priced at $1,000, you've done well with your one sale. Results that pay off lead one to ponder even more ambitious direct-mail or advertising programs. The promotions that fail to earn back what they cost suggest a variety of reasons for their failure. It is only by examining all the elements of the promotion that you may discover what went wrong.

As for direct mail, the average response to it—even to pieces designed by professionals—is about 1.4%. This need not signify success or failure. That can only be determined by knowing how much your product costs, how much your direct-mail program cost, and how many sales were made.

Naturally, there are times when expectations are tied to goals of building goodwill—to image building or public relations—rather than immediate sales. When a store or boutique uses its advertising space to ask readers to send for a gift, it is building a mailing list for future promotions. As in life, identifying realistic goals and expectations is the key to judging your promotion's success.

How to Monitor Your Promotions

After a while, it becomes impossible to keep track of inquiries without writing them down. By keeping a response notebook or file, you can begin to systematize the responses and discern more about your prospects. A sample file might contain a clip of the promotion (ad, direct-mail package, press release, flyer), the name and date of the publication that ran it (or the date you mailed it), and the names (and addresses and phone numbers) of everyone who responded. You should also keep close track of expenses incurred in creating the brochure, the number of responses, and the number of sales.

By deducting your expenses from your total sales, you can determine whether your promotion paid for itself—at least in the short term. There is a residual benefit of name recognition, goodwill, and possible future sales that is hard to calculate precisely.

There are a number of time-tested techniques that help you measure the response to a promotion, and help you keep accurate records. They include the use of coupons, reply cards, keyed addresses or telephone numbers, order forms, keying ads to a specific request, and reader response cards.

Coupons are best exemplified by local shopping circulars. By offering discounts on certain items when they are purchased using a coupon, a store can measure response to a particular promotion.

Reply cards help direct-mail readers take action because they do not require a stamp, and because they are pre-addressed.

Keyed addresses or phone numbers are another way of saying "coding." In effect, by pointing readers to an address, telephone, or box number, you can easily discern how many people responded to a particular promotion or item. Whenever a TV ad asks you to send your check to a "Department" or a special box number, the advertiser is simply trying to determine how many people responded. If the TV spot runs two hours later (with a different "Department" key) and the response is increased, the advertiser has learned something about when is the best time to show his commercials.

Whenever an ice cream parlor offers a free sundae with "a copy of this ad," they are making it easy to determine the response to a particular advertisement. This gimmick works with a variety of businesses that offer premiums to the first people to show up at a sale or opening.

Order forms are standard sales slips that are found in catalogs as well as in many ads and flyers, and *reader response cards* are used by publications to indicate to advertisers exactly what the response has been to a particular ad or press release announcing a new product.

The following case history details how one small-business woman—a handbag manufacturer—monitored her promotion and knew that it worked.

Case Study: The Handbag Promotion

A small wholesaler involved in the manufacturing of handbags realized that she needed promotional literature to give to prospects who would visit her booth at an upcoming fashion trade show. She also found herself talking with the trade press occasionally, and she recognized that a ready-made press kit would help her communicate thoroughly and effectively and would be a great time-saver.

She hired a small public relations firm to help her create the press kit. The PR company presented her with an estimate of the costs involved in creating one hundred press kits for distribution to the trade press as well as to important prospects.

The elements of the kit were the press release, a "fact sheet" containing a list of prestige accounts, and a sheet containing product descriptions and prices. These pieces of literature were to be accompanied by black-and-white or color photos of several of her handbags. (The color photos were reserved for magazines that run color.)

Costs were broken down as follows:

Fee for writing and supervising project	$750
Photographer (½ day, including film and processing)	300
Printing	50
100 8 × 10 black-and-white prints	75
100 8 × 10 color prints	175
Clerical	90
Postage	40
50 2-pocket folders, 50 envelopes and supplies	$25
Total:	$1505

The press release was sent to fashion editors in each city where the handbag manufacturer had a distributor or sales office. It also went to fashion trade magazines and style editors, as well as to important general-interest magazines throughout the United States. At last count, two of the people receiving the release via mail had called for additional information. One magazine ran the release verbatim and even used one of the photos. It is impossible to calculate precisely the benefits that this article had, but it kept the telephone ringing steadily for two days! The handbag maker ordered reprints of the article and kept them at her booth when the trade show opened. Thus, she had fifty press kits (those reserved for the trade show) to give out to the media, as well as article reprints to hand out to prospects and browsers.

Between the customer interest in her reprints and the inquiries generated from the article based on the press release, and the goodwill derived from the professionally produced press kit, the handbag manufacturer's promotion paid for itself several times over. She generated about thirty sales leads, and immediate sales totaling almost $2,800. The manufacturer, though not especially diligent about tracking her response, knows that the promotion was a short-term success. She knows that the promotion may be even more valuable in the long run, as prospects become ongoing customers for her handbags.

Follow-up

You've sent your release, placed your ad, mailed your brochure. Leads are starting to flow in. What now? If you've prepared for the leads, you'll have established a mechanism for following them up. Once your prospect has replied he expects fast action.

If your objective was direct sales, make sure that whoever fills orders knows about your promotion, and that sufficient inventories are on hand to handle the maximum number of returns you expect.

If your main objective was to get leads for your salespeople, be sure there is a system for forwarding the leads to them.

All leads should be logged in so that information like cost per lead can be calculated. Also, you need to be in touch with your sales force to determine how many of the leads convert into sales.

There may be times when you follow up on a promotion by making telephone calls. By following up on a press release or an inquiry resulting from advertisements or direct mail, you can learn firsthand how your promotion was perceived. It also gives you an opportunity to use salesmanship to turn a no into a maybe and a maybe into a yes.

Your success at follow-up depends in large part upon the people you are calling. Are they "cold prospects," people who have expressed little interest in your product but who, for example, went so far as to ask to see a catalog? Or are they "hot leads," people who understand precisely what you are selling and seem to be ready to buy right now?

Your purpose for following up may differ from promotion to promotion. Following up leads resulting from direct mail may lead directly to business. Following up on a response to a press release will tell you how an editor viewed your story, and will teach you lessons about promoting yourself in the future. Following up on responses to an ad enhances your knowledge of the market and of your particular type of customer. Anything you can find out about who answered your ad and why will be valuable to you in every future promotion.

Naturally, time won't allow you to chat with everyone who expresses some interest in your product or service. It is not necessary to get on the telephone to quiz someone about why he or she was moved to send for your catalog. However, you may wish to follow up on a small *percentage* of the inquiries you generate. In this way, while you are attempting to make the sale (or sell an idea to an editor), you'll be giving yourself an opportunity to learn which elements of your promotion seemed to make the biggest impression on those who were exposed to it.

When you follow up by phone on inquiries from letters, ads, press releases, brochures, or flyers, here are a few things to keep in mind.

1. Follow up soon.

Don't think that your ad, letter, brochure, or press release will be remembered weeks after it arrives. Answer inquiries as quickly as possible. People who have received a mailing or who have made an initial response to an ad or flyer are *leads;* they expect you to follow up.

2. Determine if the answer to the inquiry was received.

Sometimes people don't respond to your follow-up because the material you've sent to them has gotten lost in the mail. Therefore, before launching into a sales pitch, first ask your prospect whether he's received what you've sent him.

3. Then ask the caller if he's had an opportunity to look at the material.

Don't make the assumption that just because you've responded quickly to a prospect's inquiry, your prospect will be in a hurry to respond to your sales solicitations. Some people take a while to get to their mail. So before jumping to the conclusion that a letter received is a letter read, ask if the person has had an opportunity to look at the material. It gives your prospect an easy out if he has shelved it. It also gives you an opportunity to say that you'll call again in a week or so.

4. Aim the conversation.

As a salesperson, you must guide the conversation toward a goal, and that goal is to move the prospect, at whatever speed, toward a sale. Your launching pad for the call is the prospect's initial interest. From there, you must find out whether this interest is sincere, and whether the prospect is in a position to act on his interests.

How to Test a Promotion Before You Use It

We test promotions in much the same way we test anything in life: by taking a consensus among a sampling of friends and strangers. We are in the habit of checking our actions and thoughts with others every day: "How did you like *E.T.?*" "How does my résumé look?" "Does this tie go with my blue blazer?" We do this because it is less costly to ask a question than to suffer the consequences inherent in presenting a sloppy résumé or a poorly planned outfit.

Even with the finest clothes, the sharpest résumé, or the best attitude, we may not achieve some of our goals, but at least we can help put the odds in our favor, and test out our ideas with a minimum of expense or embarrassment.

There is no need to complete an entire promotional project before judging its worthiness. An idea can be tested modestly before committing a great deal of time and money to it. One promotional idea that was ill conceived had to do with a letter sent to journalists telling them of a new perfume.

A perfume manufacturer in Northern California sent a promotional letter along with a photograph of the perfume to members of the American Society of Journalists and Authors (ASJA), reasoning that, as writers, some of them might wish to include the name of the perfume in an upcoming article.

This is fuzzy thinking. The members of the American Society of Journalists and Authors are diverse in their interests. There is a directory put out by the ASJA listing its members by their areas of specialization.

The perfume manufacturer might have been more successful if he had mailed his promotional package just to ASJA members who specialize in beauty, cosmetics, and fashion.

However, if the perfume manufacturer had spoken with a few members of the ASJA before sending his package, he would have discovered that:

1. The chances that a writer is currently working on an article about new perfumes is remote. Furthermore, it's unlikely that a writer would keep his press kit on file. Writers are always swimming in paper.

2. The package failed to offer any interesting angles to the story, leaving it to the writer to develop an angle to a story about a perfume he was only slightly familiar with.

3. The package did not indicate any particular care in its presentation. The letter is presented in its entirety below:

Dear Mr. Smith:
Please consider our perfume and cologne for mention in your next issue. The perfume has been market-tested from Northern California to New York (last at the Fashion Trade Show, May-June) with great success.
We hope you feel our product is worthy of favorable mention.

Although the letter was sent to professional journalists and authors, the person writing the letter seemed to assume that they were editors as well, hence the remark about "your next issue."

The person responsible for creating and distributing the release might have gotten more from his promotion if he had taken the time and trouble to call *ten writers* on his mailing list and try to feel out how they would respond to the material. In that way, he'd discover whether they were in a position to actually use the material or would just read it and throw it away. By sending the material to writers, the perfume manufacturer miscalculated. Even the most prolific magazine-article writers can use only a small fraction of the releases they receive. Few releases contain ideas worthy of stimulating a writer to generate an article. On the other hand, editors deal with hundreds of ideas. Beauty editors could easily file the release for use when an appropriate piece on perfumes was about to be written.

Testing Promotions: A Checklist

Testing any promotion requires great patience. Every time you ask for an opinion, you must be ready to adopt new ideas. That not only takes time and money, but a good solid ego. However, a first-rate promotion can declare a dividend each time you use it, so don't give up.

Here are a few questions to ask yourself:

1. **How can you test a few people before many?**

Simple. Do some market research. Survey a few of the people you're hoping to reach and ask them their reactions to your offering. Find out whether the people you are aiming to reach are the right people, the people who can make a purchasing decision.

If you're testing an ad, try it on your friends and family before placing it. Get feedback about the ad's general effectiveness. How about its typeface? Type size? Graphic look? Does it motivate you to take action?

Before you spend money on a big ad, try a little one. Before you go national or regional, test the ad in a local paper or magazine. Keep costs down. If the ad pulls, you can always be more adventurous.

2. **How can you make sure that the elements of your package are compelling?**

Creative people are always wavering between pride in their work and a healthy doubt that they've done the very best possible. It's very difficult to see your promotions with fresh eyes, but you must try to maintain a point of view characteristic of your customer. Try suddenly picking up what you've written and seeing if it catches your attention. Ask yourself if you've helped your customer visualize how he can make use of your service.

It's important to ask people you respect to review your ads or promotions. Also, it's valuable to have people who are completely outside your industry review it. Sometimes these people can see things that pros might miss. The first-blush reaction is a truer reaction than studied reaction: After all, your prospects will judge your promotion in a matter of seconds.

3. **Can you change elements in a mailing or ad to see if that influences response?**

Of course. It's wise to keep testing. Perhaps different copy, a larger typeface, a bigger ad, or a new graphic would increase response significantly. By experimenting with intrinsic elements such as copy, design, typeface, paper stock, and type size, you keep trying to find the perfect combination of elements to catch your prospect's attention.

4. What about extrinsic factors such as changing media, sending material to a new audience, or switching mailing lists?

All of these are reasonable options, especially if you feel that your promotion is not succeeding. You should examine the mailing list and think hard about the people on it: Are they the right audience? Are they geographically right? Are other demographics right for your business? The same thinking should go into a decision to switch media: Perhaps radio would have more impact than magazines, or a local newspaper might be better for you than a trade magazine.

Building a Prospect List

Whether your promotion consists of a press release, advertisement, flyer, or direct mail, you can take the inquiries which have been generated to build a prospect list.

The names of interested people are valuable because they provide a "data base" for future promotions. They help you get to know your audience and cater to it.

Names of prospects are so valuable that business people spend thousands of dollars trying to determine which groups of consumers will yield the greatest number of prospects for their products. There is one publisher in New York City who is in the habit of taking full-page ads in the *New York Times* in which he offers a lifetime subscription to his business magazine for less than $5.

The ad pulls thousands of replies. How can he make a profit? Simple. He takes the names and addresses of those who inquire about his publication and sells those names to people who want a mailing list of people who have responded to newspaper ads. In a sense, the publisher's profit comes from building and selling mailing lists of prospects.

The reasoning is clear. By taking the time and trouble to clip a coupon and send a check, the people who respond to the publisher's ad have "qualified" themselves. That is, they've set themselves apart from the rest of the *Times'* readers by showing the initiative to respond. People like this may well be open to responding to other newspaper solicitations.

In business, you will forever be uncovering prospects only to find that they either do business with you or may do business with you in the future. There will be many others that, after shopping around, may reject your product or service in favor of someone else's.

So, in order to keep neat, accurate records of your prospects, you should rely on some type of record-keeping system that allows you the flexibility for constant updating of your files. Any filing system that allows names to be quickly and neatly added or purged will allow you to keep current on prospects that are active or inactive.

Here are a few common systems for recording prospects and tracking them:

- *Rolodex.*™ This compact revolving card file has a capacity of more than 1,000 cards. The cards may be filed alphabetically or in any arrangement that is most convenient. It allows quick access and the ability to instantly purge the file of prospects that have become inactive, or those with whom you have followed up.
- *Pressure-sensitive labels.* If you rely on frequent direct mail, you may wish to keep lists of prospect names and addresses on pressure-sensitive labels. Once you have a typed master list of prospects, you can keep adding to it and deleting names. Meanwhile, you have the ability to photocopy your master list directly onto pressure-sensitive labels. The labels are then easily transferred to envelopes or self-mailers. Label masters save you the time of retyping mailing lists each time you wish to do a mailing.
- *Index cards.* When you wish to store additional data about each prospect, index cards afford you extra space on which to make notations. Available in a variety of sizes, index cards may be stored in inexpensive metal or plastic containers, and can be arranged in any pattern you wish: geographical, alphabetical, chronological, or by product.
- *Word processor.* A word processor can electronically store your prospect list and allow you to instantly update it. Once the information has been fed into the word processor, you can easily review your files, make changes, and, with a simple command, have the word processor type out letters or envelopes to each of your prospects. Word processors are

rather expensive ($2,000–$3,000) but they can save a great deal of time for business people who have large mailing lists and who do repeated mailings.
- *Scriptomatic™ machine.* The Scriptomatic machine provides an addressing system that allows for great convenience. Scriptomatic cards prepared on an office typewriter become the basis of a filing system that allows you to keep a permanent record of a prospect while creating an addressed envelope. Changes and corrections are easy to make—just throw away the old card and slip in the new. Scriptomatic addressing machines address directly on your envelopes or other mailing materials without the need to attach labels. The key advantage of the Scriptomatic cards over label matrices is that Scriptomatic cards have room for additional information—a record of product purchases, a telephone number, and personal information. For more information about Scriptomatic machines, write Scriptomatic, Inc., 1 Scriptomatic Plaza, Philadelphia, PA 19131.

Classifying Prospects

One way to arrange prospects' names is according to their ability to become customers. We believe that the following classification describes the various "species" of prospects:
- *Hot prospect (hot sales lead).* This person responds to your promotion because he is shopping around and ready to buy. He will choose you or some other source.
- *Lukewarm lead.* This person is considering buying but may not be ready. He may seriously be seeking information now, and may buy in the future.
- *Qualified prospect.* He can afford to buy but he may not have even responded to your promotion. These are people you want to sell to but haven't as yet.
- *Brochure collector.* This person is not a qualified prospect but has responded to your promotion because he likes to receive free brochures, gifts, samples, etc. A real time-waster (includes competitors and just plain curious folk).

You can help qualify your prospects by asking questions: "Do you feel you may have an immediate need for my product?" "Does the purchasing decision for my product or service have to be cleared with other people?" "How are you currently filling this need?" These questions and others like them will help you ferret out the few hot leads in a world of many non-prospects, shoppers, time-wasters, and competitors. And, after all, those hot leads are the people we've tried to help you reach during the past seventeen chapters.

Now it's up to you.

• • •

It is only by keeping accurate records of what works and what doesn't work that we progress as promoters. Just as the scientist learns from experiments that fail, we learn what to do right only by understanding what we have done wrong. There isn't much room in business for making the same costly advertising or public relations mistakes again and again. By facing the results of your promotional endeavors, you are forced to grow, to try new things. It is just this type of growth that adds vitality to new promotions. The challenge is clear: Keep expanding your horizons while holding on to those elements of your business promotions that have proved to be winners in the past.

· Appendix ·

WHERE TO FIND MORE INFORMATION ON MANAGING, FINANCING, AND PROMOTING SMALL BUSINESS

Books

How to Promote Your Own Business deals with only one facet of running a small business—promotion. Small-business managers also need to know about such things as taxes, law, finance, human resources, management, marketing, and business start-up. The books listed below can provide you with much of the basics in these areas.

The Complete Legal Guide for Your Small Business, Paul Adams; John Wiley & Sons, 1982.
Running Your Own Show: Mastering the Basics of Small Business, Richard T. Curtin; John Wiley & Sons, 1982.
How to Start and Manage Your Own Business, Gardiner G. Greene; Mentor, 1975.
How to Finance Your Small Business with Government Money: SBA and Other Loans, Richard Stephen Hayes and John Cotton Howell; John Wiley & Sons, 1982.
Taxation for Small Business, Marc J. Lane; John Wiley & Sons, 1982.
Small Business Survival Guide, Joseph R. Mancuso; Spectrum, 1980.
People Management for Small Business, William Laird Siegel; John Wiley & Sons, 1978.
Insider's Guide to Small Business Resources, David E. Gumpert and Jeffrey A. Timmons; Doubleday, 1982.

Periodicals

There are three major magazines published specifically for small-business managers and entrepreneurs. These are:

Inc., 38 Commercial Wharf, Boston, MA 02110
Entrepreneur, 2311 Pontius, Los Angeles, CA 90064.
Venture, 35 West 45th St., New York, NY 10036.

Other publications of interest to small business include:

Business Ideas Newsletter, % Dan Newman Co., 930 Clifton Avenue, Clifton, NJ 07011.
New Ventures, 2430 Pennsylvania Avenue, Suite 106, Washington, DC 20037.

To keep up with the world of advertising and public relations, you can read any of the magazines listed below:

Advertising Age, 740 N. Rush St., Chicago, IL 60611.
Adweek, 820 Second Avenue, New York, NY 10017.
Media Decisions, 342 Madison Avenue, New York, NY 10017.
PR Journal, 845 Third Avenue, New York, NY 10022.

Finally, like all businesspeople, big and small, you'll want to keep up with the business world at large by reading *Forbes, Fortune, Business Week,* and, of course, *The Wall Street Journal.*

Reference Books

Here are some basic reference books that can help you in your business. Most are available at your local library.

Encyclopedia of Associations, Gale Research. Annual. Three volumes. Lists professional, trade, and other associations.
Bacon's Publicity Checker, Bacon's Publishing Company. Annual. Two volumes. Lists thousands of newspapers and magazines.

National Directory of Newsletters/Reporting Services, Gale Research. Four volumes.
Tax Guide for Small Business, Department of the Treasury, Internal Revenue Service. Publication No. 334.
O'Dwyer's Directory of Public Relations Firms, J.R. O'Dwyer Co. Lists 1,200 PR firms.
Standard Directory of Advertising Agencies, National Register Publishing Co. Semiannual.
Working Press of the Nation, National Research Bureau. Five volumes. Includes a listing of many free-lance writers as well as the topics they cover.
Graphic Artists Guild Handbook: Pricing and Ethical Guidelines, Graphic Artists Guild, Inc., Robert M. Silver Associates. Outlines standard fees for a wide variety of graphic arts services.
Standard Rate and Data, Standard Rate and Data Service. The most comprehensive guide to all print and broadcast media.

Sources of Information on Small Business

1. *Small Business Administration* (SBA). The SBA offers both free and low-cost pamphlets dealing with small-business promotion, finance, management, and marketing. For a list of free publications, write to Small Business Administration, P.O. Box 15434, Fort Worth, TX 76119. Ask for form SBA 115A. To obtain a catalog of low-cost pamphlets, write to Superintendent of Documents, Government Printing Office, Washington, DC 20402. Request form SBA 115B.

2. *Small Business Reporter.* A series of booklets dealing with all aspects of small business. Available from Small Business Reporter, Bank of America, Department 3401, P.O. Box 37000, San Francisco, CA 94137.

3. *SCORE* (Service Corps of Retired Executives). SCORE is a volunteer force of more than 7,800 seasoned business executives who offer their services without pay in all fifty states. Check the phone book for the listing of your local office. SCORE is sponsored by the government and under the direction of the SBA.

4. *"Dun & Bradstreet's Management Source Publications*

for Small Business." This pamphlet lists publications of interest to small-business managers. Many of the publications are available at no charge; others can be borrowed from your local library.

INDEX

Abbondanza, 12, 82–86, 88, 90, 93, 116
Accessories Magazine, 92
Accountant, 7
Account executive, 39
Action, 48, 117, 143, 156, 162, 226
Ad (advertisement), 2, 3, 7, 9, 32, 38, 39, 42, 46, 54–56, 61, 63, 65, 66, 72, 80, 121, 122, 132, 134, 138, 139, 144, 145, 147, 158–167, 169, 170, 175, 197, 201, 218–223, 226, 227
Ad agency, 2, 14, 29, 33–37, 39–41, 58, 160, 164, 175, 178, 180, 183
Advertiser, 7, 39, 87, 112, 160, 164, 167, 172, 180, 219
Advertising, 1, 2, 7–9, 11, 15, 16, 18, 22, 25–27, 30–33, 35–37, 40, 42, 46, 47, 49, 53, 54, 59, 70, 75, 76, 80, 87, 107, 112, 114, 118, 120, 123, 125, 128, 131, 132, 140, 157, 158, 160, 161, 164, 166–170, 173–182, 191, 198, 201, 205, 217, 218, 230
Advertising Age, 178
Advertising Small Business: Small Business Reporter, 26
Advertising strategy, 175
Adweek, 164, 215
Adweek Creative Services Directories, 41
All you can afford method, 28, 29
American Medical Association, 124
American Society of Journalists and Authors (ASJA), 224
American Window System, 158
Apparel, 26
Art gallery, 2
Article, 39, 42, 95, 101, 102, 104–106, 161, 192, 221, 224, 225
Artist, 33, 34, 40, 72
Association of Operating Room Nurses Congress, 202

Associations, 18
Attention, 43, 44, 46, 47, 50, 56, 96, 117, 158, 166, 183, 203, 226
Audience, 15, 18, 20, 50, 51, 53, 56, 97, 107, 162, 163, 165, 173, 178, 181, 188, 189, 192, 202, 227
Auto dealer, 7, 13
Auto supply, 26
Avis, 6
Avon, 7, 149

Backgrounder, 88
Bacon's Publicity Checker, 91, 105
Balon, Robert E. and Associates, 173
Banquet, 15
Bars, 26
Basic Book of Photography, The, 70
Bean, L. L., 133, 151
Beauty parlor, 19
Billboard, 8, 76, 80, 168
Bill stuffer, 152
Binding, 58, 59, 73, 77, 78
Biography, 88
Black-and-white, 63, 75, 164, 165, 220
Blue-line (blueprint or blues), 63
Blurb, 121
Body copy, 43, 49, 50, 54, 55, 58, 61, 62, 65, 66, 68, 69
Book-of-the-Month Club, 113, 136
Books, 231–234
Book store, 5, 26
Boston Globe, 37
Bowery Savings Bank, 50
Brand name, 6, 13
Broadcast advertising, 172, 176, 180
Broadcasting Magazine, 91
Broadcasting Yearbook, 91, 97
Brochure, 1–3, 8, 11, 15, 20, 22, 32, 36–40, 42, 46, 58, 61, 63, 67–69,

Brochure (cont.)
71, 72, 75, 77, 80, 89, 111, 113, 120, 121, 128, 130, 146–150, 152–156, 200, 204, 219, 221–223, 229
Budget, 1, 2, 6, 11, 13, 14, 25–32, 113, 117, 134, 162, 165, 170, 205
Bulk mail, 126, 127
Bulletin board, 19
Business, 12, 19, 25, 29, 46
Business plan, 12, 14, 23, 24
Business types, 9–11
Business Week, 46, 90, 136

Cable systems, 182
Calligraphy, 62
Camera-ready, 164
Candid Camera, 212
Caption, 68, 69, 155
Carter-Wallace, 26
Catalog, 2, 3, 8, 11, 14, 36, 46, 63, 75–77, 89, 111, 128, 132, 133, 138, 139, 146, 147, 149, 151–153, 156
Catering, 2, 5, 16, 19
Cents-off, 208, 209
Charter offer, 139, 140
Christmas card, 19, 31
Chrysler, 95, 179
Circular, 2, 8, 91, 151
Circulation, 168
Classified ad, 163, 217
Client, 6, 17, 39, 46, 85, 88, 96, 146, 154
Clip book, 70, 71, 160
Color, 75, 165, 220
Color separation, 63
Column-inch, 160
Commercial, 8, 10, 32, 35, 37, 42, 46, 55, 80, 95, 132, 139, 175, 177–183, 219
Commercial artist, 70
Commission, 35, 37
Communication, 6, 7, 33, 36, 80, 114, 118, 119, 132
Communication Workshop, The, 17
Community relations, 108–110
Competitor, 12, 19, 28–31, 36, 39, 104, 117, 134, 196, 197

Comprehensive (comp), 64–66
Computer company, 5, 13
Confessions of an Advertising Man, 144
Consultant, 2, 20, 46, 117, 146
Consumer, 6, 22, 57, 134, 141, 157, 163–165, 171, 177, 180, 181, 209–211, 227
Consumer companies, 26
Consumer demand, 32
Contact, 17, 37, 38, 82, 87
Contest, 8, 210
Contingency fund, 31
Cooperative advertising, 170, 171
Copier, 74, 75
Copy, 42, 54, 58, 64, 70, 121, 135, 142, 150, 153, 155, 159, 160, 164, 176, 192, 203, 226
Copywriting, 2, 33, 36, 38, 40, 42, 43, 50, 51, 55, 56, 120, 143, 150, 155
Coupon, 6, 8, 38, 46, 80, 120, 132, 141, 209, 216, 219, 227
Coverage, 174
CPM, 160, 161, 165, 166
Creative Black Book, The, 41
Credibility, 56, 88, 146
Customer, 6, 9, 13–16, 18–20, 24, 38, 44, 46, 47, 53, 109, 122, 135, 139, 141, 154, 156, 167, 179, 186, 188, 194, 212, 214, 217, 221, 226, 229

Daily News, 93
Data sheet, 152
Dating service, 18, 47, 191
Demographics, 15, 124, 227
Demographic segmentation, 13
Demonstration, 8, 197–199, 205
Design, 64, 226
Designer, 155
Direct mail, 1, 2, 8, 10, 22, 29, 46, 112–114, 117, 120, 121, 125, 126, 128, 130–132, 136, 138, 145, 197, 201, 205, 211, 217–219, 222, 227, 228
Direct Mail List Rates and Data, 125

Directories, 2, 8, 9, 147, 157, 166–168
Direct-response postcard, 128–131
Direct sale, 6, 7
Discount, 140, 208, 209
Display, 8, 38, 76, 80, 148, 183, 201–204, 206–208, 210, 214
Disposable income, 32
DOCSI Corporation, The, 178
Drawing, 70, 71
Drugstore, 2
Dry cleaner, 8
Dummy, 64
Dun & Bradstreet, 5

Editor, 8, 37, 84, 89, 90–93, 97, 101, 102, 105, 221, 222, 225
Electrolysis, 54
Encyclopedia Brittanica, 149
Entrepreneur, 5, 12, 33, 34, 90, 96, 132, 145, 232
Envelope, 117, 120, 127, 143, 144, 148, 152
Exhibit, 204, 205
Exhibit Designers and Producers Association, 204
Exhibit Schedule, 196
Exposition, 2, 11, 195, 202
Exposition of Chemical Industries, 1981, 201

Fact sheet, 88
Farm Progress Show, 202
Federal agency, 13
Feedback, 144, 226
Financial account, 35
Fitzgerald, F. Scott, 169
Florist, 2
Flyer, 2, 8, 11, 15, 16, 19, 20, 37, 42, 43, 46, 50–52, 55, 58, 63, 69, 75, 89, 111, 120, 138, 146–153, 156, 219, 222, 223, 227
Folding, 76
Follow-up, 29, 221–223
Food and Wine, 93
Forbes, 90
Fortune, 90, 91
Four-color printing, 64

Free-lancer, 2, 29, 33, 39, 40, 58, 65, 164
Fruit-of-the-Month Club, 113

GE, 6, 35, 51, 216
General Motors, 26
Geographics, 15
Geographic segmentation, 13
Gifts, 212–214
Gift store, 27
Goal, 11, 12, 16, 28, 158, 224
Gourmet, 12–14, 16, 18, 26, 53, 90, 93, 189
Graphic artist, 61, 65, 73, 74
Graphic arts, 58, 63
Graphic design, 1, 2, 29, 38, 39, 41, 58, 62, 68, 154
Graphic design studio, 33
Graphics, 54, 165, 168, 192, 203, 204, 206, 226
Gravure, 74, 76
Greeting card, 31
Gross rating point (GRP), 181
Guarantee, 140, 141

Hairgrooming, 27
Halftone, 64, 68, 73, 75, 76
Hand lettering, 62
Harvard Business Review, 31, 164
Heyward, Fred A., 45
Headhunter, 44, 45
Headline, 43, 46–49, 51, 58, 62, 63, 65, 68, 69, 85, 131, 155, 158, 160, 164, 166, 189, 203
Hertz, 6
Historical method, 28, 29
Hospital, 13
Hotel, 13
House of Guitars, 179
How to Produce an Effective TV Commercial, 180

Iacocca, Lee, 95, 179
IBM, 216
Idea, 3, 6, 7, 12, 19, 38, 42, 43, 54, 85, 86, 96–98, 102, 104, 105, 192, 222, 224, 225
Illustration, 65, 68, 70, 71, 76

Image, 6, 11, 68, 69, 106, 114, 147, 158, 163, 183, 216
Inc., 90
Index cards, 228
Industrial manufacturer, 27, 31
Insurance, 7, 21, 133, 167
Inquiries, 222, 223, 227

Jargon, 54
Junk mail, 112, 133, 162

Kaye Wholesalers, 158
Kiplinger Letter, 186
Koch Engineering Co., Inc., 67, 69

Lader & Weisberg, Inc., 158
Lawn and Garden, 165
Law and Order, 165
Layout, 64, 66, 68, 150, 157, 159, 164, 166, 189
Leads, 1, 7, 125, 164, 216, 221–223, 229, 230
LeDisco, 49
Letter, 7, 20, 21, 42, 44–46, 98, 102, 112–121, 132, 136, 138, 139, 145, 190, 201, 222, 223
Letterpress, 74–76
Lever Brothers, 35
Line art, 64, 75, 130
Line rate, 160
List broker, 125
Lists, 123–126
Literary Guild, The, 139
Loans, 5
Local shopper, 8, 9
Locksmith, 19
Logo (logotype), 64–66, 69, 72, 146, 147, 154, 201, 203, 205, 211
Lois, George, 215
Love-letter-writing, 19
Loyalty, 13

Magazine, 1, 2, 8, 9, 15, 16, 46, 73, 76, 81, 90–92, 95, 102, 106, 113, 121, 122, 132, 138, 144, 145, 151, 157, 162–165, 174–176, 181, 217, 218, 221, 227
Magazine Age, 31

Magerman Associates, Inc., 65
Mailer, 71, 72, 148
Mailing, 226
Mailing list, 18, 22, 23, 112, 114, 120–122, 124, 125, 144, 188, 225, 227, 229
Mail order, 1, 2, 41, 76, 113, 114, 132–136, 138–145, 161
Mail Order Industry Annual Report, 133
Mail stuffer, 37
Manning, Burt, 178
Market, 14, 16, 18, 27, 31, 39, 124, 165, 173, 222
Marketing, 11–13, 35, 38, 123
Marketing objective, 28, 29
Marketing Principles: The Management Process, 7
Marketing strategy, 13, 38, 39
Marketing survey, 15
Marketplace, 197, 208
Market research, 33, 36, 39, 174, 225
Mechanical, 38, 64, 72, 159, 164
Media, 2, 8, 16, 19, 33, 35–37, 55, 80, 81, 91, 92, 94, 96, 163, 165, 170, 196, 221, 227
Media kit, 166, 174
MENSA, 106, 107
Message, 11, 15, 18, 20, 43, 56, 117, 147, 152, 163, 168, 169, 181
Miller, Glenn, 173
Mobil Corporation, 108

National Computer Conference, 202
National Enquirer, 161
National Outdoor Advertising Bureau, 168
National Restaurant Show, 202
Need, 43, 44
Neiman-Marcus, 133, 151, 152
Newsletter, 1, 2, 11, 12, 63, 81, 91, 185–194
Newsletter on Newsletters, 192
Newspaper, 1, 2, 6–9, 15, 32, 47, 76, 80, 81, 84, 89–91, 101, 102, 106, 123, 124, 132, 138, 144, 157–

160, 162–164, 175, 176, 185, 217, 227
News syndicate, 92
New York Daily News, 141, 158
New Yorker, The, 143
New York Magazine, 93
New York Mets, 211
New York Publicity Outlets, 92
New York Times, The, 85, 90, 102, 227

Objective and task method, 29, 30
O'Dwyer Directory of Public Relations Firms, 41
Office manager, 14, 15
Offset, 150, 189
Offset lithography, 74, 75
Ogilvy and Mather, 144
Order form, 120, 219
Organizations, 13
Orient Express, 153

PAC-MAN, 198
Pamphlet, 38, 150, 232, 233
Pan Am, 51
Paper stock, 73, 74, 153, 155, 189, 192, 226
Party Place, The, 186, 187
Penetration, 30
Pennysaver, 162
Pepsi, 26
Personal selling, 7, 8, 215
Pfizer, 35
Photography, 1, 2, 12, 14, 15, 17, 18, 33, 39–41, 54, 58, 69, 70, 87, 88, 130, 138, 150, 153, 155, 159, 160, 165, 166, 177, 192, 203, 220, 221
Pizza, 19, 20, 44, 86
Personal objective, 30
Planning, 9, 11, 12, 20, 34, 38, 205
Platt's Oilgram, 186
Plumber, 19
Portfolio, 39
Poster, 8, 38, 58, 63, 76
Preemptible time, 182
Premium, 8, 22, 121, 139, 161, 205, 211
Presentation, 7, 20, 184, 224

Press, 16, 38, 80
Press agent, 93
Press kit, 87, 88, 220, 221, 224
Press party, 18
Press release, 1, 2, 8, 15–17, 37, 39, 42, 55, 63, 75, 81, 82, 84–94, 102, 138, 219–223, 227
Pressure-sensitive label, 228
Price, 13
Price-off deal, 8
Price reduction, 30, 140
Price sheet, 152
Prime time, 174, 180
Print, 7, 36, 38, 58, 59, 70–73, 75, 157, 170, 176, 177
Printer, 27, 73, 74, 155
Printing, 1, 2
Proctor & Gamble, 26, 131
Product, 2, 6, 12, 13, 15, 18, 22, 24, 31, 35, 39, 42–44, 48–50, 55, 57, 70, 88, 89, 92, 94, 97, 104, 112, 113, 120–122, 131–135, 138, 139, 141, 143, 147, 148, 153–157, 159, 168, 176, 180, 181, 186, 191, 196–198, 209, 216–218, 228, 230
Product improvement, 30
Product sample, 8
Product segmentation, 13
Program, 8, 12
Promotion, 1–3, 5–9, 11–14, 16, 18, 20, 23–36, 39, 40, 42, 43, 51, 53, 54, 56, 58, 59, 63, 69, 70–72, 75, 80, 95, 97, 113, 121, 132, 133, 136, 139, 141, 144, 161, 176, 186, 191, 192, 197, 198, 201, 205, 208, 210, 211, 215, 216, 217–220, 222–227, 230, 231
Promotional program, 6
Promotion Marketing Association of America, 211
Proofreading, 72
Prospect, 3, 7, 12, 13, 22–24, 38, 43, 90, 91, 107, 122, 124, 125, 130, 131, 134, 139, 143, 145, 147, 149, 150, 151, 153, 166, 175, 189, 196–201, 221–223, 226–229
Publicity, 1, 2, 7, 8, 10, 16, 19, 25, 33, 38, 39, 80, 95–97, 104, 110,

Publicity (cont.)
  111, 125, 130, 132, 138, 196, 201, 205, 211
Public relations (PR), 2, 14, 33, 37–39, 44, 46, 48, 50, 51, 58, 81, 82, 85, 91, 95, 98, 118, 122, 183, 220, 230
Public Relations Journal, 41
Purchasing agent, 40

Quality Covers, 158
Query letter, 102, 103, 105

Radio, 2, 8, 10, 15, 18, 31, 37, 81, 89, 91, 92, 95, 96, 98–100, 139, 157, 172–178, 181, 227
Ralston Purina, 35
Readability, 59, 61
Reader's Digest, 141
Real estate, 5
Recession, 32
Recognition, 11
Refund, 209
Repetition, 162, 176
Reply card, 141, 143, 219
Reputation, 6, 163, 168
Response, 130, 131, 147, 167, 217, 226
Restaurant, 2, 5, 13, 27, 46, 217
Results, 2, 144, 161, 162, 216–218
Resume, 16, 39, 224
Return postcard, 20, 22, 23
Revlon, 26
Robinson, William A., 212
Rolodex, 228
Rough, 64–66, 68, 72
Rub-on type, 62, 63
Ruff Report, 186

Saddle stitching, 77
Sales, 2, 3, 6–9, 11, 19, 22, 26, 28, 29, 31–33, 36–38, 42, 43, 46, 51, 66, 80, 117, 125, 134, 145, 147, 152, 158, 164, 166, 208, 216, 222
Sales letter, 3, 46, 63, 140, 146, 156
Sales literature, 2, 53, 138, 146–148, 150, 152–156, 188, 198, 205, 206, 210

Sales objective, 27, 29
Sales, percentage of, 26–31
Sales pitch, 19, 98, 211, 223
Sales points, 18, 51, 53, 55, 56, 68, 70
Sales Promotion Essentials, 212
Sales support, 149
Sampling, 208
Schwarz, Ted, 159
Score, 64
Scott Paper, 35
Scriptomatic, 229
Sears, 26, 151, 152
Senior citizens, 18
Service, 2, 6, 7, 12, 13, 15, 18, 20, 22, 27, 33, 42, 43, 48–51, 55, 57, 70, 88, 89, 92, 94, 97, 120, 122, 132, 147, 148, 153, 155–157, 168, 181, 186, 191, 216–218, 226, 228, 230
Sexism, 53, 54
Shelves, 214, 215
Shoppers, 162
Signs, 8, 15, 37, 38, 63, 197
Silk screen, 74, 76
Slogan, 7, 48, 51, 53
Small business, 1, 2, 5, 6, 13, 26, 27, 30, 31, 33, 34, 36–38, 48, 75, 90, 91, 108, 112, 132, 134, 148, 157, 162, 163, 165, 167, 169, 175, 179, 180, 202, 203, 216, 220, 231, 232
Smithfield, 14
Space, 8, 58, 61, 65, 67, 69, 128, 141, 159, 160, 165, 191, 214
Space Invaders, 198
Speaking, 106–108
Specialty magazine, 18
Sponsor, 7, 80, 172
Spot, See "commercial"
Society for Technical Communication, 123
Soft-sell, 186
Sound effects, 177
Standard Directory of Advertising Agencies: The Agency Red Book, 40, 41
Standard Industrial Classifications, 123, 124

Index

Standard Rate and Data, 166
Steelmaker, 13
Stenography, 16
Stock, 64
Storyboard, 180
Strange Wine, 183
Streetcar Named Desire, A, 49
Style, 42, 59, 68, 153, 215, 221
Subways, 8
Subscription list, 122
Successful Meetings, 196
Successful Promoter, The, 159
Sugar Ray Leonard, 50

Take-one, 169
Target marketing, 13, 20, 35
Taste, 54
Teaching, 110, 111
Technical terms, 54, 55
Telephone book, 8
  (also, see "Yellow Pages")
Television (TV), 2, 8, 10, 15, 22, 32, 36, 41, 46, 55, 80, 81, 91, 92, 95–97, 132, 139, 157, 172, 174–183, 219
Testimonial, 141
Testing, 223, 225, 226
Thomas Publishing Company, 167
Thomas Register, 167
Thompson Cigar Company, 136, 137, 141, 143
Time, 85
Tips, 2, 3, 30, 35, 51, 65, 73, 120, 128, 139, 152, 175, 176, 200
Tissue, 65
Today Show, The, 85
Tonight Show, The, 85, 96, 107
Training, 20–22
Travel, 2, 8, 43, 50–52, 148
Trade journal, 30, 91, 92, 196

Trade press, 220
Trade show, 2, 8, 11, 76, 80, 183, 195–200, 202–207, 215, 221
Trade Show Bureau, 197, 199, 203
Trade Show Convention Guide, 196
Transit advertising, 169, 170
Type, 58–62, 65, 68, 72, 75, 150, 155, 159, 167, 189, 226
Type-of-business segmentation, 13
Typewriter, 62, 63
Typing, 12, 14, 53

U.S. Gross National Product, 5
U.S. Small Business Administration, 5
United Way, 109
Unit of Sale, 27, 29
University, 13

Venture, 90
Videotape, 96, 175, 183

Wall Street Journal, 37, 86, 161
Weil Olds, 177
Westinghouse, 6
White, Hooper, 180
Win Newsletter, 98
Women's Wear Daily, 92
Word processor, 228
Wrigley's Gum, 11
Writer, 16, 33, 39, 40, 44, 54, 81, 101, 104, 117, 224, 225
Writer's Digest Books, 164
Writer's Market, 105

Xerox, 74, 125

Yale University, 57
Yellow Pages, 41, 122, 124, 166, 167

ⓟ Plume

BUSINESS SAVVY

(0452)

☐ **HOW TO PROMOTE YOUR OWN BUSINESS by Gary Blake and Robert W. Bly.** A practical primer to the ins and outs of advertising and publicity, complete with actual case histories, illustrations, charts, ads and commercials, samples of flyers, brochures, letters and press releases. This is the only promotional guide you'll ever need to make your business a solid success. (254566—$10.95)

☐ **QUALITY WITHOUT TEARS: The Art of Hassle-Free Management by Philip B. Crosby.** Now, from the author of *Quality is Free* comes another must for managers. Crosby pinpoints "the secret enemies" of quality and shows how quality can be produced without twisting arms. "Outstanding . . . brings home the point that no one can afford to blunder along anymore."—*Productivity* (256585—$8.95)

☐ **RESUMES THAT WORK by Tom Cowan.** The complete guide to selling yourself successfully—whether you're seeking your first job, changing jobs, returning to work or changing careers. Includes 126 sample resumes, plus special hints on cover letters and interviews and up-to-date information on the entire spectrum of today's job market. (254558—$9.95)

☐ **WRITING ON THE JOB: A Handbook for Business & Government by John Schell and John Stratton.** The clear, practical reference for today's professional, this authoritative guide will show you how to write clearly, concisely, and coherently. Includes tips on memos, manuals, press releases, proposals, reports, editing and proofreading and much more. (255317—$9.95)

☐ **YOUR GUIDE TO A FINANCIALLY SECURE RETIREMENT by C. Colburn Hardy.** Revised and Updated. Make sure your retirement years are golden. Learn how to set up the best IRA's, how to buy (and avoid) various types of insurance, how to plan your estate, how to invest savings and other ways to make you richer tomorrow—if you start planning today. (256216—$8.95)

All prices higher in Canada.

Buy them at your local bookstore or use this convenient coupon for ordering.

NEW AMERICAN LIBRARY
P.O. Box 999, Bergenfield, New Jersey 07621

Please send me the PLUME BOOKS I have checked above. I am enclosing $_____ (please add $1.50 to this order to cover postage and handling). Send check or money order—no cash or C.O.D.'s. Prices and numbers are subject to change without notice.

Name_____

Address_____

City_____State_____Zip Code_____

Allow 4-6 weeks for delivery.
This offer subject to withdrawal without notice.